MAJORITIES AND MINORITIES

NOMOS

XXXII

NOMOS

Harvard University Press
I   *Authority* 1958, reissued in 1982 by Greenwood Press

The Liberal Arts Press
II   *Community* 1959
III   *Responsibility* 1960

Atherton Press
IV   *Liberty* 1962
V   *The Public Interest* 1962
VI   *Justice* 1963, reissued in 1974
VII   *Rational Decision* 1964
VIII   *Revolution* 1966
IX   *Equality* 1967
X   *Representation* 1968
XI   *Voluntary Associations* 1969
XII   *Political and Legal Obligation* 1970
XIII   *Privacy* 1971

Aldine-Atherton Press
XIV   *Coercion* 1972

Lieber-Atherton Press
XV   *The Limits of Law* 1974
XVI   *Participation in Politics* 1975

New York University Press
XVII   *Human Nature in Politics* 1977
XVIII *Due Process* 1977
XIX   *Anarchism* 1978

NOMOS XXXII

Yearbook of the American Society for Political and Legal Philosophy

MAJORITIES AND MINORITIES

Edited by

John W. Chapman, *University of Pittsburgh*

and

Alan Wertheimer, *University of Vermont*

New York and London: New York University Press · 1990

Majorities and Minorities: Nomos XXXII
edited by John W. Chapman and Alan Wertheimer
Copyright © 1990 by New York University
Manufactured in the United States of America

Library of Congress Cataloging-in-Publication Data
Majorities and minorities / edited by John W. Chapman and Alan
Wertheimer.
p.   cm.—(NOMOS ; 32)
Includes bibliographical references.
ISBN 0-8147-1433-1
1. Majorities.   2. Minorities.   I. Chapman, John William, 1923–
II. Wertheimer, Alan.   III. Series: Nomos ; 32.
JF1061.M35   1990
323—dc20   89-13214
                                                                CIP

CONTENTS

CONTRIBUTORS

JOSEPH H. CARENS
Political Science, University of Toronto

THOMAS CHRISTIANO
Political Science, The University of Chicago

RUSSELL HARDIN
Political Science, The University of Chicago

JOSEPH CHARLES HEIM
Political Science, California University of Pennsylvania

MONICA HERK
Political Science, Princeton University

JENNIFER L. HOCHSCHILD
Political Science, Princeton University

ANDREW LEVINE
Philosophy, University of Wisconsin, Madison

DIANA T. MEYERS
Philosopy, University of Connecticut

JONATHAN RILEY
Political Science, Tulane University

FREDERICK ROSEN
Political Science, University College, London

IAN SHAPIRO
  Political Science, Yale University

ROBERT L. SIMON
  Philosophy, Hamilton College

JEREMY WALDRON
  Law, Cornell University

PREFACE

This thirty-second volume of NOMOS grew out of the meetings of the American Society for Political and Legal Philosophy held in conjunction with the American Political Science Association in Chicago in September, 1987. The topic, "Majorities and Minorities: Political and Philosophical Perspectives," was selected by vote of the membership of our society. Alan Wertheimer served as chair of the program. The original program consisted of three papers, two of which appear in this volume. The commentators were invited to submit revised versions of their comments or to submit new papers on the issues under consideration. In addition, the editors solicited papers on topics that were not discussed at the meeting.

This is the first volume in the NOMOS series to be edited under the ASPLP's new policy. John Chapman is now serving as the Editor of NOMOS. The chair of each program will serve as Associate Editor of the resulting volume.

J.W.C.
A.W.

INTRODUCTION

ALAN WERTHEIMER

"If majorities are often wrong, why is it right for them to rule?,"[1] asks Elaine Spitz. It is certainly not right, in any fundamental sense, says John Rawls: "the procedure of majority rule, however it is defined and circumscribed, has a subordinate place as a procedural device."[2] Indeed, if anything characterizes the American disposition toward majorities and majority rule, it is a considerable skepticism. For no sooner do we say majority rule then we add the crucial, "but there must be protection for the rights of minorities." The presuppositions of majority rule, the justification of majority rule, the status of majorities and minorities as social groups, the desirability of institutional constraints on majorities—all are long-standing issues in political philosophy. This volume seeks to continue exploration of these issues.

There is nothing sacrosanct about the way in which the contributions to this volume have been organized. The organizing themes could have been different, and several contributions straddle the themes we have chosen. On the assumption that the contributions can and should speak largely for themselves, this introduction simply attempts to provide a road map for the issues that are raised.

In Part 1, Joseph Heim explores the presuppositions of the view that the wishes of the majority and the rights of the minor-

ity should have any sort of special status. He argues that concern with majorities and minorities is a relatively recent idea
and is predicated on a "neutral state" (or, perhaps more accurately, a secular state; for a secular state could be committed to
a non-neutral or perfectionist conception of "the good"). If the
purpose of a state is "confessional," if the state is dedicated to
promoting a particular religious creed, then no reason exists to
respect the views of the majority of the population (as opposed
to those who are authorized to interpret that creed) or respect
the rights of minorities who reject that creed. Heim maintains
that toleration of minorities was originally based on a principle
of benevolent generosity rather than on a theory of minority
rights and that the latter idea took a long time to develop. In
addition to analyzing the history of these ideas, Heim is right to
imply that a conception of the purpose of a political community
must precede questions of the role of majorities and minorities
within it.

The next two chapters take up the status of utilitarian justifications of majority rule from a historical and analytical perspective. If a society should wish to maximize happiness, and if
individual votes are good proxies for individual happiness, then
it has reason to abide by the votes of the majority. On the other
hand, to defend majority rule on utilitarian grounds also raises
the familiar objections to utilitarianism as an ethical theory; that
it is insensitive to considerations of justice and individual rights.

The main point of Frederick Rosen's contribution is to defend classical utilitarianism against these sorts of objections.
Consider the claim that utilitarianism might justify enslaving a
minority for the benefit of the majority. According to Rosen,
Bentham maintained that we have no reason to think that happiness accruing to the majority from the enslavement of the
minority would exceed unhappiness felt by the minority. Moreover, Bentham maintained that the most important, and equally
held, interests are our interests in security, and these require
considerable protection for what we may call the rights of minorities. Thus, says Rosen, utilitarianism would not justify punishment of the innocent, for this would severely undermine our
sense of security. Indeed, what Bentham called our interests in
security is but another name for what Mill would later call our

interest in liberty, an interest that he sought to protect against the "tyranny of the majority."

Jeremy Waldron asks whether any fundamental relation arises between a deontological or rights-based view of morality (as opposed to utilitarianism) and institutional protection for individual or minority rights against the votes of the majority. He argues that there is no fundamental relation. Whereas concern over majority tyranny has typically focused on the need to constrain the "outputs" of a majority rule procedure, Waldron asks us to look more closely at the "inputs," at the sorts of views or "preferences" (to use the current terminology) that are counted in the first place. Waldron's case rests on a contrast between a Benthamite and a Rousseauian model of voting. The Benthamite model assumes that voters are psychological egoists concerned with maximizing their own (individual) welfare. The Rousseauian model assumes that each voter is choosing not what is good for himself but what he thinks is good for the polity. And what he regards as good for the polity may already include recognition of individual and minority rights. In the Benthamite model, the interests and rights of the minority might need protection from the majority. But if each individual is voting what he regards as best for the community, as Rousseau urged, then nothing tyrannical happens when one is in a minority except that one's view as to what is right is not the dominant view. One need not fear that one's interests or rights will not be respected. Waldron argues that the Rousseauian model offers a reasonably accurate picture of (at least some) individual voting. And to the extent this is so, then arguments for constraints on the majority—for example, judicial review—will fail.

Part 2 focuses on conceptual and procedural problems of majority rule. Ian Shapiro begins by defending majority rule against what he believes are three major objections and by reminding us that majority rule was originally attractive because it was an ideology of opposition, an ideology that was not about government, but rather about displacing entrenched elites, undermining the powerful, and empowering the powerless. The reductionist fallacy claims that majority rule does not aggregate individual preferences in the way the market does. Although the reductionist objection is technically correct, he does not believe it is an important objection because, among other things, the "unanimity" alternative, to which majority rule is often compared, is neither plausible nor defensible. The constitutionalist objection claims that because majority rule can damage minorities the scope of majority rule must be restricted. This objection, says Shapiro, obscures the fact that the inherent hostility of majority rule towards minorities is one of its appealing properties. Moreover, the claim that courts should protect rights against legislatures cannot be sustained without an independent theory as to what rights are desirable and why courts, more than other political institutions, are likely to protect those rights. Finally, the instability objection holds that majority rule is vulnerable to "cycling" and may fail to produce equilibria. Shapiro argues that courts also are vulnerable to cycling because they, too, employ majority rule to make decisions. Moreover, he claims, instability may be less undesirable than is often supposed.

Diana Meyers's article, which had its origins in a commentary on an earlier version of the previous chapter, probes the conception of the person that underlies commitment to democracy. She argues that public-choice theory (which is also discussed by Shapiro, Hardin, and Christiano) assumes that individuals are "desire-generators" and takes no account of the sources of those desires. On the other hand, radical participation theory, which can be seen as an attack on the "atomistic individualism" underlying economic approaches to political phenomena, seems to assume that the self is simply and completely the product of one's socialization. On this view, the self is a "desire-sponge." After rejecting both views, Meyers opts for a conception of the self as a "self-defining agent." On this view, individuals are equipped with a set of skills that enable them continually to define and redefine themselves. And whereas this conception of the self must allow for individuals to voice their preferences, Meyers argues that society cannot respect the integrity of its members if it allows questions centering on "vital qualities" to be decided by majority rule.

Although majority rule has, on occasion, been defended on utilitarian grounds (see chapters by Rosen and Waldron), Thomas Christiano asks whether majority rule, as a specific procedure, can be defended on egalitarian grounds, whether there is any strong connection between the sort of procedural equality inherent in majority rule and a more fundamental commitment to political equality. Christiano argues that there are several properties that qualify majority rule as an egalitarian procedure: one person–one vote; anonymity; and neutrality. But, like Waldron, Christiano is concerned with the "inputs" into a majority rule procedure. Whereas Waldron contrasted Benthamite (or egoistic) preferences with Rousseauian (or moral) preferences, Christiano draws a contrast between "separable preferences" and "nonseparable preferences," and argues that whereas most voting procedures are designed to deal with "separable preferences," politics is actually most concerned with nonseparable preferences. Given that, and given that most voting procedures encourage strategic manipulation, Christiano argues that it is no violation of the principles of political equality that individuals have more power regarding some decisions and others have more power regarding others. On his view, bargaining not only is consistent with political equality but is required by it. In the final analysis, Christiano argues that we must distinguish between equality in a collective decision process and equality in a collective decision procedure, and it is with the former that we should be concerned.

Russell Hardin's "Public Choice Versus Democracy" explores the implications of public-choice theory for the conceptual coherence of and case for democratic theory in general and majority rule in particular. Hardin maintains that public-choice theory has two main findings: (1) we cannot determine what a collectivity prefers in any reliable way on the basis of individual preferences; and (2) even when we can reach a solution that all individuals might recognize as the best account of their collective preference, those same individuals may not be motivated to contribute to the collective solution. Moreover, the combination of these two difficulties intensifies the problem, because few collective-action solutions are uniquely preferred. For example, even if we all agree that it is in our collective interest to reduce pollution, we may disagree as to how it should be done. It is bad enough that we should be coerced into providing what we do want; it is even worse to be coerced into contributing to a solution that we do not want. After probing these difficulties for

democratic theory, Hardin asks whether they can be overcome.
His answers are not reassuring.

Part 3 begins with Robert Simon's analysis of the tension
between our commitment to pluralism and our commitment to
equality of opportunity. Simon contends that cultural differences among ethnic groups may be such that members of some
groups have a higher rate of educational, occupational, and
economic success than others. In an earlier version of this chapter, Simon argued that this was true of Asian-Americans. If a
commitment to pluralism entails that we permit and even encourage such differences, then pluralism may compromise the
principle that morally arbitrary and uncontrollable factors in an
individual's background should not be allowed to affect his or
her life chances. On the other hand, not to permit such differences is to preclude the diversity that is necessary to the liberal
ideal of allowing different ways of life and, indeed, of providing
different ways of living so that people can reflectively choose
among them.

Joseph Carens's chapter, which began as a discussion of an
earlier version of Simon's chapter, holds that the question is not
whether group differences should be allowed, but when these
differences are just and when they are unjust. Carens maintains
that we cannot say a cultural difference is legitimate without
understanding its history and social context. For Carens, the
advantages of Asian-Americans are not illegitimate because they
have not traditionally enjoyed power and privilege in our society, but we cannot say the same for the rich, for whites, and for
men. In the final analysis, says Carens, a society that permits
relatively few inequalities among individuals may be the one in
which cultural differences are most likely to flourish.

Andrew Levine's "Electoral Power, Group Power, and Democracy" began as a commentary on a paper by Randall Kennedy entitled "Group Rights to Minimal Electoral Power" in
which Kennedy argued for the constitutionality and desirability
of strategies specifically designed to enhance the political power
of blacks. Levine argues that once we see that representative
democracy is not best understood as an approximation to direct
democracy and that there is no important sense in which the
majority rules (a point also made by Rosen), then no prima facie

case obtains for a principle of "one person–one vote," a principle that would exclude the strategy that Kennedy advocated. Levine maintains that it would be one thing if citizenship were fully and equally enjoyed, for then one person–one vote would provide for maximal popular control. But given that nothing like that equality exists, and given that we have always recognized some legitimacy in group rights, (for example, the rights of states) nothing is inherently illegitimate in the recognition of the rights of racial groups to electoral power, particularly if the point is not to rectify past injustice but to empower persons who are now relatively powerless.

Part 4 focuses (more or less) on the American experience with majority rule, both philosophically and socially. Jonathan Riley defends the antimajoritarian features of the American political system against proposals to build into the system more majority rule, or unencumbered representative democracy. Two questions arise: (1) are antimajoritarian constraints desirable? (2) and if so, what form ought they take? Riley says that we need to distinguish between two conceptions of popular sovereignty, the ideal that lies behind majority rule. On a majoritarian interpretation, antimajoritarian constraints obviously are not desirable. But on a consensus reading of popular sovereignty, constraints look more attractive. If we opt for consensus, then the question is not whether we require constraints, but whether we should rely on moral constraints, as in parliamentary regimes, or whether we should give such constraints the force of law, as in the American Constitution. Riley rejects the popular claim that constitutional constraints are to be disparaged as meaningless just because they can be overridden. Moreover, he argues, by making it more difficult to change laws, antimajoritarian constraints increase the "security of expectations," which is itself an important component of justice.

Jennifer Hochschild and Monica Herk have contributed the most empirical piece to the volume. Their question is this: What do we know about the beliefs of whites and blacks that can help us determine how best to achieve the philosophical goals we share? The problem, they maintain, is that while whites have become more egalitarian and optimistic over the last two or three decades, blacks have become more pessimistic. Moreover, whites' beliefs in equality are complicated by such concerns as the rate of change, social distance, status, and mechanisms of change. They argue that the total effect of white resistance to racial change is much greater than professed egalitarianism would suggest and that progress in the status of black Americans will not occur without strong, indeed "heavy-handed," governmental action.

NOTES

1. Elaine Spitz, *Majority Rule* (Chatham, N.J.: Chatham House, 1984), ix.

2. John Rawls, *A Theory of Justice* (Cambridge: Harvard University Press, 1971), 356.

PART I

HISTORICAL
INTRODUCTION

1

THE DEMISE OF THE CONFESSIONAL STATE AND THE RISE OF THE IDEA OF A LEGITIMATE MINORITY

JOSEPH CHARLES HEIM

The issue of majorities and minorities within a common political community is a recent topic in Western political thought. Indeed, prior to the early nineteenth century, this issue scarcely existed; it found no resonance in the public and educated discourse before that day. In the advanced Western states, any examination of majority-minority problems is premised on the idea of a neutral state, empowered to act by the results of universal franchise, responding to the concerns of all members of society within its borders. No idea could have been further

The author wishes to thank Dr. John Chapman; Mr. Richard Langhorne, Fellow of Saint Johns College, Cambridge; Mr. J. F. Burnet, Fellow of the author's own Magdelene College, Cambridge, as well as devoted servant of the Church of England's Diocese of Ely; Reverend John Berry of Fisher House, Cambridge; Brother James Branson, O.P., and Reverend Kenelem Foster, O.P., of Blackfriars, Cambridge; Suzanne Heim, Toby Orford, Geoffrey Nuttall, Paula Nuttall, David Smith, Mark Clarke, and Richard Cottam, Robert Hickey, and Andrew Blanar of the University of Pittsburgh for their helpful comments and suggestions.

removed from the men who exercised the responsibility and care of government in the eighteenth and early nineteenth centuries.

For these men, the Louis XIVs and the Frederick the Greats, the Edmund Burkes and the young William Gladstones, the state was by its very nature confessional, that is, it was restricted and dedicated to preserving the position of the adherents of the dominant religious creed. Political liberties were the exclusive prerogative of the members of the established church. Anglicans in England, Lutherans in Prussia, Catholics in France, Spain, and Austria, and Orthodox Christians in Russia were the only members of the political community. The criterion of loyalty, the precondition for the exercise of rights, was narrowly circumscribed. Therefore, refusal of submission or subscription to the prevailing articles of faith was seen as an act of disloyalty, or, at best, evidence of loyalties elsewhere. As long as the terms of allegiance were so conceived, any idea of a legitimate minority sharing equal political rights remained impossible. The question of majority-minority relations, a central concern of political and legal philosophy in an increasingly democratic age, did not arise until the passing of the confessional state.

The essential feature of the confessional state was religious uniformity, which all of the major European states sought to attain throughout the seventeenth and eighteenth centuries. At the Treaty of Westphalia the German states solved their problems by agreeing to put Catholics and Protestants into different states, while Louis XIV revoked the Edict of Nantes and expelled the Hugenots from France.[1] This desire for uniformity was not solely a Continental quest; shortly after his restoration in England, Charles II proclaimed that "we deny a fitting liberty to those other sects of our subjects, whose consciences will not allow them to conform to the religion established by law."[2] This was consolidated by Parliament's passage of the Test and Corporation Acts, sacramental provisions that required those appointed or elected to public office to take communion in the Anglican Church.

These principles were reflected in the governing institutions. Far from being a lingering or sentimental remnant from an earlier era, monarchy was the main pillar in the edifice of the confessional order. Feudal kings could scarcely have imagined the powers their eighteenth-century successors enjoyed—powers that emerged when the sovereign was accorded the new task of preserving religious uniformity in the state. Enshrined as law by the coronation oath, this became a raison d'être of monarchy, and the renewed legitimacy so created goes a considerable distance toward explaining the persistence of kings and princes. Adoption of the principle of uniformity became inseparable from the advocacy of an important governmental influence, if not outright control, by the crown. As the ultimate guarantor of a religiously based state, the crown naturally inserted its authority into the other vital institutions of the state—the army, the navy, the church, the judiciary and legal establishment—to ensure that they acted to further the prescribed design. Representative bodies, where they existed, were drawn only from the ranks of those belonging to the established church; ratification, rather than questioning, characterized their actions in regard to the religious nature of the state.

Policy, too, was shaped by the prerequisites of uniformity. Free movement of peoples did not exist, and immigration was allowed only on those rare occasions when the immigrants were likely to assimilate to, or not differ markedly from, the religious beliefs of the majority. Even the early American colonies, composed predominantly of those unable to acquiesce in religious disadvantage, established confessional policies such as restriction of the franchise to certain denominations.[3] In all of the European states, a resident, regardless of his church membership, was responsible for taxes and tithes for the upkeep of the established church. Likewise, no European state was without penal laws whereby persons not of the faith of the established church were subject to a variety of disabilities and controls.

The confessional state displayed remarkable resiliency and durability; it was as dominant a feature of the European landscape in the 1820s as it had been in the 1660s.[4] Aside from France, where it was briefly toppled in the years from 1789 to 1799 (but it might be added, quickly re-established by Napoleon with his Concordat and Organic Articles),[5] the confessional state remained impervious to violent internal assaults. The eventual admission of those persons not of the established faith, or as they were often then called, "dissenters," "sectaries," or "aliens," into the exercise of political liberties, and the consequent dismemberment of the confessional state, was brought about by a transformation in the world view of the governing circles of the old order.

This transformation was fostered, in large measure, by the diminishing threat posed by nonadherents of the majority creed. By the mid-eighteenth century, the European states were homogenous in terms of the religious affirmations of their inhabitants, and minorities had become very small in number, if not minuscule. It was a period, as its art and architecture suggest,[6] when the elite was secure in its position and confidence, a time when the civilized temper of the age encouraged it to abandon the crude and no-longer-needed measures of the past.

In this situation, lessening of restrictions on minorities could be countenanced and acts of toleration entered official policy.[7] The toleration espoused by the various monarchies of Europe in no way challenged the fundamental basis of the confessional order. Toleration was distinctly not emancipation; it acknowledged no political rights, and it did not recognize the idea that a political community could accept differences in the composition of its members. Primarily, toleration was a measure of relief: punitive practices relating to ownership and inheritance of property, religious assembly, and education, were eased or lifted. By these concessions, daily life was made less burdensome for the member of a religious minority, who nevertheless remained unable to take even the first steps toward civic equality. The manner in which the policy of toleration was created illuminates the intentions of its designers; far from being the result of a popular assertion of rights, eighteenth- and nineteenth-century toleration laws were acts of benevolent generosity given by the increasingly cultured and enlightened men who were ministers of the crown.

Toleration was implemented because it was championed by the proponents and governors of the confessional order; certainly they had no wish to bring about its demise. Yet, toleration was a step, albeit an unintentional one, in that direction. Toleration fostered the illusion among the rulers of the old order that the confessional state could, with proper safeguards and guarantees, be maintained even with the admission of some religious minorities, who, after all, had behaved in a nonthreatening manner and had even shown a willingness to assimilate the characteristics of a majority.

Later, collapse of the traditional eighteenth-century European balance of power brought alterations of the confessional state in its wake. Confronted with intense external threat and impending dissolution, the confessional state diluted its purity by the entrance of religious minorities into those institutions— army, navy, and the diplomatic service—vital to national survival. This effort to garner new sources of state strength hastened the molding of a new, national identity. Admittedly, this was a consequence of the fear of foreign conquest and overthrow; nevertheless, the beginnings of a "national" outlook marked an erosion in the idea of a community based on religious persuasion.

Ideas of civic equality and religious liberty fertilized the field previously plowed by the legacy of toleration and national struggle. The advance of ideas of political liberty from the salons and drawing rooms to the chancelleries and parliaments was made possible by the willingness of certain segments of the confessional elite—in England, the Whigs and on the Continent, "the liberals"—to adopt the ideas and formulate them as an intended government program. Despite their willingness, these men remained a minority; their ideas converted few of those needed to change the confessional order. The confessional state was weakened instead because these ideas gained credence at the same time another equally significant, intellectual movement influenced the governing orders of the confessional state.[8]

The justification of the confessional state was always both theological and political. Whiggery and liberalism were secular challenges; they denied that political community could be limited to a particular creed. This argument made little progress among the dominant group of men responsible for the care of the confessional state; they believed the established order was religiously endowed and sanctioned. It was this religious conviction that was called into question by the Oxford Movement, or Tractarianism, in England, and Ultramontanism in France and throughout Europe.[9] These ways of thought and feeling denied that the state had a right to control or interfere in the affairs of the established church. Moved by deep piety and devotion, the Tractarians, for example, argued that the confessional state, by reducing the Church to an agency of the state, had put on it in the eloquent words of John Keble, "shackles of gold," that hindered it from accomplishing its divine mission.

The intellectual assault on the confessional state was twofold, and in the end it was this double blow that eliminated the possibility of a confessional state, even one provided with guarantees, coinciding with the extension of political emancipation to members of previously excluded groups. This irreconcilability was the key to the emergence of majority-minority relations in the west; it was also the reason why certain political institutions—monarchy, in particular—have ceased to exist, or have been relegated to areas where they are devoid of actual power. A clear example of this development is England, where the fortunes of Catholic Emancipation were the central domestic concern for nearly forty years.

England, which bequeathed the idea of parliamentary government to the world, was also, in spite of this, or perhaps in addition to this, an exemplary confessional state.[10] The monarch was charged by his coronation oath to uphold the Protestant constitution and defend the established Church.[11] All the Hanoverian monarchs took this oath seriously, none more so than George III. Indeed, he held that preservation of religious uniformity in the state was an inviolable sacred trust. On that ground, he did what no English king has done since: he exercised his prerogative and, at a time when active war with France was looming, he dismissed a government that enjoyed substantial support in Parliament and contained one of the most powerful collections of ministers ever assembled—Lord Grenville's "Government of Talents" of 1803.

Parliament, too, was a bastion of the established order and Anglican supremacy. A striking testament of its religious orthodoxy was that it accepted no measure of toleration beyond the limits of Trinitarian Christianity. No measure of Roman Catholic (or any other) emancipation passed the Commons until the end of the second decade of the nineteenth century; even then, it was held off another decade by the Lords. That august body, where all Anglican bishops were entitled to sit, was, after the monarchy, the main bulwark of the confessional state; correspondingly, it, too, suffered a real diminution of power with the passage of emancipation.

Roman Catholics were a tiny minority. Located in outlying areas, they formed a predominantly rural community, heavily dependent upon a Roman Catholic squirearchy and aristocracy.[12] They posed no threat at all, and measures of toleration were extended in 1779, whereby they were admitted to the army and entitled to become officers,[13] and in 1791, the last remaining penal disabilities of the sixteenth and seventeenth centuries were abrogated. For the established order, the difficulty with the question of Catholic Emancipation lay not with outcomes a tiny, enfranchised minority was likely to effect, but with its impact on the ultimate principle of state uniformity that buttressed the confessional order.

According to Edmund Burke, perhaps the most eloquent apologist for the confessional order, the preservation of uniformity was dependent upon a church defined by its ability "to exclude from her voluntary society any member she thinks fit, or to oppose the entrance of any upon such conditions as she thinks proper,"[14] so forming an exclusive union with the state. Burke held that

> in a Christian commonwealth the Church and State are one and the same thing, being different parts of the same whole. . . . Religion is so far, in my opinion, from out of the province or the duty of a Christian magistrate, that it is, and it ought to be, not only his care, but the principal thing in his care; because it is one of the great bonds of human society, and its object the supreme good, the ultimate end and object of man himself.[15]

For twenty years after the fall of Pitt's Government, stalemate ensued over the issue of Catholic Emancipation. The issue was further complicated by the question of guarantees: What measures would ensure the privileged position of the established Church once Catholics entered Parliament, under whose authority the Church derived its legal status? Other contentious difficulties arose over the issue of securities: the extent of state and monarchical control of the Catholic Church in England, and the regulation of would-be Catholic public officials.[16]

It was on the issue of the established Church, however, that the secular thrust of the Whig challenge to the confessional state became apparent. Unlike his Tory counterpart, the Whig saw no divine sanction for a particular, doctrinal church. Charles James Fox, a great Whig orator, openly argued for a church "establishment founded in the opinions of the majority of the people."[17] From this line of reasoning, it was not too far to claim that "the state had no business with preserving the purity of Christianity."[18] The Whigs sought to empty political life of religious mandates: their goal was the removal of the rationale, that allowed religious barriers to impede the extension and exercise of political liberties. The focus of government had to be shifted from the religious concerns of the confessional state; rather, as Macaulay stated, "We consider the primary end of government as a purely temporal end, the protection of the persons and property of men."[19]

Catholic Emancipation found support even within the Tory ranks,[20] though not necessarily for the same reasons. The eruption of the Irish question into British politics played no small part; Catholic Emancipation offered a way of dealing with this: newly admitted Irish Catholic Members of Parliament (MPs) would be swamped by the more numerous English Anglicans at Westminister.[21] The subordination of the church's interests to those of the confessional state began to arouse discontent; a major reason for the acceptance of the Repeal of the Test and Corporation Acts in 1828 was that it purified the communion rite of the Anglican Church, because reception would no longer be undertaken for the profane purpose of political advancement.[22]

A dwindling group remained in the breach, firmly opposed to any movement in the direction of emancipation. Lord Eldon, one of the longest sitting Lord Chancellors in English history, continued to stand by the same principles that he advocated when Catholic Emancipation first entered into the parliamentary agenda. "The British constitution was not based upon the principle of equal rights to all men indiscriminately, but of equal rights to all men conforming to, and complying with, the tests which that constitution required for its security."[23]

The diehards, however, were soon consigned to the political wilderness. The great mass of Tories accepted Catholic Emancipation in the belief that with its guarantees and securities, which ranged from oaths that required would-be Catholic MPs to maintain the position of the established church to restriction of their private correspondence with foreigners, Emancipation posed no danger to the continued existence of the contemporary order. Indeed, perhaps the best theoretical defense of the confessional state, aside from Coleridge's *On the Constitution of the Church and State* (1828), was written after the passage of Catholic Emancipation.[24]

William Gladstone's *The State in Its Relations with the Church* (1838) was the attempt of a young, High-Church Tory to show that the confessional state was rooted in natural law, and that it, therefore, served the best interests of the Church as well as the State.[25] Gladstone's position was ably dismantled by John Keble, one of the leaders of the Oxford Movement, who pointed out the dangers the Church faced when it was connected with an authority whose purpose was secular, and how civil power was likely to usurp ecclesiastical authority in this situation.[26]

Not only Gladstone was convinced by Keble's argument: the passage of Catholic Emancipation marked the beginning of the end of the direct connection between the sacred and the secular in public life. The admission of religious minorities into the exercise of civil rights and political liberties was a mortal blow; the combination of this conception and a state based on the principle of religious uniformity was untenable and contradictory. In the aftermath of Catholic Emancipation, the future and legitimacy of political institutions had to be defined anew.

Lord John Russell, a Whig statesman, early recognized that a state no longer based on religious exclusion had no vital need of an institution charged with preserving uniformity. The absence of a religious duty or sanction meant there was nothing sacred about a king and royal authority.[27] The issue of majority-minority relations was ushered onto the stage of public life as the previous institutional setting underwent unparalleled alteration.

The question of majority-minority relations, therefore, emerged from a larger political consideration: the composition of the political community and its state. It was, like the question of parliamentary reform and political representation, a legacy of the passing of the confessional state. The admission of religious minorities into the exercise of political privilege wrought profound change in Western political thought and practice. In a fundamental way, the idea of what comprises political community, and what institutions best serve its purposes, was given a new foundation.

NOTES

1. On the French state's religious policy during the reign of Louis XIV, see Ernest Lavisse, *Louis XIV*, 2 vols. (Paris: Plon, 1976), and L. Martin, *Les Origines du Gallicanisme* (Paris: Bloud, 1939). The indispensable source for understanding the religious temper of this time remains Ronald Knox, *Enthusiasm: A Chapter in the History of Religion with Special Reference to the Seventeenth and Eighteenth Centuries* (Oxford: Oxford University Press, 1950).

2. "His Majesty's Declaration to all his loving subjects, 26 December 1662," in *The Stuart Constitution 1603–1688: Documents and Commentary*, ed. J. P. Kenyon (Cambridge: Cambridge University Press, 1966), 403–4.

3. On this, see James H. Kettner, *The Development of American Citizenship 1608–1870* (Chapel Hill: University of North Carolina Press, 1978), and Perry Miller, *Orthodoxy in Massachusetts 1630–1650* (Cambridge: Harvard University Press, 1933). In this light, it is interesting that Thomas Jefferson considered his work in fostering religious freedom in public life as significant as his work on the Declaration of Independence and the founding of the University of Virginia. See Dumas Malone, *Thomas Jefferson and the Rights of Man* (Boston: Little, Brown, 1951).

4. In general, see William Doyle, *The Old European Order 1660–1800* (Oxford: Oxford University Press, 1978); and Max Beloff, *The Age of Absolutism* (London: Hutchinson's University Library, 1954); and Mary Fulbrook, *Piety and Politics: Religion and the Rise of Absolutism in England, Württemberg, and Prussia* (Cambridge: Cambridge University Press, 1983).

5. The Declaration of the Rights of Man of 1789 struck down all

religious barriers to the exercise of political rights; significantly, during the Restoration Period, Article V of the French Charter of 1814 reaffirmed this principle.

6. Two examples of how this was the case in England are James Lees-Milne, *Earls of Creation: Five Great Patrons of Eighteenth Century Art* (London: Hutchinson, Ltd., 1986), and John Steegman, *The Rule of Taste from George I to George IV* (London: Century Publishing, 1987).

7. For this, see Wilbur Jordan, *The Development of Religious Toleration in England*, 4 vols. (Cambridge: Harvard University Press, 1932–1936), and U. Henriques, *Religious Toleration in England 1787–1833* (Toronto: University of Toronto Press, 1961).

8. On the origins and diffusion of liberal ideas, see especially Paul Hazard, *La Crise de la Conscience Européene 1680–1715*, 3 vols. (Paris: Bolvin, 1935), and Ira Wade, *The Intellectual Origins of the French Enlightenment* (Princeton: Princeton University Press, 1971).

9. For the Oxford Movement and its ideas, the best introduction remains R. W. Church, *The Oxford Movement: Twelve Years 1833–1845* (London: Macmillan, 1892). On individuals, particularly noteworthy are Georgina Battiscombe, *John Keble: A Study in Limitations* (London: Constable, 1963), Henri Bremond, *The Mystery of Newman* (London: Williams and Northgate, 1907), and Owen Chadwick, *Newman* (Oxford: Oxford University Press, 1983). Of specific interest are Terence Kenny, *The Political Thought of John Henry Newman* (Oxford: Oxford University Press, 1957), and William Peck, *The Social Implications of the Oxford Movement* (London: Macmillan, 1933). In addition, the complete *Tracts for the Times* was reprinted in six volumes in 1969 by the AMS Press of New York. For Ultramontanism, see E. E. Y. Hales, *Revolution and the Papacy 1769–1846* (London: Eyre and Spottiswoode, 1960), and Owen Chadwick, *The Popes and European Revolution* (Oxford: Oxford University Press, 1981).

10. The most recent account of this is J. C. D. Clark, *England 1688–1832: Ideology, Social Structure, and Political Practice During the Ancien Régime* (Cambridge: Cambridge University Press, 1985). Also worthwhile is Ian Christie, *Stress and Stability in Late Eighteenth Century Britain: Reflections on the British Avoidance of Revolution* (Oxford: Oxford University Press, 1984).

11. Interestingly, vestiges of the confessional state emphasis on exclusivity continued to linger in the English coronation oath until the modern age. As late as Edward VII in 1901, the monarch was required to condemn and publicly denounce particular religious practices and beliefs. The coronation oath was finally changed in this respect when

Parliament passed the Accession Declaration Act of 1910. See Arthur Berridale Keith, *The King and Imperial Crown: The Powers and Duties of His Majesty* (London: Macmillan, 1936), 6–7.

12. On the Catholics in England, see Philip Hughes, *The Catholic Question 1688–1829* (London: Burns Oates, 1929); Bernard Ward, *The Dawn of the Catholic Revival*, 3 vols. (London: Longmans, 1909–1911); Edward Norman, *The English Catholic Church in the Nineteenth Century* (Oxford: Oxford University Press, 1984).

13. Robert Keith Donovan, "The Military Origins of the Roman Catholic Relief Programme of 1778," *Historical Journal* 28 (1) (January 1985): 79–102.

14. Edmund Burke, "Speech on the Acts of Uniformity," in *The Works of the Right Honourable Edmund Burke*, vol. 7 (London: F. C. and J. Rivington, 1808), 10–11, 15, 17.

15. Edmund Burke, "Speech on a Motive Made in the House of Commons by the Right Honourable C. J. Fox, May 11, 1792, for Leave to Bring in a Bill to Repeal and Alter Certain Acts Respecting Religious Opinions, Upon Occasion of a Petition of the Unitarian Society," in *The Works of the Right Honourable Edmund Burke*, vol. 7, 43.

16. The Vatican was prepared to concede quite a large degree of control to the English Crown. On this, see Hales, *Revolution and the Papacy;* and J. T. Ellis, *Cardinal Consalvi and Anglo-Papal Relations* (Washington D.C.: Catholic University of America Press, 1942).

17. Charles James Fox in debate of 2 March 1790, in *Parliamentary History*, vol. 28 (London: Hansard's, 1790), 397.

18. Charles James Fox in debate of 2 March 1790, in *Parliamentary History*, vol. 28, 399.

19. Thomas Macaulay, "Gladstone on Church and State," in *The Works of Thomas Babington Macaulay*, vol. 6 (London: Longmans, 1866), 372.

20. The best account of the immediate politics of this issue remains G. I. T. Machin, *The Catholic Question in English Politics 1820 to 1830* (Oxford: Oxford University Press, 1964).

21. On the positions of the political groups of the period, see G. I. T. Machin, "The Duke of Wellington and Catholic Emancipation," *Journal of Ecclesiastical History* 14 (1963): 190–208; G. F. A. Best, "The Whigs and Church Establishment in the Age of Grey and Holland," *History* 45 (1960): 101–18, and Richard Brent, *Liberal Anglican Politics: Whiggery, Religion, and Reform 1830–1840* (Oxford: Clarendon Press, 1987).

22. Machin, *The Catholic Question.*

23. T. Twiss, *Lord Eldon*, vol. 1 (London: Longmans), 492–93.

24. Coleridge, Samuel Taylor, *On the Constitution of the Church and State* (Princeton: Bollingen Press, 1978 [most recent edition]).

25. On Gladstone's political theology, see esp. Perry Butler, *Gladstone: Church, State, and Tractarianism* (Oxford: Oxford University Press, 1984); and Agatha Ramm, "Gladstone's Religion," *Historical Journal* 28 (Fall 1985): 327–40; and Boyd Hilton, "Gladstone's Theological Politics," in Michael Bentley and John Stevenson, eds., *High and Low Politics in Modern Britain* (Oxford: Oxford University Press, 1983), 28–57.

26. Perry Butler, *Gladstone: Church, State, and Tractarianism*, 101–10.

27. On this, Lord John Russell, *Essay on the Constitution* (London: John Murray, 1823), chap. 23.

2

MAJORITIES AND MINORITIES: A CLASSICAL UTILITARIAN VIEW

FREDERICK ROSEN

A traditional criticism of utilitarianism has focused on its alleged inability to provide an adequate theoretical foundation for securing individual rights and the protection of minorities. The very phrase, "the greatest happiness of the greatest number," has been interpreted as a clear declaration of majority ascendancy. This criticism may be traced to the heart of utilitarianism in John Stuart Mill's notion of the "tyranny of the majority," which Mill regarded as a partial criticism of the utilitarian theory of government that he inherited from Jeremy Bentham and James Mill. The object of this chapter is to examine the problem of majority rule and minority rights from the perspective of the classical formulation of utilitarianism, especially that of Bentham and to a certain extent John Stuart Mill, and to suggest that many common criticisms of their approach to majorities and minorities are without foundation.

I. MAJORITIES AND MINORITIES IN PRACTICE

Classical utilitarianism[1] addresses the relation between majorities and minorities on two levels, the practical and the theoretical. On the practical level, the majority is a device that may be useful in making decisions, but no more important than other devices. Bentham, for example, was interested in the distinction between comparative and absolute majorities in his *Constitutional Code*, but he was far more interested in the distinction between open and secret voting and even in the use of chance or lot in reaching decisions.[2] Nor, as a democrat, was he especially committed to the idea of majority rule. All government, including representative democracy, was minority government, that of the "ruling few" over the "subject many." Representative democracy was considered superior to other forms of government, not because of a supposed ascendancy of the majority, but because it was able to make a "ruling few" more accountable to the "subject many" than other forms of government. Where Bentham criticized the doctrine of the separation of powers for allowing a minority veto of legislation, his criticism was based more on the link he saw between minority control and the operation of "sinister interests" than on any commitment to "majority rule."[3]

To emphasize Bentham's indifference to the concept of majority rule, consider the following passage that appears in manuscripts written as a commentary on the first Greek constitution (the Constitution of Epidaurus of 1 January 1822) that excluded Muslims and Jews from citizenship and office.

> The exclusion put on this occasion upon so large a part perhaps the largest part of the existing population is at present it would seem an unavoidable arrangement but it is a highly deplorable one. It entails upon the country the existing division, reversing only the position of the condivdent races. It places the Turks under the Greeks [as] the Helots were in under the Spartans, in the situation that the Protestants in France were in under the Catholics, in Ireland the Catholics under the Protestants, in the Anglo-American United States the Blacks under the Whites. In no country can such schism have place but in point of morality and felicity both races are, in howsoever shapes, sufferers by it: the oppressors as well as the oppressed.

To lessen the opposition of interests—to bring them to

coincidence as speedily as is consistent with security should therefore be an object of constant care and endeavour.[4]

The first point to be noted is that Bentham's position does not depend on whether or not those excluded constitute a minority or a majority. In the examples that he provides some are oppressed minorities under majorities and others are oppressed majorities under minorities (e.g. the Catholics under the Protestants in Ireland). Second, Bentham's remedies for this perhaps "unavoidable" exclusion in Greece has no special reference to majorities and minorities. Both oppressors and oppressed, in his view, suffer from such an arrangement. The oppressors have no security against discontent and rebellion; the oppressed suffer indignity and are vulnerable to direct attack. Bentham recommended the accommodation of the Moslems and Jews within the state in a way that would not threaten Greek security, but would eventually lessen the hostility between these groups. In one example he argued that the Turkish community might be allowed to become citizens and be given the vote, but if they tended to outnumber the Greeks in too many electoral districts, the voting age for non-Greeks might be increased.[5] Although such an arrangement, he admitted, would not be perfect, it might reduce the mutual fear and hostility that would arise from total exclusion, and would allow the new Greek state to move toward granting equal rights for all. Bentham saw in this sort of position the combination of what he called "self-regarding prudence" with "effective benevolence," the latter being "effective" so long as the former was recognized and secure.[6] In another example he assumed that the Greeks would be trained in the use of muskets and in European methods of warfare. Rather than keep the Turks completely disarmed he proposed that they should be allowed swords and pistols so that they might be able to defend themselves without having the power to threaten the overall security of the Greeks.[7] Here again, he sought to combine "effective benevolence" with "self-regarding prudence," but this combination did not involve any special awareness that he was dealing with majorities and minorities.

II. Interests, Security, and Equality

The phrase, "self-regarding prudence," evokes the idea of self-interest, and it is from the concept of an interest that we might best examine on a theoretical level the utilitarian approach to majority rule. Bentham may again be taken as the archetypal figure in classical utilitarianism. For the individual every object of motivation creates an interest so that each person would seem to have an incalculable number of interests. Furthermore, each might be motivated by different goals and desires so that his interests will be not only difficult to calculate but also potentially subjective. Although not denying these difficulties with the concept of an interest, Bentham would have argued that the most important interests are those that individuals share with others, and, for purposes of legislation, these might be reducible to a few essentials, the most important of which is security. Each person has an interest in his own security, which for Bentham is so fundamental that all other interests are subordinate to it. John Stuart Mill followed Bentham in recognizing the importance of security in his own account of utilitarianism.

> Nearly all other earthly benefits are needed by one person, not needed by another; and many of them can, if necessary, be cheerfully foregone, or replaced by something else; but security no human being can possibly do without; on it we depend for all our immunity from evil, and for the whole value of all and every good, beyond the passing moment; since nothing but the gratification of the instant could be of any worth to us, if we could be deprived of everything the next instant by whoever was momentarily stronger than ourselves.[8]

In this passage Mill brought together in characteristic manner many of the important ideas Bentham had associated with the idea of security. First, like Bentham, Mill accepted that security is the most important element in human existence and something no one can do without. Second, he saw that although individuals may seek a wide diversity of objects, and what one wants another does not, everyone wants security. Third, security is largely conceived as a negative idea insofar as it is realized by preventing pain and evil. To have security is to be free from something, for example, invasion, illness, or interference. Fourth, the importance of security is underlined by the fact that without it only direct and immediate pleasures can be enjoyed. All of one's plans for the future, one's expectations and hopes, depend on security. The emphasis Bentham placed on security of expectation was shared by Mill. Finally, insofar as everyone has an interest in security, that is to say, this interest is shared equally, there is a clear link through security between equality and interests.

Each person in a society thus has an interest in security, and the advancement of security may be regarded as being in the general interest. Many different and complex governmental policies are part of the advancement of security, including protection against invasion, crime, famine, hunger, illness, oppression, and the abuse of power. For Bentham, each individual has an equal interest in security and the object of all individuals should be to maximize it. This is not to say what people actually do, as many individuals think that it is in their interest to create insecurity for others so long as they gain immediate benefits for themselves. Nevertheless, the only interests that can be maximized for everyone are those that everyone shares, such as security, and it is ultimately in the interest of each individual to advance the common interest, as in the long run his own interests will also be furthered. Conversely, where individuals pursue their own interests in opposition to the general interest, they eventually run into conflict with other members of society.

The emphasis on the idea of security by both Bentham and Mill has many ramifications, only two of which will be considered here.[9] The first is that in a political context Bentham's greatest happiness principle means mainly the maximization of security applied equally to all members of a given society. Although the object of legislation is to maximize the happiness of all members of society, that object in turn means to effect the maximization of security. Furthermore, as was evident in the passage concerning the Greeks and Turks, no one is secure unless everyone is secure.

Although Bentham clearly understood what he meant by the greatest happiness principle, and especially the link with security, he also realized that there might be some public confusion over the meaning of the principle. In particular, the phrase, "the greatest happiness of the greatest number," might imply the happiness of the greater at the expense of the lesser number. In his "Article on Utilitarianism," written for Perronet Thompson to use in his reply to Macaulay in the *Westminster Review*, Bentham attempted to clarify the meaning of this phrase and posed the following example: "Number of the majority, suppose, 2001: number of the minority, 2000. Suppose, in the first place, the stock of happiness in such sort divided that by every one of the 4001 an equal portion of happiness shall be possessed. Take now from every one of the 2000 his share of happiness, and divide it anyhow among the 2001."[10] Bentham believed emphatically that the redistribution of happiness from the 2,000 to the 2,001 would produce a great loss of happiness, for "such is the nature of the receptacle, the quantity of unhappiness it is capable of containing during any given portion of time is greater than the quantity of happiness."[11] What Bentham meant by this statement is not entirely clear, but he felt that the point was self-evident, as he indicated in the next paragraph.

> At the outset, place your 4001 in a state of perfect equality in respect of the means, or say instruments, of happiness — and in particular power and opulence: every one of them in a state of equal liberty, every one independent of every other, every one of them possessing an equal portion of money and money's worth: in this state it is that you find them. Taking in hand now your 2,000, reduce them to a state of slavery, and, no matter in what proportion, of the slaves thus constituted divide the whole number with such their property among your 2,001. The operation performed, of the happiness of the whole number, 4,001, will an augmentation be the result? The question answers itself.[12]

In other words, the happiness to be obtained by its redistribution from the minority to the majority would be small in comparison with the unhappiness to be felt by the minority by their reduction to slavery. Bentham also noted that the smaller the minority, the smaller the amount of happiness might be gained by the majority.[13] If the 4,000 reduced one person to slavery for the sake of confiscating his property, the amount gained by 4,000 would be miniscule, and would bear no comparison with the pain and unhappiness generated by such an action. Furthermore, the pain would not be confined to the person who lost his property but would be suffered by everyone in the society as they see their own property threatened with confiscation.

By the greatest happiness principle, Bentham clearly meant an equal distribution of pleasure or its equivalent (or an equal reduction of pain) to all members of society or to all of those concerned with an action.[14] He used the greatest happiness of the greatest number as a secondary principle so that where happiness could not be distributed equally (for whatever reason) the distribution would be made equally (or as equally as possible) to the greatest number.

When one combines Bentham's conception of security (and especially security of expectation) with his formulation of the greatest happiness principle, his approach to the relation between majorities and minorities becomes more clear. The greatest happiness in politics and legislation effectively means the maximization of equal security to all members of society. Security means, for the most part, protection against pain, and this distribution of pain is the special province of the legislator who, given the varieties and the subjective nature of much pleasure, cannot possibly know what will provide pleasure for each member of society. The province of the legislator is the protection of each individual in society against the pains from which he, together with all other members, wishes most to be protected. This is the realm of security that is the main constituent of the greatest happiness principle. In the relation between security and happiness, security of expectation plays the key role. For both Bentham and Mill, the disappointment of settled expectations (such as the sudden reduction of an individual from citizen to slave) creates such pain and is so fundamental an injustice that it can never be justified on the grounds of the augmentation of happiness elsewhere.

Not all utilitarians would agree with this emphasis on security. In "An Outline of a System of Utilitarian Ethics," J. J. C. Smart accepts that a sheriff in a small town might justify the arbitrary execution of an innocent man as a scapegoat in order to prevent serious riots and widespread loss of life.[15] Bentham would not accept such an execution as the utilitarian outcome, however, because he was not concerned simply with measuring the number of people who may be killed, as though the calculation of pain is equivalent to the calculation of the number of dead citizens. To execute anyone in a society as a scapegoat would so threaten security of expectation that the action would seriously diminish the happiness of every other person. If one is executed as a scapegoat today, anyone else might be treated similarly tomorrow. No one could be secure in his basic expectation of life in the society. The happiness purchased by the execution of the scapegoat would be small change in comparison with the price to be paid in the threat to fundamental security. Nor would the prospect of widespread rioting and death outweigh the death of the scapegoat, as both would equally threaten fundamental security.

III. POPULAR SOVEREIGNTY AND MAJORITY RULE

The second aspect of the utilitarian emphasis on security to be considered here is Bentham's idea of security against misrule, which means, in effect, the protection of the majority (or subject many) from the misrule of the minority (or ruling few). We might begin with Bentham's conception of a constitutional democracy where sovereignty is placed in the hands of the people. Throughout his writings on constitutional democracy, Bentham was careful to distinguish between the exercise of sovereignty (constitutive power) and the exercise of the powers of government (operative power).[16] The effective power to make and execute laws is operative power and even the sovereign power in the state is dependent upon operative power. Constitutive power is defined by Bentham not as the power to make a constitution (for that belongs to operative power) but in a more limited manner as the power to choose and dismiss those who hold operative power. For Bentham, this power is especially apt in a

democracy where the people may have little time and inclination to rule but have the capacity to choose their rulers and
every opportunity to consult their interests in doing so.

That Bentham, as a utilitarian, distinguished between constitutive and operative power reflects on his conception of individual interest leading to an equal security for all members of
society. As few people have the leisure, inclination and knowledge to rule, individual interest is secured best by maximizing
control over those who do rule. Securing their interests means
in effect enhancing constitutive power which is achieved in the
control of the "ruling few" by the "subject many."

Given the nature of constitutive power, which at one point
Bentham conceived as a power of patronage[17] (to choose and
dismiss one's rulers), it would be inappropriate to confuse his
idea of popular sovereignty with majority rule. Although it is
true that the majority of the legislature determines the laws,
subordinate executive and judicial branches carry them into
effect and ensure compliance. In addition, although the legislature is chosen by the majorities of constituents in various electoral districts, the majority of the people do not actually rule.
Bentham takes great pains through the distinction between constitutive and operative power to prevent this misconception. He
believes in popular participation in government and even sees
(contrary to the views of some critics)[18] the moral benefits of
such participation, but participation on its own is not ruling in
the sense of making and enforcing legislation.

To see democratic government as majority rule creates a confusion that obscures the fact that even in a democratic government all ruling is in effect minority rule and the task of democratic constitutionalism is to secure the majority from misrule
and oppression under a system of minority rule. In advocating
popular sovereignty, Bentham advocated one means by which
the abuse of power might be controlled or checked. The confusion of popular sovereignty in a constitutional democracy with
majority rule, however, is commonplace. For example, it plays
an important role in John Rawls's attempt to link his two theories of justice with practice in the context of constitutional democracy.[19] The principle of equal liberty (the first principle of
justice) is succeeded by the principle of participation that posits

an equal liberty of participation by the members of the society. In the context of constitutional government, this principle becomes the majoritarian principle that is in turn limited by constitutional devices designed to protect minorities. Rawls's conception of constitutional government is, therefore, a system that satisfies majority aspirations while protecting minority interests, and such a system reflects the more distant Rousseauian origins of this approach to politics. For Rousseau, the majority (the Lawgiver notwithstanding) actually rules with all of the people forming the legislative power in the state. Rawls proposed no such direct democracy. But Rawls's position only makes sense if, to use Bentham's terms, there is no difference between the possession of constitutive and operative power. Not only would Bentham argue that such a distinction is crucial to an understanding of constitutional democracy, but he would also contend that not to make the distinction obscures the important fact that constitutional democracy, like other forms of government (for example, monarchy and aristocracy), must exercise minority rule with the government to be regarded as any other ruling elite. The phrase "majority rule" or the "majoritarian principle," once removed from the context of direct democracy, becomes misleading and even dangerous if it implies a measure of direct popular control over government. Popular control in a representative democracy may be achieved in any number of ways, but "majority rule" is not one of them.

IV. Democratic Despotism

In a recently published essay, Pedro Schwartz, though accepting many of the arguments that appear in this chapter, contends that the direct consequence of Bentham's system of constitutional democracy (whether intended or not) is to enhance "democratic despotism."[20] In part, Schwartz is defending the theory of government rejected by Bentham, that is, the theory based on the social contract, the separation of powers, federalism, direct limitations on legislative powers, checks and balances, and bicameralism. On another level he is suggesting that the very logic of classical utilitarianism and legal positivism, especially in Bentham's thought, inevitably leads to a despotic system of government. As for the first criticism, based on Bentham's rejection of such doctrines as the social contract and the separation of powers, Schwartz did not doubt that Bentham intended to provide different securities for these traditional institutions and practices long associated with individual liberty in the tradition of Locke and Montesquieu. He was skeptical, however, of Bentham's complete acceptance of political democracy not only as the basis of good government but also as being fully compatible with the protection of individual liberty. Schwartz reflects a long tradition of European liberalism that sees liberty and democracy as largely opposed ideas and his criticisms of Bentham, though more contemporary in form, are reminiscent of Elie Halévy's similar criticisms of Bentham's so-called "Jacobinism" which were written at the beginning of the twentieth century.[21] Nevertheless, Bentham was well aware of the problem of combining security with equality and democratic policies at the time of the French revolution and strongly emphasized the greater importance of security. By the 1820s, with the model before him of the successful operation of a wide suffrage without any threat to the security of property in the various states of the United States, Bentham believed confidently that elementary security was compatible with political democracy so long as numerous checks or securities were introduced to protect the people from the abuse of power by government. He differed from Macaulay, who thought the export of democratic institutions to Europe would threaten security of property.[22] Bentham's theory of interests led directly to the conclusion that with each person's interest in security, and with security of property being fundamental to such personal security, the introduction of political democracy could mean an enhanced security for the individual rather than its diminution. Like John Stuart Mill, who followed, he accepted democracy and then built into the constitutional system numerous means by which intelligent, accountable, and responsible government could be established within the democratic regime. The very notion of a representative constitutional democracy symbolizes Bentham's opposition to "democratic despotism."

The rejection of many notions regarded by Bentham's contemporaries as crucial to liberty and security, such as the separation of powers and bicameralism, was based not on a disregard for liberty and a taste for despotism, but on the belief that more effective securities could be devised that were also more compatible with a system of representative democracy. Bentham believed that the traditional institutional securities, as, for example, the separation of powers, evolved to provide security and limited government under monarchies and aristocracies. While these regimes still existed he did not propose to abolish such practices, but they would be inappropriate under representative democracy and might even operate to make it less successful in securing the liberties of the people. Bentham was clearly arguing within the tradition he was criticizing, and if he rejected some of the constitutional proposals of Locke and Montesquieu, he did not reject the goals of widespread security that they had sought. He attempted to replace them with new instruments in the context of a constitutional democracy, and if the new means were not as successful as the old, Bentham would have been the first to advocate returning to those he had rejected.

The experimental character of Bentham's theory is of crucial importance to rebutting Schwartz's contention that Bentham perhaps unwittingly favored "democratic despotism." If Bentham rejected the separation of powers, for example, it was because he could show that the consequences of its practical application in the new context of representative democracy were not as beneficial as others had supposed. But his advocacy of other practices was subject to the same test and to a willingness to alter arrangements when other practices could be shown to be better on utilitarian grounds. It is important not to confuse Bentham's experimental and theoretical approach to constitutional democracy with more dogmatic ideologies that perhaps arose at the same time.

Furthermore, those like Schwartz, who link Bentham's theory of democracy with "Enlightened Despotism," are unaware of the more direct connection in his theory with the constitutionalism of Montesquieu and Delolme.[23] Consider, for example, Bentham's placing in the *Constitutional Code* ultimate operative power in the state in a single legislative chamber, elected on the basis of universal suffrage. Here, if anywhere, we find the core

of what might be called "democratic despotism." All other powers in the state are subordinate to this democratically elected
legislative body. There is no opposition from another legislative
chamber, an independent executive or judiciary, or another tier
of state or local government. Though, apparently, whatever the
legislature decides becomes law, the matter is not as simple as
this brief sketch suggests. The tradition in which Bentham was
writing provides an account of executive power that is analogous to that provided by Bentham of legislative power. For
Montesquieu, and especially for Delolme, one of the great
strengths of the British constitution lay in the power held by the
king in that he dominated all aspects of executive government
and could not be challenged or have his power usurped by any
other body in the state. Nevertheless, despite his enormous
power, including his immunity from prosecution, his power was
checked in one important respect, as the funds for his activities
had to be voted by the House of Commons. In the same manner, Bentham's legislature in the *Constitutional Code* has great
power in the state and its legislative powers cannot be usurped
by any other power. Nevertheless, like the king in the British
constitution, in one important respect its power is checked, as it
depends entirely on the votes of the people. Just as the House
of Commons could not equal the power of the monarch without
disbanding the constitution so as to acquire executive power
itself, the electorate or public opinion tribunal in Bentham's
system could not have the powers possessed by the legislature
without radically altering the constitution. Nevertheless, just as
the control of the House of Commons over the monarch was
effective, though indirect, so was the power of the electorate
over the legislature in Bentham's system intended to be equally
effective though also indirect. For this reason he depicted the
power of the legislature as "omnicompetent" rather than "omnipotent."[24]

Nor does Bentham's legal positivism lead, even unwittingly,
to "democratic despotism." His theory of democracy, with the
people sovereign, does not embrace the view that law is "whatever the sovereign wills," and as G. J. Postema has recently
argued, even his theory of law does not embrace this view.[25]
From his earliest writings Bentham regarded sovereign power

as capable of being limited, divided, and functionally distinguished within a constitutional system. In his democratic theory, the people, though sovereign, do not make laws, and the legislature, though the source of legislation, is omnicompetent and not sovereign. It must also share its power functionally with the executive and judicial branches even though these branches are in principle subordinate to the legislature. Furthermore, Bentham was perfectly willing to see his *Code* adapted to a federal system and to place clear restraints on the legislature (in suggesting that its members meet educational qualifications before standing for office). These limitations on the omnicompetent legislature are compatible with Bentham's legal positivism, because it is a mistake to conflate an account of the formal source of a law with an account of political power in a state. Only such a conflation would allow one to see Bentham's theory of democracy as despotic because of the nature of legal positivism.

V. Tyranny of the Majority

The final theme considered here is the extent to which classical utilitarianism allowed or accommodated what John Stuart Mill has called "the tyranny of the majority." Did Bentham anticipate Mill's attempt to correct this new threat to human well-being posed by the coming of popular politics, or did Mill see the need to call attention to the "tyranny of the majority" partly because of the consequences of Bentham's own approach to democratic government? To answer both of these questions in the affirmative may seem contradictory. Nevertheless, although Bentham's theory of constitutional democracy may, in Mill's opinion, have enabled majority tyranny to develop, Mill also adopted a number of concepts, prominent in Bentham, that would lay the foundations for resisting majority tyranny. In his 1838 essay on Bentham, Mill depicted critically the political arrangements of Bentham's *Constitutional Code* as placing the people under the "absolute authority of the majority of themselves" and refers to the influence of this authority as extending to "the despotism of Public Opinion."[26] These strong comments extend Mill's criticisms of Bentham's political ideas in the 1833 essay, "Remarks on Bentham's Philosophy," where he was con-

cerned with Bentham's supposed failure to give sufficient attention to tradition, habit, and the different conditions of different
people, and reflect the influence of Alexis de Tocqueville, whose
Democracy in America he reviewed for the first time in 1835.[27]
Once he had read Tocqueville, he clearly linked Bentham's
conception of a constitutional democracy with the notion of
democratic despotism, if not majority tyranny.

Nevertheless, when Mill invokes the "tyranny of the majority"
in the introductory chapter of *On Liberty*, he makes no direct
reference to Bentham or to his theory of government.[28] Perhaps at this later period, other aspects of Bentham's political
thought have become more influential, as is apparent in the
emphasis on security in *Utilitarianism*. Bentham's notion of security provides at least the legal framework within which individuality can best develop, and security, for Bentham, is merely
another name for the idea of civil liberty.[29] Indeed, one might
argue that Bentham's conception of security would favor and
advance the cause of individuality more surely than any other
concept of civil liberty discussed in the latter half of the eighteenth century. Furthermore, in the early *Fragment on Government* (1776), Bentham had already conceived of liberty of the
press and liberty of public association (two important ingredi-
ents of Mill's conception of liberty) as part of the very definition
of a free constitution and linked these freedoms directly with
security.[30] He continued to uphold these freedoms later in life
as being as important in a democracy as in a free state generally.

We have already seen that it would be a misconception to
regard Bentham's theory of constitutional democracy as embodying the idea of majority rule and such a conception could
not, therefore, lead to "majority tyranny." Inasmuch as Bentham stressed the importance of an educated government service (including educational qualifications for members of the
legislature), he clearly intended that government should consist
of educated men whose opinions and policies would not simply
reflect the majority of the electorate.[31] It is arguable that Bentham made a greater provision for competence in public office
in his *Constitutional Code*, which could oppose majority opinion
in society, than Mill did in his *Considerations on Representative
Government*.[32]

Perhaps the only link in Bentham with Mill's conception of the tyranny of the majority may be found in Bentham's emphasis on the importance of public opinion in society. If Mill sought to protect the individual from the stultifying effects of public opinion, Bentham saw in public opinion, and in what he called the public opinion tribunal, the main institution that could represent the public interest and advance the strategy of reform. Where Mill resists public opinion, Bentham seems to defer to it as embodying the greatest happiness principle.[33] Nevertheless, when Bentham emphasizes the importance of public opinion he is mostly considering issues that are not directly relevant to the problem of resisting majority tyranny as Mill saw it. Public opinion is, for Bentham, a force that is not controlled by government, and it can play the important role of acting in opposition to it.[34] Since it possesses none of the power of government, it cannot be corrupted in the same sense that government officials can be corrupted. Bentham conceives of public opinion as a critical force in society, not simply reflecting mass opinion but working through the press and institutions such as the jury system to advance the public interest and to change laws and government practices. He is well aware of the strength of what he calls "sinister begotten prejudice" that enables sinister interests to thrive with impunity while the great mass of people support government policies and especially wars that are wholly opposed to their interests. Not all expressions of the public are expressions of the public interest but public opinion does have the capacity to be an independent force in society representing the public interest. The public opinion tribunal, as Bentham conceives it, is a judicial body that judges and criticizes laws and policies, and while accommodating the views of the people generally, it is linked fairly directly to educated, critical opinion. This intelligent and critical opinion in society would tend to uphold Mill's own principle of liberty, and he would probably address his own essay to it in the first place.

On closer examination of Bentham's conception of public opinion, it is clear that the public tribunal was not conceived as a stultifying defender of dominant class interest that Mill sought to oppose. To assume that it was is to confuse the public opinion tribunal with the notion of "sinister begotten prejudice." Like

Marx, Bentham believed that the interests of the ruling class led to the formation of a superstructure of ideological mystification through which allegiance was obtained for policies that were actually opposed to the interests of the people. "Sinister begotten prejudice," for Bentham, would persist in a representative democracy, as those in power sought to protect their power and positions. Its force was limited by the general accountability of rulers to the ruled established through elections and by the influence of the public opinion tribunal. If Mill (following Tocqueville) believed that democracy led to the tyranny of the majority, Bentham saw the tyranny of the majority present in any regime through the force of sinister begotten prejudice. He also provided the theoretical framework for understanding how totalitarian states of the twentieth century could mobilize support, when its policies were not in the interests of those whose support is obtained. In these nondemocratic states, the tyranny of the majority can be even stronger than in the democracies criticized by Mill and Tocqueville.

Bentham did not give his attention solely to the protection of the people from the excesses and abuses of government, as he upheld the importance of privacy. In his defense of liberty of the press, for example, he proposed that in place of the current practice, where severe punishments were handed out for criticism of public officials and much smaller ones for defamation of private individuals, he would reverse the process so that the private individual would be secure against libel and defamation, but no punishment could be imposed for criticism of a public official except for false or groundless defamation.[35] Bentham proposed a strong legal framework to protect the liberty of the private individual, and he also proposed abolishing the numerous offenses that limited the freedom of consenting adults to enjoy unconventional pleasures so long as no harm was done to others.[36] Rather than see Mill's opposition to majority tyranny as a correction of or deviation from classical utilitarianism, it might better be seen as an important development within that tradition. Mill developed a new notion of social liberty that he welded to Bentham's idea of civil liberty as security and created the classic defense of the individual against the pressures of society.

NOTES

1. By "classical utilitarianism" I mean the utilitarian philosophy of Jeremy Bentham and, to a considerable extent, that of John Stuart Mill. In adopting this phrase I do not intend to suggest that Bentham was the first utilitarian or that the ideas presented here are those held by many contemporary moral philosophers. By presenting an historically accurate view of the most characteristic version of utilitarianism, I hope that some common though erroneous views, amounting to caricature, may be exposed and avoided.

2. See *Constitutional Code,* vol. 1, ed. F. Rosen and J. H. Burns, in *Collected Works of Jeremy Bentham* (hereinafter *CW*), J. H. Burns, J. R. Dinwiddy, and F. Rosen, gen. eds. (Oxford: Clarendon Press, 1983), 157–58, 317–21, 329–37.

3. Bentham Manuscripts, University College London (hereinafter UC), cxxvi. 8.

4. UC xxi. 192. See also F. Rosen, "Bentham's Constitutional Theory and the Greek Constitution of 1822," *Balkan Studies* 25 (1984), 31–54.

5. UC cvi. 393.

6. See this distinction used in *Deontology together with A Table of the Springs of Action and Article on Utilitarianism,* ed. A. Goldworth (Oxford: Clarendon Press, 1983), 249–81.

7. UC cvi. 393–94.

8. John Stuart Mill, "Utilitarianism," in *Essays on Ethics, Religion and Society,* ed. J. M. Robson in *Collected Works of John Stuart Mill* (hereinafter *CWM*), J. M. Robson, gen. ed., vol. 10 (Toronto: University of Toronto Press, 1969), 251. See F. Rosen, "Bentham and Mill on Liberty and Justice," in *Lives, Liberties and the Public Good, New Essays in Political Theory,* ed. G. Feaver and F. Rosen (London: Macmillan, 1987), 121–38.

9. For the fullest account of the theme of security in Bentham's thought, see G. J. Postema, *Bentham and the Common Law Tradition* (Oxford: Clarendon Press, 1986), 147ff; P. J. Kelly, *Utilitarianism and Distributive Justice: Jeremy Bentham and the Civil Law,* Ph.D. thesis, University of London, 1988, 121ff.

10. *Deontology, CW,* 309–10.

11. Ibid., 310.

12. Ibid.

13. Ibid., 309.

14. Most writers on utilitarianism assert that Bentham believed the right action to be that which produced the greatest amount of happi-

ness without regard to how it was distributed. This view has been challenged in F. Rosen, *Jeremy Bentham and Representative Democracy, A Study of the Constitutional Code* (Oxford: Clarendon Press, 1983), 211–20.

15. J. J. C. Smart, "An Outline of a System of Utilitarian Ethics," in *Utilitarianism, For and Against,* ed. J. J. C. Smart and B. Williams (Cambridge: Cambridge University Press, 1973), 69ff.

16. UC cxiii. 4, 6. See "Economy as Applied to Office" in *First Principles Preparatory to Constitutional Code,* ed. T. P. Schofield *CW* (Oxford: Clarendon Press, 1989), 3–122.

17. UC cxiii. 4.

18. See Carole Pateman, *Participation and Democratic Theory* (Cambridge: Cambridge University Press, 1970), 19–20.

19. J. Rawls, *A Theory of Justice* (Oxford: Clarendon Press, 1972), 221ff.

20. P. Schwartz, "Jeremy Bentham's Democratic Despotism," in *Ideas in Economics,* ed. R. D. Collison Black (London: Macmillan, 1986), 74–103.

21. See E. Halévy, *La formation du radicalisme philosophique,* 3 vols. (Paris, 1901–1904), trans. as *The Growth of Philosophic Radicalism,* trans. M. Morris (London: Faber and Faber, 1928). See F. Rosen, "Elie Halévy and Bentham's Authoritarian Liberalism," *Enlightenment and Dissent,* 6 (1987):59–76.

22. See J. Lively and J. Rees, eds. *Utilitarian Logic and Politics* (Oxford: Clarendon Press, 1978), 120.

23. See Montesquieu, *De l'Esprit des Lois* (1748), xi. 6; J. L. Delolme, *La Constitution de l'Angleterre* (1771).

24. See *Constitutional Code, CW* vol. 1, 41–42.

25. See Postema, *Bentham and the Common Law Tradition,* 218–62.

26. J. S. Mill, "Bentham," *CWM,* vol. 10, 106–7.

27. See J. S. Mill, "Remarks on Bentham's Philosophy," *CWM,* vol. 10, 16–17; "De Tocqueville on Democracy in America," in *Essays on Politics and Society,* ed. J. M. Robson, *CWM,* vol. 18 (Toronto: University of Toronto Press, 1977), 156, 175–78, 200.

28. "On Liberty," *CWM,* vol. 18, 219–20.

29. See F. Rosen, "Bentham and Mill on Liberty and Justice," *Lives, Liberties and the Public Good,* 122–26. For a different view, see D. G. Long, *Bentham on Liberty: Jeremy Bentham's Idea of Liberty in Relation to His Utilitarianism* (Toronto: University of Toronto Press, 1977), 115–18.

30. *A Comment on the Commentaries and A Fragment on Government* ed. J. H. Burns and H. L. A. Hart (London: Athlone Press, 1977), *CW,* 485.

31. See J. Steintrager, *Bentham* (London: Allen & Unwin, 1977), 97–116; F. Rosen, *Jeremy Bentham and Representative Democracy*, 195–199.

32. Cf. D. Thompson, *John Stuart Mill and Representative Government* (Princeton: Princeton University Press, 1976).

33. See *Constitutional Code CW*, vol. 1, 36.

34. See F. Rosen, *Jeremy Bentham and Representative Democracy*, 19–40.

35. Jeremy Bentham, *On the Liberty of the Press and Public Discussion* (London: William Hone, 1821), 12.

36. See L. Crompton, *Byron and Greek Love, Homophobia in Nineteenth-Century England* (London: Faber and Faber, 1985), 19ff, 251–83.

3

RIGHTS AND MAJORITIES:
ROUSSEAU REVISITED

JEREMY WALDRON

1.

The distinction between political theory and political philosophy often seems artificial. The two terms pick out much the same discipline pursued under the auspices of different academic departments. But one topic where there has been a considerable divergence of emphasis between political theorists and political philosophers—or between those who study political morality in philosophy departments and those who study it in departments of political science—is the topic of fundamental rights. Those who believe in rights hold the view that individuals and minorities have certain interests that they can press, certain claims they can make against the rest of the community that are entitled to respect without further ado. Of course this view is controversial: some believe that individuals and minorities have rights in this sense, others do not, and even among those who do consider-

I should like to thank Robert Cooter, John Chapman, Kristin Luker, Kim Scheppele, Philip Selznick, Susan Sterett, and Jackie Stevens for their help in discussing these issues. An earlier version of this chapter was read in the Department of Philosophy, State University of New York at Binghamton. I am grateful to the other participants for their comments and suggestions.

able disagreement exists about the nature of those rights. The divergence I am interested in, between political philosophers and political theorists, involves two different ways of characterizing that controversy.

For philosophers, the controversy has usually been characterized as a choice between individual rights and some version of utilitarian theory. They have taken the controversy to be one about justification. Is utilitarianism, as it claims to be, an adequate theory of political justification, or does it need to be supplemented (or indeed replaced) by an independently grounded theory of individual rights?

For political theorists, the contrast is characteristically not with utilitarianism but with majoritarian democracy. Political theorists are interested in forms of political decision making, and they take the argument to be about political legitimacy. Is there nothing that cannot be made legitimate by a majority decision? Or should we recognize limits, based on individual rights, on what a majority can commit a society to do?

The contrast between justification and legitimacy may appear bewildering at first, particularly since both are used here in a normative sense.[1] To ask whether a decision is justified is to ask whether it is, on the merits, the right decision; it is to look at the reasons weighing in favor of the course of action decided upon. To ask whether a decision is politically legitimate, however, is to raise a procedural question; it is to ask whether it was taken in the way such decisions ought to be taken.[2] We need a distinction between justification and legitimacy, particularly in a democratic context, because we need some way of distinguishing between the reasons voters have for voting as they do, and the reasons officials have for implementing a certain decision after the votes are counted. I may vote in a popular initiative for California to have a lower speed limit because I think saving lives matters more than fast cars; that is what I think about justification. But I believe the speed limit should stay as it is if most people in the state disagree with me; that is what I think about legitimacy. Clearly, the fact that the majority approves of something is not a good reason for someone to vote in its favor (indeed, if everyone voted on the basis of reasons like that—"I vote for what the majority thinks"—voting would collapse as a practice). Reasons for supporting a proposal of something are logically distinct from reasons for acting in politics on the basis of the fact that people support a proposal. Both are normative, but they capture different stages or levels of normativity in relation to political decision making.[3]

Rights, then, can be seen—and are seen characteristically by philosophers—as an issue in the theory of justification. And they can be seen—and are seen characteristically by political theorists—as located in the theory of legitimacy. In this chapter, I develop some ideas about the relation between these two ways of conceptualizing the issues. What is the relation between rights versus utility, on the one hand, and rights versus democracy, on the other?

2.

An obvious starting point is to ask about the connection between utilitarianism and majoritarian democracy. Do they in any sense amount to the same thing? When philosophers say that rights are "trumps" over utility (to use Ronald Dworkin's term), and political theorists say that rights are "trumps" over majoritarian democracy, are they in effect identifying the same target, the same suit, as it were, to be trumped?[4]

If you screw up your eyes and suspend a few critical questions, you can see a kind of connection. Suppose the votes cast on some issue represent individual preferences. Several alternative courses of action can be taken, and as good democrats we decide to adopt the course that attracts the greatest number of votes. That can sound a bit like trying to maximize the satisfaction in the constituency, under a familiar utilitarian formula. In both cases, the fact that a course of action promotes the satisfaction of some preference counts in its favor; and when it becomes apparent that not all preferences can be satisfied, we opt to satisfy as many of them as we possibly can, given the choice that we face. As democrats, we follow the will of the majority; as utilitarians, we try to promote the greatest happiness of the greatest number. The two may amount to the same thing if votes are a reliable guide to individual happiness.

Something along these lines laid the basis for the utilitarian theory of democracy put forward by Jeremy Bentham in his later years. Throughout his career, Bentham had adhered to the principle of utility, which he described in 1789 as "that principle which approves or disapproves of every action whatsoever, according to the tendency it has to augment or diminish the happiness of the party whose interest is in question . . . if that party be the community in general, then the happiness of the community: if a particular individual, then the happiness of that individual."[5] But Bentham was also a psychological egoist, and assumed that people always act to further their own satisfactions: they seek their own happiness and avoid their own pain. For a long time, he failed to face up to the implications of this egoism so far as those who made decisions in the name of the community were concerned. Considered in the abstract, a legislator's decisions affect the whole society, and so the standard of social utility is the appropriate criterion of justification. But considered from the legislator's point of view, the political choice represents an opportunity to augment or diminish his own happiness, and that is what Bentham's psychological theory predicts will matter to him. We should expect then that a legislator will always approve or disapprove of laws that affect the whole community according to their tendency to promote his own happiness, for that is the happiness of the party whose interest is—psychologically—in question.

The cruelest of Bentham's biographers have suggested that he confronted this difficulty only after years of having what he took to be his eminently sensible utilitarian proposals for legislative reform trashed by the legislators to whom they were sent. Slowly it dawned on him that maybe these people were not particularly interested in promoting the general happiness along the lines he suggested (though there were other explanations available that did not, in all modesty, occur to Bentham). So eventually he turned his mind to consider what political structures would have to be like to establish some reliable coincidence between the personal interest of the legislator and the general happiness of society (and some greater receptivity to schemes and proposals like his own).[6]

About 1817, almost thirty years after the publication of *An Introduction to the Principles of Morals and Legislation*, Bentham

began writing in favor of representative democracy based on
what he called "virtually universal" suffrage. He rejected direct
democracy on the Athenian model on the grounds that legislation required special skills, but opted for democratic accountability through general elections on the grounds—reminiscent
of Aristotle—that though it takes an expert cobbler to make a
shoe, the only person who can judge whether it pinches is the
person who wears it.[7] The idea was that each voter would express his opinion, based on experience, on whether this legislator's continuing in office was likely to benefit him, and the sum
of these opinions based on voters' self-interest would be a rough-
and-ready guide to whether the legislator's actions would in fact
promote the aggregate interest of the community. Since the
legislator was interested in remaining in office, he would have a
personal incentive to act in a way that would benefit those with
the power to decide his future.

It is a rough-and-ready theory indeed, and its difficulties are
plain enough. For one thing it faces problems of implementation exactly like those that evoked it in the first place. Representative democracy is a no more convincing deus ex machina than
a benevolent legislator. If people are egoists, why expect constitution writers to opt for a system of representative democracy?
(Remember Bentham was writing some fifty years before the
Second Reform Bill.) And if, by some happy chance, a representative system is set up, why should one expect people to sustain
it or to do what is necessary to prevent its corruption?[8]

Other difficulties concern the democratic process itself. If
decision making is egoistic and prospective, the utilitarian argument relies on the assumption that each voter is a good judge of
his own future self-interest. But on any account (including Bentham's) people are not reliably prudent. Their decisions about
savings reflect this, and one imagines that electoral decisions will
be similarly distorted in favor of overconsumption.[9] Moreover,
an electoral outcome can correspond only very roughly to a
social utility function. Voting cannot possibly be made to reflect
the intensity of the satisfaction or dissatisfaction anticipated by
individuals with respect to some law. Yet intensity of satisfaction
is a crucial dimension in the Benthamite hedonic calculus.[10]

Deeper difficulties also arise. As a predictive theory, Bentham's psychological eogism is almost certainly false. People, whether they are voters or politicians, do not make decisions purely on the basis of self-interest. They are occasionally (I think, often) motivated by their sympathies for others, their own perception of what would be conducive to the general good, or adherence to some other moral ideal. This sounds as though it ought to make things better, since it mitigates the centrifugal force of egoism in politics, but in fact it makes things worse for the Benthamite theory of democracy. So long as each voter decides on the basis of his own interest, some chance exists that a majority decision might correspond roughly to the aggregate happiness of society. But if large numbers are voting on the basis of what they think the aggregate happiness demands, then the whole thing falls apart. If some are voting that way and some are voting selfishly, adding those votes to one another is like adding chalk and cheese. And if all are voting selflessly, on the basis of their personal perceptions of the general welfare, then we have no aggregative reason for thinking that the majority decision tells us anything new at all. Aggregation over individual votes makes some sort of sense from the utilitarian point of view if votes represent individual preferences. But it makes no sense at all from that point of view if votes represent utilitarian opinions.

3.

It looks as though we might want to set up an ideal-typic contrast between two different models of democracy or democratic decision making. The first model is the Benthamite model, which I have already outlined and criticized. The important points about the Benthamite model are that individual votes represent individual satisfactions, and majority vote-counting approximates a social welfare function with individual satisfactions as its arguments.

I wish to contrast that with something I shall call the Rousseauian model of democratic decision making. The reference, of course, is to the discussion of the "general will" in books 2 and 4 of *The Social Contract*.[11] I am going to simplify in a way that will outrage scholars of Rousseau, but the detail of his work

is not what matters here. For my purpose, the important feature
is not Rousseau's distinction between democratic laws and democratic government, nor his preference for direct democracy
over representative institutions, but rather his views about what
citizens are doing when they cast their votes in a democratic
polity.

> When a law is proposed in the people's assembly, what is
> asked of them is not precisely whether they approve of the
> proposition or reject it, but whether it is in conformity with
> the general will which is theirs; each by giving his vote gives
> his opinion on this question, and the counting of votes
> yields a declaration of the general will. When, therefore,
> the opinion contrary to my own prevails, this proves only
> that I have made a mistake, and that what I believed to be
> the general will was not so.[12]

Ignore for the moment the presumption that the majority must
be right. The important point is that when voting the Rousseauian citizen is expressing an opinion about what the general
will requires (which on Rousseau's view, means what conduces
to the common good of all in society), an opinion that it makes
sense to assess as correct or mistaken.[13] If the individual vote is
different from the majority verdict, one of them, at least, must
be wrong. On the Benthamite model, however, an individual's
vote and the majority verdict can differ without any contradiction whatever. All it shows is that the individual in question may
not be among the "greatest number" whose satisfactions are to
be advanced.

That is the contrast I want. Bentham's voter is taken to be
expressing a preference of his own; his vote represents a possible individual satisfaction. Rousseau's voter is not supposed to
express his personal preference; rather he affirms his personal
belief about the best way to promote the general good. The
Benthamite political system sums votes as utilitarianism sums
satisfactions, while the Rousseauian political system counts votes
to determine the preponderance of opinion. What we have is
the divergence that Rousseau pointed to when he distinguished
between the general will and the will of all: "the general will

studies only the common interest while the will of all studies private interest, and is indeed no more than the sum of individual desires."[14]

A further question concerns what the general good, the proper object of individual voting, amounts to on the Rousseauian account. Are people supposed to be thinking utilitarian thoughts, thoughts about the greatest happiness of the greatest number, as they struggle to express the general will? Or are they, as Rousseau sometimes suggests, supposed to be turning their attention to the common good, that is, rules or practices that benefit everyone? The idea of the general good, and accordingly that of the general will, are vague enough to cover either of these criteria and a number of others besides. I want to leave this question open at this stage.[15]

It would be wrong to pretend that the ideal types of decision making defined here are ever to be found in pure form. But they may represent extremes on a spectrum. Given that democracies make social decisions functions of individual decisions, a theory of democracy is Benthamite to the extent that it takes individual decisions to represent personal satisfactions or interests and Rousseauian to the extent that it takes individual decisions to represent opinions or beliefs about the general good.

I have made a long detour away from the subject of rights. The question with which I began is whether the notion of rights as trumps over utility is in the end the same as the notion of rights as trumps over democracy. My answer is that they can be assimilated only to the extent that democractic decision making is seen as a Benthamite process, and even then the assimilation is fraught with difficulty. Still, if democracy is Benthamite, then right-based reasons for concern about certain utilitarian justifications may cash into right-based reasons for concern about certain democratic outcomes. But if democracy is more Rousseauian, then the idea of trumping democracy will be quite different from the idea of trumping utility, and we shall have to say rather more complicated things about the relation between them.

4.

It is time I said more about the idea of individual rights. In the first instance, the idea of rights is a claim about political justifications: it is, to be blunt, a claim that there are limits on what can be justified. In social and political life, individuals and groups inevitably will suffer disappointments, frustrations, losses, setbacks, defeats, and even harms of various sorts. No one can get everything he wants. Rights imply limits on the harms and losses that any individual or group may reasonably be expected to put up with; they indicate that certain losses and harms are simply not to be imposed on any individual or group for any reason. These are harms and losses that may not be traded off against a larger mass of lesser considerations in the way the utilitarian calculus allows. It follows, clearly enough, that rights impose constraints on the ends we may pursue and the means we may adopt in politics. Even for the sake of the greater happiness or the pursuit of some other noble goal, we must not impose the losses or inflict the harms that are specified. The job of rights is to stake out these limits.

So far, that is an abstract conception. It gains content when someone tells us what the limits are. And it becomes a theory when we are given an indication of why these losses and harms are not to be imposed, and why the reasons we might have for wanting to impose them are inadequate. The modern analysis of rights made an enormous leap forward when it was realized that talk about natural rights or human rights is not a way of giving those answers but a way of promising to give them.[16] As Richard Rorty put it, "to say that certain people have certain rights is merely to say that we should treat them in certain ways. It is not to give a *reason* for treating them in those ways."[17] The reasons will be rooted in some account of what is required as a minimum if individual men and women and individual communities are to have any prospect of flourishing or any chance at all of a decent life. A theory of rights will identify certain human interests—some related to freedom, others perhaps to other aspects of well-being—and show the moral importance of those interests receiving a guaranteed level of protection and satisfaction. Different theories will do this in different ways, and they will identify different, though usually overlapping, sets of interests as the proper objects of this special concern.

Rights are not a simple matter. We are used to thinking of them in terms of relatively simple slogans: "Free speech," "The free exercise of religion," "Due process," "Life, liberty, and property," "No cruel and unusual punishment," and so on. But, as the history of judicial debate on these matters strikingly illustrates, such ideas cannot be captured as easily as that. As the criterion of human flourishing and a decent life is complex and subtle, so the idea of what is required as its minimum condition will be accordingly complex and subtle. Most important, it is something on which people, even with the best will in the world, are likely to disagree. We must not confuse the enthusiasm that exists for certain slogans, the amendments to the 1787 U.S. Constitution, for example, with any deep consensus about what rights we have or what they really involve. Use of simple phrases and well-known formulations are perhaps inevitable in the politics of human rights, but it is in the deeper concerns and in the arguments that are associated with the formulations that we will find the substance of a particular theory. Certainly the more or less universal acceptance of a slogan as something to pledge allegiance to tells us little or nothing about the depth or the detail of political or moral consensus.[18]

When considering the tasks involved in the articulation of a theory of rights, and in its application to the real world, the notion that a right reflects a solid and unquestioned consensus becomes ludicrous. In a theory of rights, one has to give an account of the moral importance of some interest, and one has to address the relation between that account and other justificatory theories that might be deployed against it. There is possible moral conflict between rights and other considerations, or among rights themselves. People can certainly disagree about these matters without abandoning the idea of rights, and certainly without lapsing back into preoccupation with self-interest. We may be tempted to see trenchant and apparently irresolvable disagreements about rights as nothing more than disguised conflicts of interest. But the complexity of the subject gives excellent reason for resisting that temptation.

Above all the fact that a moral argument is subtle, complicated, difficult, and controversial does not mean it cannot be about rights. Though rights talk is customarily contrasted with certain styles of moral reasoning, for example, the sort of trade-off calculations that a consequentialist engages in, it still has a special complexity, and with it a controversial character of its own. We cannot evade these difficulties in any theory of justification: political life is messy in the moral demands that it generates.

These complexities and controversies give rise to serious questions about what we should do politically when advocates of rights disagree. So long as rights are merely an aspect of justificatory debate, complexity and controversy can thrive. Some will say that a certain social practice or decision violates rights, others will say that it does not, and they will argue back and forth in journals and class-rooms, in newspapers and caucuses, about what respect for rights requires. The real problems arise when some issue of rights is what we have to make a social decision about. For then we have to ask: Should this decision be made by a majority, as other social decisions are made? Or should it be made using some other principle of political legitimacy?

5.

I said earlier that political theorists think of rights, not merely as an aspect of the theory of political justification, but as part of the theory of legitimate decision making. Certain decisions, they may say, are not to be taken on a majoritarian basis: there are certain things a majority must not do.

Sometimes these views about legitimacy follow straightforwardly from theories of justification. Thinkers such as Madison, Tocqueville, and John Stuart Mill, for example, held that if something done by a despot or an elite would count as tyranny, it would still be tyrannical when done in the name of a majority: "the power to do everything, which I should refuse to one of my equals, I will never grant to any number of them."[19] Some actions are so wrong that not even the principle of majority-rule can legitimate them.

Sometimes the conception of legitimacy is more procedural, however, and based on a concern for the decision-making process. John Hart Ely, for example, argues that rights are best understood as constraints designed to sustain, enhance, and facilitate the processes of representative democracy.[20] Between these poles of substance and procedure is a set of ideas about what is required to sustain the allegiance of all groups in society: What guarantees must be offered in order to prevent their secession or rebellion?[21]

Whatever the foundation of rights may be in a theory of political legitimacy, this question arises: How are we actually to prevent the decisions that rights prohibit? If we believe that there can be no justification for imposing certain harms or losses on individuals, or if we believe that imposition of certain harms or losses must be prevented to protect the integrity of the democratic process or to sustain the allegiance of all sections of society, how are these results to be brought about? To say that rights impose limits on political legitimacy is so far mere talk. How can that talk be translated into appropriate political outcomes?

In the United States, it is natural to think immediately of institutionalizing rights as constraints on political decision making. The Bill of Rights lays it down as a matter of principle that certain laws are not to be passed and certain official actions are not to be tolerated. The courts have taken it upon themselves to declare when these principles are violated and to nullify the application of any law or official regulation that falls foul of them. And these determinations are now accepted as authoritative within the political system and in the country at large. Rights-based constraint on democratic decision-making is now established as a working political practice.

It is perhaps more difficult to see that these institutionalizations are not the only or the inevitable upshots of the arguments about legitimacy. We tend to think that those who express concern about the dangers of the tyranny of the majority or about the threat to individual or minority rights must be proposing something like a Bill of Rights enforced by judges as the institutional prescription. The proposal is understandable given the ambiguity of the word "rights," which is used sometimes to characterize moral arguments and sometimes to depict arrangements of positive law. But it is not a necessary move at all.

Institutional solutions other than a Bill of Rights may be enter-
tained: for example, Madison opted for checks and balances
and the separation of powers, not for a Bill of Rights in any
shape or form.[22]

Consider also the noninstitutional alternatives. John Stuart
Mill proclaimed adherence to a principle of individual liberty
that was "entitled to govern absolutely the dealings of society
with the individual in the way of compulsion and control," and
he expressed his fear of "an increasing inclination to stretch
unduly the powers of society over the individual both by the
force of opinion and even by that of legislation."[23] But his
remedy was not to set up institutional checks and balances or
embody his harm principle in a Bill of Rights. Instead, the aim
of his work was to educate public opinion about the importance
of respecting individual liberty.

> The disposition of mankind, whether as rulers or as fellow
> citizens, to impose their own opinions and inclinations as a
> rule of conduct on others is so energetically supported by
> some of the best and some of the worst feelings incident to
> human nature that it is hardly ever to be kept under re-
> straint by anything but want of power; and as the power is
> not declining, but growing, *unless a strong barrier of moral
> conviction can be raised against the mischief,* we must expect, in
> the present circumstances of the world to see it increase.
> [emphasis added][24]

Mill's analysis of the main threat to individuality is similar:

> The combination of all these causes forms so great a mass
> of influences hostile to individuality that it is not easy to see
> how it can stand its ground. It will do so with increasing
> difficulty *unless the intelligent part of the public can be made to
> feel its value*—to see that it is good there should be differ-
> ences, even though not for the better, even though, as it
> may appear to them, some should be for the worse. [em-
> phasis added][25]

Admittedly, the target of Mill's concern was as much the
tyranny of public opinion as majoritarian legislation, and so far

as the former is concerned of course only moral restraint can be effective. But Mill seems to have believed, and I think quite properly, that a change in public opinion was necessary to protect individual interests from legal and political attack. "Unless a strong barrier of moral conviction" can be raised in favor of the idea of individual rights, "unless the intelligent part of the public [Mill's audience] can be made to see its value," then individual liberty and with it social progress would be swept aside by the legal and social pressures of mass society.

6.

Something like the sort of consensus that Mill was seeking to create or evoke is probably necessary anyway, even if institutional constraints are the main line of defense. The point is the same as one noted earlier about Bentham's theory of democracy. Institutional constraints and Bills of Rights do not appear magically out of the air; they have to be politically agreed upon and instituted like every other legal and political arrangement. Once instituted, they must be accepted, respected and enforced; otherwise they will be what Madison referred to as "a mere demarcation on parchment," which, as the constitutional experience of most of the regimes in the world demonstrates, is no protection whatever against tyranny and oppression.[26]

It is tempting to say that institutional constraints of right, and constitutional provisions generally, must command unanimous support, for it is their job to set the terms on which majoritarian competition is subsequently to take place. In pure theory, that looks attractive. The constitutional framework can be presented as the terms of a social contract based on the consent of all, and then, within that framework and according to those terms, subsequent political disagreements are to be resolved by procedures, such as majority-rule, that are agreeable to everyone.[27]

But in practice we know it is impossible to secure unanimous agreement on anything, and certainly not on a topic as divisive as individual rights. Even so, to be institutionalized and sustained, a Bill of Rights must command some sort of consensus, at least at a superficial level. Certainly it will need wide public support, directly or indirectly, to be enacted and to last for more than one or two administrations. This is reflected in the demanding provision made for constitutional amendment. Once we see that the decision to institute constraints of right is itself a political decision, we see the possibility and indeed maybe the necessity for the majority, at least on some occasions, willingly to embrace restraints on its collective power.

It follows that any theory that holds that the majority is always liable to abuse its power cannot be used as an argument in favor of a Bill of Rights. This theory would be too pessimistic, for it would preclude the possibility of a majority ever initiating and sustaining institutional constraints on itself, except by accident. Any theorist of rights who is at all optimistic about the possibility of protecting rights in a democratic system has to rest his hopes in the last resort on being able to convince a sufficient number of his fellow citizens, at least on occasion and probably consistently, that respect for rights is important.

7.

I distinguished earlier between Benthamite and Rousseauian conceptions of democratic decision making: a Benthamite voter votes according to his own interest, while a Rousseauian votes what he thinks the general good requires. But in section 3, the question of what the phrase "the general good" means in the Rousseauian model was left unresolved.

Whatever the general good is supposed to mean for Rousseau or anyone attracted to this model of democracy, it must surely represent an adequate basis of justification. When voters turn their minds to the general good, when they try to express through their votes the general will, they must aspire to make political decisions that are just. This means, among other things, that they aspire to make political decisions that strike a proper balance between the interests of the various members of society. If the issue affects interests that may appropriately be dealt with in an aggregative way, then they will seek a utilitarian verdict. But if it concerns interests that have the special importance associated with rights, then they aim for a decision that is sensitive to that special importance.

In other words, if the philosophical theorist of rights is correct at the level of political justification, then social utility cannot always be the appropriate object of the general will. Certain things must not be done, even in the name of social utility, and each person's thinking about the general good, each person's Rousseauian decision making, will, it is hoped, reflect that consideration.

This is an important difference between Benthamite and Rousseauian conceptions of democracy. In Benthamite democracy, individual votes represent nothing more than individual satisfactions; they express nothing at all about the proper balance that is to be struck between the individual and society. Any concerns about that balance have got to be, as it were, external to the voting process. But in Rousseau's model, votes already deliver an opinion about the proper balance between the two. Weighing is intrinsic to what is going on in the individual voter's decision. There might, therefore, be some greater difficulty in justifying external institutional constraints of right in a Rousseauian democracy, because rights should be taken account of by citizens as a matter of course.

It is no good to say, in a hard-headed spirit, that Rousseau's model is too idealistic, and that pragmatically it makes more sense to assume that people will vote and behave politically as Bentham predicted. As discussed in section 6, that cannot be true all the time or there would be no hope of ever actually institutionalizing the constraints of right that this very model cries out for. And we know anyway, from our own experience of politics, that it is *not* true much of the time. People often vote on the basis of what they think is the general good of society. They are concerned about the deficit, or about abortion, or about Nicaragua, in a way that reflects nothing more about their own personal interests than that they have a stake in this country.[28] Similarly, they often vote in a way that takes into account their conception of the special importance of certain interests and liberties. They vote in a way that is sensitive to the idea of rights as they understand it, rather than merely on the basis of what they take to be their own self-interest. If one wants to be a hard-headed "realist" in politics, one should follow the evidence where it leads, and not simply assume selfish motivations when experience reveals that they are in play only some of the time.

In particular, though it is certain that voters behave in a Benthamite fashion some of the time and in a Rousseauian fashion some of the time, we have no evidence to support any correlation of this pattern with the distinction between those areas where we have and those areas where we do not have institutional constraints of right. There is no evidence at all to suggest that the issues covered by the Bill of Rights, for example, are issues on which people would otherwise be most likely to vote in a Benthamite way. My hunch is that the contrary is true. When they are given the chance, these are issues on which voters are least likely to be Benthamite, precisely because these are areas where we as a society have had some measure of success in "raising the strong barriers of moral conviction" that Mill talked about. Voters and their representatives are deeply aware that these are matters they should not be deciding purely by consulting their own interests.[29]

8.

For voters to ask themselves in Rousseauian fashion what the general good of the society requires is one thing; it is quite another for them to agree about that. Even if "the general good" were interpreted in a utilitarian way, we should expect disagreement, because people have varying beliefs, different information, and differential capacities to engage in complex consequential calculations. Indeed, one of the hopes held out for the Benthamite model of democracy is that voting outcomes would provide information about aggregate welfare that would otherwise be unavailable to a student of social utility.

I hope the argument in section 4 established that voters are also likely to disagree about individual rights, even if they all take them seriously, even if they all turn their minds conscientiously in that direction. The contents of particular rights, relations between rights and other moral considerations, and relations among rights generate issues of explanation, defense, and moral and political reasoning that are unlikely to yield any easy consensus through political deliberation. On any particular issue of right, several conflicting conceptions are bound to emerge, each attracting adherents who try to persuade the others as the debate goes along.

It is possible that these disagreements are driven by underlying conflicts of interest, but that is unlikely to be the case in any straightforward sense. People disagree about the proper scope of free speech in modern society, even when their own interests are not at stake. Or, if their interests are at stake, those interests cannot be understood in Benthamite terms because they are informed by the perceived importance, at a social and political level, of certain values and principles that define their social role. Think, for example, of a journalist protecting his sources, or a priest arguing for a particular conception of First Amendment freedoms.

The abortion debate provides a striking example. The moral issues involved in the question of whether abortion should be permitted and facilitated are almost intractably contentious, because they involve deep, subtle, and challenging questions about the way we value life and its relation to the way we value autonomy and individual control. No one but a moral idiot thinks the issue is easily resolved, and so we do not have to appeal to any underlying conflict of interests to explain the depth and intensity of this particular row over rights. True, some have tried to frame the issue as a conflict of interest between the sexes. But that is simplistic. When more perceptive accounts have been given of the motivations of the contestants, the interests they have at stake are revealed as deep and clashing world views, about the ideal forms of individuality, procreation, sexuality, lifestyle, and social structure. Though it is easy to categorize the pro-choice and pro-life activists as "interest-groups," it is pretty clear that the issue between them is more a Rousseauian disagreement about the basic principles of social life than a Benthamite clash of different and incompatible claims to satisfaction.[30]

9.

When society divides on the existence, meaning, or limits of some individual right, as it almost always does, what is to be done? What ought to happen in a democracy, when the voters, having asked themselves Rousseauian questions and addressed them conscientiously, come up with different answers? Presumably the rival views will attract different degrees of popular support, and there may be one view that attracts more support than any of the others. Is this the one that should prevail?

The question is hard to answer. At least one of the traditional arguments in favor of majority rule does not work in Rousseau's model. But it is also important to see that the traditional objection to majority rule, the worry about the tyranny of the majority, does not apply either.

The traditional argument in favor of majority rule that does not work in a Rousseauian context is, of course, the Benthamite argument. As long as votes represent individual satisfactions, then a rough utilitarian argument favors trying to satisfy as many of them as possible. Since each vote represents a possible satisfaction, and since the aim is to maximize satisfaction, then each vote provides in itself an independent reason for action. But if votes offer opinions about the general good, including opinions about how satisfactions should be pursued and distributed in society, then no such maximizing reason for acting in accordance with the preponderance of opinion exists. A view that something should be done is not in itself a reason for doing it. Do not say that acting in accordance with the greatest preponderance of opinion is at least a way of maximizing the amount of satisfaction that people get from having their opinions acted on. The people concerned may well regard *those* satisfactions as in themselves quite trivial in comparison to the issues, including the issues of satisfaction, that form the subject matter of their opinions.

Rousseau's own comments on the matter are sketchy and unsatisfactory. In one passage he argues that unanimity is the mark of the general will and that "the more . . . that public opinion approaches unanimity, the more the general will is dominant; whereas long debates, dissensions and disturbances bespeak the ascendance of particular interests."[31] But as we have just seen, this is a mistake given the difficulty of even the most fundamental issues to which public opinion must speak. Rousseau did acknowledge that unanimity is no guarantee that citizens are genuinely addressing themselves to issues of the general good. "Fear and flattery," he said, "can change voting into acclamation; people no longer deliberate, they worship or they curse."[32] The "will-of-all" can also be unanimous.

Rousseau's settled position appears to have been this: *if* there is disagreement, and *if* in spite of that disagreement you can be sure that citizens are nevertheless addressing the issue of the general good, then, "the votes of the greatest number always bind the rest." He went on immediately to say that "this is a consequence of the [original social] contract itself."[33] But that remark is obscure. I can see nothing in Rousseau's earlier analysis of the social contract to which it could be a reference.

The only convincing argument in favor of majority rule consistent with Rousseau's thinking is the argument developed by Condorcet: if voters are independently addressing a question, that is susceptible to a right and a wrong answer, and if the average probability of each voting for the correct answer is greater than 0.5, then the probability that the answer determined for the group by a majority procedure will be correct tends to certainty as group size increases.[34] Recently Condorect's theorem has been presented as an explanation for Rousseau's conviction that the general will would usually emerge from majority voting.[35] But the application of the theorem must be tempered by Condorcet's own view that, independently, as group size increases, the average individual competence is likely to decline and to have fallen well below 0.5 before one reaches even the size of a citizen assembly in a small Rousseauian *polis*.[36] And, of course, the theorem implies that if average competence is below 0.5, then the chances of the majority being right decline to zero as group size increases.

Maybe something about the dynamics of argument can sustain average competence at a level where Condorcet's theorem produces favorable results. When a proposal is first mooted, some people will be for it and others against it. At this stage the distribution is random; there is no reason to think that the side that happens to have the largest number of supporters is correct. But suppose a debate now ensues, and people on both sides try to convince their opponents with arguments. If the issue is one where rational argument is possible, and if the people involved in the debate are susceptible to rational argu-

ment and immune to mere rhetoric ("fear and flattery" as Rousseau puts it) and not motivated by particularistic interest, then
we would expect that at the end of the debate the chances of
any given person arriving at a correct answer would be greatly
enhanced. We should not think that this violates the independence condition on Condorcet's theorem. Provided that the
probability of each individual's reaching a correct decision can
be determined independently at the end of the deliberation and
before the votes are cast, what that probability is a result of does
not matter in the least.

Though there are no knock-down arguments in favor of majority rule in a Rousseauian polity, it is important to see that the
traditional objections to, and misgivings about, majority-rule are
almost entirely inappropriate in this context. The justificatory
burden is to that extent lighter.

The most common misgiving is that in democratic decision
making, minorities or individuals may suffer oppression at the
hands of a majority. That is an acute danger where the votes of
those who compose the differing factions represent the particular interests or satisfactions of the voters. In that case, for a
majority to prevail means nothing more than that the interests
of the minority are sacrificed to those of the larger group. But
nothing similar need happen between majorities and minorities
in the Rousseauian case. There, each vote represents an individual opinion on a matter of common concern including, where
appropriate, an opinion on the proper balance to be maintained
among the various individual and minority interests. Nothing
tyrannical happens to me merely by virtue of the fact that my
opinion is not acted on. Provided that the opinion that is acted
upon takes my interests, along with everyone else's, properly
into account, the fact that the opinion is not mine is not in itself
a threat to my freedom or well-being.

Of course, if I disagree with the majority, I will not think that
all interests have been properly taken into account or that the
general good is being correctly discerned. And I may think
consequently that a serious threat to my interests is posed. But
that need not be the subject of the disagreement. If all parties
are approaching the decision in a Rousseauian spirit, the issues
on which they disagree need not reflect differential levels of

concern for their own respective interests. It is true that *A* may differ from *B* and *C* about the proper regard that is due *A*'s interests; but *A* may also differ from B and C about the proper regard that is due *B*'s interests. He may think that *B* and *C*, the majority, are underestimating the importance of some interest they have but he lacks.

An example may help. Many women dissent from the feminist position on gender equality and independence, and some men do not. Suppose those of both sexes who are sympathetic to the feminist position happen to be in a minority. Then some members of the minority, the "feminist" men, may describe the disagreement by saying that some people in the majority, nonfeminist women, are not paying sufficient regard to their own interest in freedom and well-being.

The more important point is this. Even if the issue on which A, the minority, differs from *B* and *C* is the proper level of respect due *A*'s interest, there is no reason to take *A*'s view of the matter any more seriously or think it any more likely to be correct than the opinion shared by *B* and *C*. Again, with the proviso that all are approaching the matter in a Rousseauian spirit. The majority is not necessarily right, but on a matter concerning the rights of minorities it is not necessarily wrong either. Indeed, as I remarked in section 6, the majority could not always or typically be wrong about such matters, or we would have no hope of ever getting political respect for the rights of minorities.

What respect, then, is owed to minority opinion in a Rousseauian polity? The provocative answer is none at all, so far as political action is concerned. If there is some sort of argument for the legitimacy of majoritarianism and if votes really do represent opinions on the proper balance of interest in society and not interests themselves, then the majority view should simply prevail, and the minority regard their view as defeated. Since it is defeat in a debate about a matter of common concern, not in a struggle of interests, they should be able to reconcile themselves without much difficulty.

But the response is a little glib. Respect is owed to minority opinions as opinions. They should be aired in debate, and be given an effective opportunity to win supporters. And they should not be suppressed after the debate, either, because the citizenry may have to consider the matter again sometime and because liberal respect is owed to people simply as the proponents of opinions. Both from the point of view of the general good, and from the point of view of respect for persons, dissident thinking should be tolerated. But toleration is not the same as allowing an opinion to prevail to any extent. It is one thing to allow an opinion to exist and do its work in argumentation, quite another to allow it to be decisive or even to operate as a vector in political action.

Again the difference in significance between minority opinions as Rousseau conceives them and minority interests in a Benthamite democracy is striking. In a Benthamite world, proponents of rights want minority interests to prevail and to be decisive to a greater extent than the utilitarian calculus would allow. If I have a right to emigrate, then my interest in choosing whether or not to emigrate is to prevail even though social utility might be promoted by denying it. In this respect, rights are like vetoes; or to put it another way, they make individuals dictators on the issues they cover. In a Rousseauian democracy there may still be rights, but since they are the subject matter of individual opinions, they should never be identified with the individual opinions. There is no case then for allowing minority opinions to prevail, though individual opinions may and probably will make a case, a moral case, for allowing certain minority interests to prevail. In both types of democracy, of course, individual voting must be protected; in the Benthamite model, individuals must be allowed to assert their interests, and in Rousseauian democracy, individuals must be allowed to voice their opinions. But in addition, in the Benthamite model, certain individual voices must be allowed to prevail despite the fact that they are in the minority; in the Rousseauian model such a requirement is not needed.

10.

I started thinking about these issues by pondering a question almost everyone interested in constitutional law asks sooner or later. When the people of a state, several million of them, have addressed an issue, directly or through their representatives, and passed a law on something they take to be a matter of public importance, what is the justification for allowing a handful of judges to second-guess their deliberations and strike down their law? Many of the proposed justifications turned out to be unsatisfactory.

It is because the courts are a forum of principle, we are told, and they sustain and uphold the importance of principle in our political process.[37] But does anyone deny that a voter or a legislator is as capable of acting on principle as a judge? For example, does anyone seriously think that the legislators of Texas were not, at least by their own lights, acting on principle when they passed the laws that were struck down in *Roe v. Wade*?[38] They disagreed with the principled reasoning of a majority in the Supreme Court, of course, but in an area as troublesome as abortion, it is ludicrous to infer from the fact of disagreement that only one body could be alive to issues of principle.

Much the same can be said about the claim that review by a tiny elite is necessary to protect individual and minority rights. That sounds plausible only so long as it is reasonable to think that proper regard will not be paid to individual rights in the democratic and representative processes. If we view the political process in a Benthamite light we will jump quickly to that conclusion. But if we accept that voters and legislators are as obsessed with rights as everyone else in this country, we may incline to a more Rousseauian outlook. If voters and legislators are capable, as they undoubtedly are, of at least sometimes focusing their deliberations on the general good, and on some sense of the proper balance that should be held among individual interests in society, and if those deliberations sometimes inform their political decision making, then by instituting a practice of judicial review, we are allowing the opinions of the people on a certain matter to be overridden by the opinions of nine judges on exactly the same matter for no better reason than . . . well, what?

Is it that the judges are wiser and have a better understanding of the general good and of this proper balance than the people or their representatives? Do not say that they know more about the law. One of the issues at stake here is whether there should be a body of judicial doctrine on these matters. We allow majority voting by judges without regard to their comparative wisdom. What is the justification for denying the benefit of that decision procedure to the mass of others who may have thought as honestly and as high-mindedly about the issues as the judges have?

A third, unconvincing response is to point to the defects in the democratic and representative process. There are all sorts of concerns about electoral systems, political corruption, difficulties in voter registration, districting, and in general the very considerable looseness that exists between the popular will and its representation in state and federal legislatures. The concerns are legitimate, of course. But it is hard to see why giving a veto to a handful of judges is the appropriate remedy, that is, it is hard to see why that is not simply a way of making matters worse. We cannot justify one defect in the democratic system simply by pointing to others.

A fourth argument is one we have touched on already. Even if judicial review is not an appropriate way of ameliorating defects in the democratic process, it may nevertheless be a way of keeping the process open and ensuring that all have access to the public forum. Rights such as free speech, for example, do not so much cut across the ordinary processes of democracy. Rather they embody democratic values in themselves, and they help to ensure that our system remains true to its own procedural aspirations.[39] The argument is a good one. We have already seen it urged in favor of rights in a theory of legitimacy. But for the reasons I have been outlining, it does not necessarily make a case for judicial intervention. It is true that the processes of democracy must be sustained and policed, but this is something with which citizens and their representatives should be concerned. Just as they are capable of considering matters of principle that go beyond their own personal interests, so they are capable of taking care of the integrity of the democratic process that goes beyond the particular purposes for which that process is being used from time to time. A concern for the fairness and integrity of the process is something that Rousseau's ideal citizen will exhibit along with everything else. He does not need a judge to do it for him. As far as I can see, the only argument that justifies the role of courts in Rousseau's conception of politics is to see them essentially as participants in, and facilitators of, democratic political debate.[40]

Though we talk easily enough about democracy and the emergence of a majority view, we should remember that political debate is not always something that simply happens. Sometimes the impetus comes from the people and arises out of their experience and concerns. But often what happens is that a subject is raised first by some small interest or pressure group and only becomes a real issue for national political debate when the rest of the community is forced to take notice of it. This may happen through skillful politicking, or as a result of symbolic protest or mass demonstrations that are difficult to ignore. That, for example, is how the Campaign for Nuclear Disarmament and other peace groups in Britain and Europe forced the issue of nuclear weapons onto the political agenda. In a system with something like a Bill of Rights, it may also come about through litigation. An issue that might otherwise have remained a marginal minority concern can be imposed on the attention of society as a whole by being brought before a court connected to some human right that in the abstract at least enjoys widespread support.

The clearest illustration of this process is the campaign in the 1950s and 1960s for civil rights and desegregation in the United States. Without a Bill of Rights, the issue of school desegregation might well have remained an irritant in the local politics of the South. By bringing it before the Supreme Court and by raising questions in that forum about whether segregation was compatible with the constitutional guarantee of "equal protection," civil rights leaders were able to initiate a campaign and a debate that changed the face of racial politics in America. And certainly, there is no doubt at all that, as Ronald Dworkin puts it, the debate "would not have had the character it did but for the fact and symbolism of the Court's decisions."[41]

But although it is true that their decisions sometimes drive citizens to confront issues they may have wished to avoid, the Supreme Court's role in this process should not be exaggerated. I think that Ronald Dworkin is wrong when he argues that

judicial review "forces political debate to include argument over
principle," as though principles would naturally be absent from
debate without the Court's intervention.[42] We have already seen
that people are perfectly capable of thinking in principled terms;
they do not need judges to teach them to do it. Or, if there is a
case for saying that principles have tended to drop out of electoral politics, it is mainly a self-fulfilling prophecy. If we say to
each other often enough that courts are the forums of principle,
and legislatures and elections are simply processes in which
interests confront one another in an unprincipled way, then we
may end up with legislators and voters who answer to this
denigration of their political performance. If we insist that politics is about principle at every stage in the process, then the case
for giving special authority to the courts to look after individual
rights looks much less convincing.

11.

The upshot of my argument is that we should revise the way we
think about rights to accomodate the possibility, perhaps the
certainty, that voters and representatives in a democratic system
will approach their responsibilities in a Rousseauian spirit. If we
accept that as a reality, we should recognize that rights may
already be weighed in majoritarian decision making. If so, the
standard opposition between the democratic process and rights
as external institutional constraints would have to be discarded.
The concept of rights as trumps does make sense, at the level of
justification, in relation to aggregate utility, and it also makes
sense at the level of decision making in relation to Benthamite
democracy. But at that level it does not make sense in relation
to Rousseauian democracy, for there everything relevant to political justification may already have been considered. Trumps
cannot trump trumps, and trumps may already have been played
in Rousseauian democratic deliberation.

  We do not know, of course, and often we cannot tell, when
political decision making is Benthamite and when it is Rousseauian. Often it will be mixed, and sometimes in the minds of
individual voters the two modes are hopelessly entangled. I
have insisted (section 7) only that electoral and legislative deci-

sion making is sometimes Rousseauian, and that it is not uniformly or predictably Benthamite in those cases where external constraints of right are usually imposed. So long as this is the case, we should not think of individual rights and majoritarian democracy as necessarily antithetical to one another.

Let me end with a final comment in the spirit of Rousseau. We should perhaps take more seriously than we do the element of insult involved when a people or its representatives are told that they are incapable of making good laws, or that the laws they make must be subject to review by a specialist judicial elite. People fought long and hard in this country as well as Europe for the right to participate in politics on roughly equal terms. It cannot be that they were fighting purely in a Benthamite spirit to have their interests taken into account along with everyone else's, though of course that was important. They were also fighting to be allowed a say in the shaping of a good society, of the community in which they in common with others were to make their lives—to have their opinion count for something on such matters. They wanted to be able to address the great questions of the general good, including the question of the balance of individual rights and the integrity of the process in which they were protected, and not have those issues snatched away from them on the grounds that they are not fit to deal with them. They wanted to embark on the great art of legislation, not to be confined by constitutional constraints to petty, pork-barrel politics.

It is sobering to detect the similarity between many of the arguments in favor of external constraints of right and the arguments that were traditionally advanced for aristocracy and against democratic forms of government. Plato, for example, despaired deeply of the capacity of the common people and their chosen leaders to understand and address the issue of justice.[43] If, despite our democratic pretensions, we see politics as a Benthamite contest, if we remove issues of right from the jurisdiction of the people and pass them to judges, it is presumably because we share this pessimism of the ancients. What I have wanted to argue is that nothing in the idea of rights warrants this animus against democracy.

NOTES

1. I am not using "legitimacy" in the Weberian sense of something that as a matter of fact is widely approved of and accepted as valid: see Max Weber, *Economy and Society* (Berkeley: University of California Press, 1968), 31–38.

2. My distinction between justification and legitimacy is similar to Ronald Dworkin's distinction between justice and fairness in *Law's Empire* (Cambridge: Harvard University Press, 1986), 177–78.

3. This surely is part of the solution to the famous "paradox of democracy": Richard Wollheim, "A Paradox in the Theory of Democracy," in *Philosophy, Politics and Society,* ed. Peter Laslett and W. G. Runciman, 2d series (Oxford: Basil Blackwell, 1969), 153–67.

4. Ronald Dworkin, *Taking Rights Seriously* (London: Duckworth, 1977), ix; see also Ronald Dworkin, "Rights as Trumps," in *Theories of Rights,* ed. Jeremy Waldron, (Oxford: Oxford University Press, 1984), 153–67.

5. Jeremy Bentham, *Introduction to the Principles of Morals and Legislation,* ed. J. Burns and H. L. A. Hart (London: Methuen, 1982), chap. 1, secs. 2–3 12.

6. See the discussion in David Lieberman, "Historiographical Review: From Bentham to Benthamism," *The Historical Journal* 28 (1985), 199–217.

7. The analogy is found in a Bentham manuscript in the University College collection in London; my source is Ross Harrison's excellent discussion in *Bentham* (London: Routledge & Kegan Paul, 1983), 209. (Chap. 8 of Harrison's book is a superb discussion of Bentham's democratic theory.) Cf. Aristotle, *The Politics,* translated by T. A. Sinclair (Harmondsworth: Penguin Books, 1962), book 3, Chap. 11, 125: "There are tasks of which the actual doer is not either the best or the only judge . . . it is the diner not the cook who pronounces upon the merits of the dinner."

8. See the discussion in Harrison, *Bentham,* 215–23.

9. For a modern discussion, see Samuel Brittan, "The Economic Contradictions of Democracy," *British Journal of Political Science,* 5 (1975): 135–61.

10. The classic discussion is Robert Dahl, *A Preface to Democratic Theory* (Chicago: University of Chicago Press, 1956), 48.

11. Jean-Jacques Rousseau, *The Social Contract,* trans. Maurice Cranston (Harmondsworth: Penguin Books, 1968).

12. Ibid., book 4, chap. 2, 153.

13. Ibid., book 2, chaps. 3–4, 72–76.

14. Ibid., book 2, chap. 3, 72.

15. The point is taken up again in section 7 of this chapter. For the differences between conceptions such as "general good," "common good," "social good," "public interest," and "the good of all," see Brian Barry, *Political Argument* (London: Routledge & Kegan Paul, 1965), Chaps. 11–15. See also John Rawls, *A Theory of Justice* (Oxford: Oxford University Press, 1971), 61 ff.

16. Much of the impetus here come from Bentham's critique of natural rights: see Jeremy Waldron, *Nonsense Upon Stilts: Bentham, Burke and Marx on the Rights of Man* (London: Methuen, 1987), 36 ff.

17. Richard Rorty, "Solidarity or Objectivity?," in *Post-Analytic Philosophy*, ed. John Rajchman and Cornel West (New York: Columbia University Press, 1985), 14. I am grateful to Jeffrey Lange for this reference.

18. For the claim that acceptance of the slogan represents consensus on a certain concept, and that it tells us little about the detailed conception of particular rights, see Ronald Dworkin, *Taking Rights Seriously*, 134–36.

19. Alexis de Tocqueville, *Democracy in America* (New York: Arlington House, 1835–40) part 1, chap. 15, 249. See also Alexander Hamilton, James Madison, and John Jay, *The Federalist Papers*, No. 10 (New York: Mentor Books, 1961), 77 ff; and John Stuart Mill, *On Liberty* (Indianapolis: Bobbs Merrill, 1956), 6 ff.

20. John Hart Ely, *Democracy and Distrust: A Theory of Judicial Review* (Cambridge: Harvard University Press, 1980).

21. See, for example, Robert Dahl, "Procedural Democracy," in *Philosophy, Politics and Society*, eds. Peter Laslett and James Fishkin, 5th series (Oxford: Basil Blackwell, 1979), 97–133.

22. See Hamilton, Madison, and Jay, *The Federalist Papers* no. 47, 300 ff.

23. Mill, *On Liberty*, chap. 1, 13, 18.

24. Ibid., chap. 1, 18.

25. Ibid., chap. 3, 90.

26. Hamilton, Madison, and Jay, *The Federalist Papers* No. 48, 313.

27. For a modern contractarian argument along these lines, see Rawls, *A Theory of Justice*, 221–34.

28. Of course, what people think about the general good will be colored by their own experiences and concerns. But it is surprising (from a cynical view) how often one's expression even of one's own particular concerns (as a parent or as a member of a labor union or as a farmer) is already qualified to take account of what is thought

to be its proper relation to other interests in society and the general good. I am grateful to Philip Selznick for discussions on this question.

29. It is worth noting Ronald Dworkin's argument that the areas covered by rights are the areas where individual voting is most likely to be dominated by external rather than personal preferences—the areas where voting is least likely to conform to the pure Benthamite model. (Dworkin does not adduce any evidence for this, and it is not clear whether it is supposed to be an empirical claim or a normative claim about the proper function of rights.) Dworkin's theory diverges from mine, however, in his insistence that external preferences dominant in a decision process are a reason in favor of setting up institutional constraints of right. See Ronald Dworkin, *Taking Rights Seriously*, 231–38, 275–76, and 357–59. See also Dworkin's essay "Rights as Trumps," 153.

30. See Kristin Luker, *Abortion and the Politics of Motherhood* (Berkeley: University of California Press, 1984), esp. chaps. 7–8.

31. Rousseau, *The Social Contract*, book 4, chap. 2, 151.

32. Ibid., book 4, chap. 2, 152.

33. Ibid., book 4, chap. 2, 153.

34. Marquis de Condorcet, "Essay on the Application of Mathematics to the Theory of Decision-Making," in *Condorcet: Selected Writings*, ed. Keith Michael Baker (Indianapolis: Bobbs Merrill, 1976), 33–70.

35. Bernard Grofman and Scott Feld, "Rousseau's General Will: A Condorcetian Perspective," *American Political Science Review*, 82 (1988), 567–76. See also: Brian Barry, "The Public Interest," in *Political Philosophy*, ed. Anthony Quinton (Oxford: Oxford University Press, 1967), 112–26.

36. Condorcet, "Essay on the Application of Mathematics," 49.

37. See, for example, Ronald Dworkin, *A Matter of Principle* (Cambridge: Harvard University Press, 1985), Chap. 2.

38. *Roe v. Wade* 410 U.S. 113, 93 S. Ct. 705 (1973).

39. See Ely, *Democracy and Distrust*, esp. Chaps. 4–6.

40. The role might be analogous to that of "the lawgiver" in Rousseau's theory—a mythic figure who teaches the people to subordinate its will to its reason, and to recognize what it desires (Rousseau, *The Social Contract*, book 2, chaps. 6–8, 83–88).

41. Dworkin, *A Matter of Principle*, 70. I am grateful to Susan Sterett for urging me to reconsider the role courts play in the initiation and enhancement of democratic debate.

42. Ibid., 70.

43. Plato, *The Republic*, translated by Desmond Lee (Harmondsworth: Penguin Books, 1974), 280–83 and 372–81 (book 6, 487b–89c; and book 8, 555b–62a). See generally Paul Corcoran, "The Limits of Democratic Theory," in *Democratic Theory and Practice*, ed. Graeme Duncan (Cambridge: Cambridge University Press, 1983), 13–24.

PART II

CONCEPTUAL AND PROCEDURAL ISSUES

4

THREE FALLACIES CONCERNING MAJORITIES, MINORITIES, AND DEMOCRATIC POLITICS

IAN SHAPIRO

I. An American Subject

Minorities and majority rule is our subject—and it is a peculiarly American one. The tricky task for this constitutional democracy is to devise "ways of protecting minorities from majority tyranny that is not a flagrant contradiction of the principle

Thanks are due to John Chapman and Alan Wertheimer for inviting me to deliver an earlier version of this chapter to The American Society for Political and Legal Philosophy in September 1987, and for the helpful comments I received from them and the two commentators, Diana Meyers and Frederick Schauer. Subsequent versions were presented to a seminar sponsored by the Center for Philosophy and Public Policy and the University of Maryland Politics Department, and to the New England Political Science Association's Annual Meeting in the Spring of 1988 in Cambridge, Massachusetts. Particularly helpful were the comments of Stephen Elkin, Joe Oppenheimer, and Karol Soltan in Baltimore, and those of Jeffrey Abramson, Josh Cohen, and Shannon Stimson in Cambridge. Useful suggestions, some of which have been heeded, have also been received from Lea Brilmayer, Jay Budziszewski, Jules Coleman, Robert Dahl, David Lumsdaine, Barry Nalebuff, Douglas Rae, Susan Rose-Ackerman, Rogers Smith, and Steven Wizner. The research assistance of Debra Morris and Grant Reeher is acknowledged. While working on this article I have of majority rule." The terms of the problem are set, John Hart Ely elaborates, by the fact that "a majority with untrammeled power to set governmental policy is in a position to deal itself benefits at the expense of the remaining minority." In Bruce Ackerman's words, "no modern contractarian has succeeded in vindicating majority rule without, at the same time, undermining the foundation of individual rights." As William Riker and Barry Weingast reiterate, majority rule "affords no protection against arbitrary actions or against actions directed at benefiting the temporary majority at some minority's expense." [1]

Yet at other times and in other places this property of majority rule made it simultaneously attractive to the disenfranchised and frightening to entrenched elites. For the English Chartists in the 1830s and 1840s, majority rule with universal suffrage was an oppositional ideal. In a society based on hereditary wealth and political privilege, majority rule was desired precisely to dispossess a minority of ill-gotten gains, and nineteenth-century liberals like Mill and Tocqueville, who endorsed expansion of the franchise, were for this reason ambivalent about it. [2]

From the beginning the American preoccupation with majority rule was different. The problem was to domesticate and institutionalize an idea whose historical use had been to destabilize institutions. In the context of a society that, if not fully pluralist, appeared to lack one fundamental socioeconomic cleavage characteristic of nations with a feudal past, [3] Americans would be first to confront the fact that the minority harmed by the workings of majoritarian process need not be a rich and powerful elite, it could be a dispossessed racial or religious minority. American democratic theorists continue to be preoccupied with the logical properties of majority rule and its fairness from a neutral or "God's-eye-view" standpoint, and they are often deeply troubled by discoveries that majority rule can generate arbitrary outcomes as a result of cyclical majorities,

received support from the Griswold Fund and the Social Science Faculty Fund at Yale, the Guggenheim Foundation, and the Center for Advanced Study in Palo Alto. Part of my support at the Center was paid for by National Science Foundation grant number BN 587-00864. I am grateful for all this support.

strategic voting, and control of the agenda. Yet my central contention here is that a great deal of this concern is misplaced. Specifically, my goal is to debunk three fallacies that dominate contemporary discussions of majority rule, minorities, and democratic politics. The *reductionist fallacy* is that of regarding it a defect of majority rule that it fails to "amalgamate" individual preferences in ways analogous to idealized models of the market's amalgamation of economic preferences. I argue that appropriately revised expectations about decision rules expose the reductionist fallacy for what it is, yet still justify a presumption in favor of majority rule. To commit the *constitutionalist fallacy* is to claim that because majority rule can damage the interests of minorities, or because it is vulnerable to manipulation, or both, its scope should be restricted by anti-majoritarian constitutional devices. With reference to the historical purposes of majority rule and some contemporary illustrations, I argue that inherent hostility toward some minorities is one of its appealing properties, and that the only constitutional limitations to it that can be defended by appeal to democratic theory are those geared toward realizing its purposes. The *instability fallacy* involves holding it to be a defect of majority rule that it is vulnerable to cycling and may fail to produce equilibria. In light of considerations drawn from the theory of power, I argue that instability is often a desirable property of majority rule.

II. The Reductionist Fallacy

The origins of the reductionist fallacy lie in the economic modeling of political processes, and specifically in the influential attempt by Buchanan and Tullock—canonized in 1987 by Buchanan's receipt of the Nobel prize for economics—to analyze decision rules from the standpoint of a set of political analogues of the Pareto system. Prefiguring a style of theoretical argument that would later be made famous by John Rawls, they asked the question: what decision rules would mutually disinterested citizens choose at a constitutional convention when everyone is uncertain "as to what his own precise role will be in any one of the whole chain of later collective choices that will actually have to be made." Whether selfish or altruistic, each agent is forced by the circumstances "to act, from self-interest, *as if* he were choosing the best set of rules for the social group."[4] Thus considered, they argued, no reason exists to prefer majority rule to the possible alternatives. Collective decision making invariably has costs and benefits for any individual, and an optimal decision rule would minimize the sum of "external costs" (the costs to an individual of the legal but harmful actions of third parties) and "decision-making costs" (those of negotiating agreement on collective action). The external costs of collective action diminish as increasingly large majorities are required; in the limiting case of unanimity rule every individual is absolutely protected since anyone can veto a proposed action. Conversely, decision-making costs typically increase with the proportion required, since the costs of negotiation increase. The choice problem at the constitutional stage is to determine the point at which the combined costs are smallest for different types of collective action, and to agree on a range of decision rules to be applied in different future circumstances.[5]

At least three kinds of collective action can be distinguished requiring different decision rules. First is the initial decision rule that must prevail for other decision rules to be decided on. Buchanan and Tullock "assume, without elaboration, that at this ultimate stage . . . the rule of unanimity holds." Next come "those possible collective or public decisions which modify or restrict the structure of individual human or property rights after these have once been defined and generally accepted by the community." Foreseeing that collective action may "impose very severe costs on him," the individual will tend "to place a high value on the attainment of his consent, and he may be quite willing to undergo substantial decision-making costs in order to insure that he will, in fact, be reasonably protected against confiscation." He will thus require a decision rule approaching unanimity. Last is the class of collective actions characteristically undertaken by governments. For these "the individual will recognize that private organization will impose some interdependence costs on him, perhaps in significant amount, and he will, by hypothesis, have supported a shift of such activities to the public sector." Examples include provision of public education, enforcement of building and fire codes, and maintenance of adequate police forces. For such "general legislation" an individual at the constitutional stage will support less inclusive decision rules, though not necessarily simple majority rule, and indeed within this class different majorities might be agreed on as optimal for different purposes. "The number of categories, and the number of decision-making rules chosen, will depend on the situation which the individual expects to prevail and the 'returns to scale' expected to result from using the same rule over many activities."[6]

In that class of potential collective actions not covered by unanimity rule, there is an important sense in which the particular majority or minority is unimportant, since Buchanan and Tullock envisage a regime in which logrolling and vote trading are ubiquitous. Although prevailing norms prohibit open buying and selling of votes, more subtle forms of vote trading go on in democratic systems all the time, and they produce more efficient results in the literal Paretian sense that more people end up higher on their utility functions than would otherwise be so. If logrolling is disallowed, they argue, this can be based only on the assumption that all voters have equal, interpersonally comparable, utility scales on all issues, an assumption that is "wholly different from that which is employed in economic analysis."[7]

What makes this reductionist argument defective? To see this we must attend to the role played in it by unanimity. Buchanan and Tullock argue that unanimity as a decision rule has the unique property that if decision-making costs are zero, it is the only rational decision rule for all proposed collective action.[8] This argument confuses unanimity qua decision rule with unanimity qua social state. From the standpoint of the constitutional convention we have to assume that we are as likely to be ill-disposed toward any future status quo as well-disposed toward it, and in cases where we are ill-disposed a decision rule requiring unanimity will frustrate our preferences. Buchanan and Tullock assume throughout that it is departures from the status quo that need to be justified, but as Rae has shown, this is not warranted. Externalities over time, or "utility drift" (Rae's term), may change our evaluations of the status quo. We may feel in certain circumstances that failures to act collectively, rather than

collective action itself, should shoulder the burden of proof.[9]
We may change our minds for other reasons, foreseen or unforeseen, or a status quo that I reject may have been the product
of unanimous agreement of a previous generation, by which I
do not wish to be bound. Indeed Rae has shown formally that if
we assume we are as likely to be against any proposal as for it,
which the condition of uncertainty at the constitutional convention would seem to require, then majority rule or something
very close to it[10] is the unique solution to Buchanan and Tullock's choice problem.[11]

Here I am concerned less with these analytical weaknesses
than with unanimity's appeal as an ideal for Buchanan and
Tullock. Notice first what it says about their expectations from
decision rules. By arguing that decision-making costs are the
only obstacles to unanimity, they take a quite benign view of
political differences, such that if enough time *is* spent on negotiation, unanimity is assumed to be attainable. Although it is
characteristic for economists to assume all disutilities to be com-
pensable—so that at some price every individual will want a
policy she did not previously want, some exchange that will
leave her on as high an indifference curve as before enactment
of the policy—in politics we cannot assume this. Even in strict
interest-group politics, the narrowness of the interest being protected or advanced may mean that no substitution-equivalents
exist that can make compensation, and hence unanimity, possible in principle. The substitution-equivalent for those who
opposed desegregation probably did not exist. Where votes are
judgments about what public policy ought to be, the theory
fares yet less well. Involvement in a war in the Persian Gulf or
Central America or the teaching of religion in public schools
are generally embraced or rejected as matters of principle. To
hold by assumption that unanimity in such cases is always possible through negotiation requires either a whiggish rationalism,
a belief that if only we all talked for long enough all our disagreements would vanish, or a reductionist economism that
requires all politics simply to be individual utility maximization.

The whiggish rationalism is well illustrated by Robert Paul
Wolff, who also argues that only unanimous direct democracy
can ensure that the autonomy of no individual is ever violated.[12]

Wolff's argument is vulnerable analytically for exactly the same reasons as is Buchanan and Tullock's,[13] but he makes his expectations from social decision rules far more explicit. He distinguishes the natural world, the "irreducibly *other*" that stands apart from man, "against him, independent of his will and indifferent to his desires," from the social world that often appears to be apart from man but ultimately is not. The natural world "really does exist independently of man's beliefs or desires, and therefore exercises a constraint on his will which can at best be mitigated or combatted." The social world "is nothing in itself, and consists merely of the totality of the habits, expectations, beliefs and behavior patterns" of the individuals who live in it. For this reason "it ought to be in principle possible for a society of rational men of good will to eliminate the domination of society. . . . It *must* be possible for them to create a form of association which accomplishes that end [the "general good"] without depriving some of their moral autonomy. The state, in contrast to nature, cannot be ineradicably other."[14] Yet there are many aspects of the natural world we are perfectly able to control despite their "otherness," from the temperature of our bathwater to the genetic structure of our beings. Conversely, we often cannot control by-products of our actions even if we are aware of them.

The other strategy, of economistic reduction, confronts different difficulties. First, as we saw, it may be that as a normative matter people regard their preferences as nonnegotiable. The limiting case of this is Nozick's problem with his independents, those anarchists who refuse to join any state under any circumstances. Although Nozick devoted plenty of ink to arguing that these people could be forcibly included if adequately compensated and still be said to have consented, I have shown elsewhere that his arguments fail.[15] This kind of example might be thought a little tendentious, because the hard-boiled anarchist is a difficulty for any contractarian theory; but it is useful analytically because it reveals that the primary value enshrined in compensation arguments is utilitarian efficiency, not consent or individual autonomy. Such arguments do not, therefore, establish unanimity as the optimal decision rule from the standpoint of individual rationality. Only if one assumes, implausibly, that every preference of every voter has its price can we say that enough negotiation would lead to consensus.

Even that assumption runs into serious difficulties deriving from different capacities to negotiate. Buchanan and Tullock never confront this, since they defend unqualified unanimity rule only in the theoretical case where decision-making costs are zero. However, this runs together the mere costs of doing business with the substantive compensation that would have to occur if such business was done. Peoples' expressed preferences are, to a degree, a function of their resources. One must anticipate that no matter how much time is spent negotiating, the bag lady from Manhattan may not have the resources to compensate the businessman and buy off his potential opposition to a welfare program. She may have nothing he wants.

This example illustrates some of the analytical difficulties that arise from modeling political decision making on the Pareto system. The central purpose of microeconomic theory is to predict prices, and from this standpoint it makes perfect sense to be indifferent to the moral meaning of the choices being made in a market system. If our question is simply whether the businessman and the bag lady will trade, and at what price, we can see why it makes sense to say that voluntary action (and hence unanimity rule) dictates that no transaction will occur. But to suppose that this amounts to a justification for not departing from the status quo on the ground that there is no way to do so under unanimous agreement, is obviously quite different and not persuasive in the absence of independent argument.

As with Wolff's argument, the Pareto system in its pure form also fails to speak to the question of externalities. If Buchanan and Tullock's political use of it is to be salvaged, it must be argued that despite the existence of externalities (which undermine the significance of voluntary transactions even from the standpoint of pure efficiency), the burden of persuasion remains on those who advocate collective action. Buchanan and Tullock try to establish a theoretical preference for private externalities over those generated by collective action, on the grounds that the former can be internalized through the market. "The fact that collective action, under most decision-making rules, involves external costs," they argue, creates a prima facie presumption against it.

> The private operation of the neighborhood plant with the smoking chimney may impose external costs on the individual by soiling his laundry, but this cost is no more external to the individual's own private calculus than the tax cost imposed on him unwillingly in order to finance the provision of public services to his fellow citizen in another area. . . . [T]he initial definition of property rights places some effective limits on the external effects that private people may impose on each other. By contrast, the individual rights to property against damaging state or collective action are not nearly so sharply defined in existing legal systems. The external costs that may be imposed on the individual through the collective-choice process may be much larger than those which could ever be expected to result from purely private behavior within *any* accepted legal framework.[16]

So, although "[t]he continuation of private action, within the restriction of property ownership as defined, may impose certain spillover costs" on him, in the absence of "the protection of something approaching the unanimity rule," he "may rationally choose to bear the continued costs of private decision making." Here we see the rationale for Buchanan and Tullock's claim that individual rights should get special protective treatment in the choosing of decision rules.

> The individual will anticipate greater possible damage from collective action the more closely this action amounts to the creation and confiscation of human and property rights. . . . This implication is not without relevance to an interpretation of the economic and social history of many Western countries. Constitutional prohibitions against many forms of collective intervention in the market economy have been abolished within the last three decades. As a result, legislative action may now produce severe capital losses or lucrative capital gains to separate individuals and groups. For

the rational individual, unable to predict his future position, the imposition of some additional and renewed restraints on the exercise of such legislative power may be
desirable.[17]

We have seen that unanimity as a decision rule does not
ensure the assent of all once omissions, Rae's "utility drift," and
other unforeseen eventualities are taken into account. But what
of this more general argument that collective action is particularly dubious in the area of property rights, since it creates more
severe externalities than private action? Assuming that the unanimity test for collective action is an analytical parallel of compensation in welfare economics (since compensation can be interpreted "as that payment, negative or positive, which is required
to secure agreement"), Buchanan and Tullock argue by reference to Pigou's classical smoking chimney that noncollective
action allows for the internalization of external costs. In that
example smoke from an industrial plant fouls the air and imposes external costs on the residents of surrounding areas. "If
this represents a genuine externality," they argue, "either voluntary arrangements will emerge to eliminate it or collective
action with unanimous support can be implemented." If the
externality is real,

> *some* collectively imposed scheme through which the dam-
> aged property owners are taxed and the firm's owners are
> subsidized for capital losses incurred in putting in a smoke-
> abatement machine can command the assent of all the par-
> ties. If no such compensation scheme is possible (organiza-
> tion costs neglected), the externality is only apparent and
> not real. The same conclusion applies to the possibility of
> voluntary arrangements being worked out. Suppose that
> the owners of the residential property claim smoke dam-
> age, however slight. If this claim is real, the opportunity
> will always be open for them to combine forces and buy out
> the firm in order to induce smoke-abatement devices.[18]

In the case of a real externality, then, organization costs aside,
it would make no difference whether unanimous collective ac-

tion was undertaken, or whether the costs of the externalities were internalized through market transactions. A privatized system and a purely voluntary collectivized system (unanimity rule) have the advantage of enabling us to distinguish real from apparent diseconomies, but once we move into the realm of coercive collective action, this disappears.

Here we can see the deep implausibilities attending the reductionist fallacy. Again, as a set of analytical assumptions merely to predict the conditions under which compensation through sidepayments will occur, there is nothing morally objectionable about Pigou's chimney. But once this is treated as a normative model for the requirements of collective action, it becomes clear that it is doubly misleading. First, it creates the impression that the "scientific" or morally neutral way of dealing with externalities collectively is to approximate the outcomes of a well-functioning competitive market. Second, the assumptions about the market rest on a series of fictions that are never present in actual markets.

To begin with the distinction between real and apparent externalities, there is a neat theoretical simplicity to the claim that if the transaction does not occur voluntarily, then that is decisive evidence that the externality was not real. But things are seldom so simple. Consider the claim that if the working classes did not like capitalism, they would get together and buy the capitalists' factories from them, and since they do not we know that they do not really dislike the system. If this reasoning seems disingenuous, it is for its willful disregard of the resources problem, and its concomitant insensitivity to all distributive questions. This is inherent in the structure of the compensation tests to which Buchanan and Tullock refer. The early welfare economists devised these hypothetical tests to find a way of discussing Pareto-noncomparable outcomes that increased overall welfare, but they were wholly insensitive to distributive questions, holding only that transactions that increase net social product are to be preferred, whether or not this involves redistribution.[19] As Buchanan and Tullock employ the compensation argument, it depends critically on revealed preferences, because externalities that are not internalized in private transactions are declared not to be real. Yet to reveal a preference in a competitive system, one must have the resources to reveal it; the market is sensitive only to preferences backed up by dollars. But it seems a little much to maintain that residents around a major airport who claim to find the noise intolerable cannot really find it so, otherwise they would have bought the airport, and then to treat this standard as the model that collective action should try to emulate.

Second, just as unanimity *qua* decision rule can give a single individual veto power in decisions for or against collective action, the same thing can occur in private markets. Buchanan and Tullock's a priori preference for private action rests on the presumption that "[m]ore often, the external costs imposed by private action will be concentrated on a minority group of the total population, and other individuals in the group will receive some external benefits as a result of these external costs."[20] Yet as their own example of Pigou's chimney makes clear, there is no good theoretical reason to believe either of these empirical claims. It may well be a minority, even a monopolist, who imposes externalities on a majority. Instead of localized smoke-creating in one neighbourhood, suppose that it is toxic chemicals that are damaging the ozone layer, the destruction of tropical forests at a rate that is affecting critically the production of gases essential for long-term human survival, or the local externalities of the actions of multinational corporations in the Third World, of which the activities of Union Carbide in Bhopal, India, are a paradigm instance. In such circumstances it may be that only collective action can prevent a minority from imposing external costs on a majority; under a private regime the majority will be powerless to prevent the external effect. As for the collateral benefits to third parties, unless we make a leap of Mandevillean faith that individual profit maximization will typically have positive external effects, these are no more likely to be positive than negative.

A third problem concerns the failure of Buchanan and Tullock's analysis to grapple with voluntary collective action problems other than those connected to decision-making costs. Consider circumstances where the benefits to the victims of negative externalities from potential preventative collective action, minus total decision-making costs, exceed the current benefit of the action to the perpetrator, but no change from the status quo will occur voluntarily. There are many reasons in game theory as to why this can happen, the most common having to do with the prisoner's dilemma and freeriding. It is by no means clear that the structure of choice situations will always permit the incentives of self-interested individual rationality to work to the mutual benefit of those who would benefit from voluntary collective action. Here again, "coercive" collective action may actually be superior, even in terms of individual rationality, to unregulated private action.

Buchanan and Tullock's use of the Pareto principle in evaluating decision rules reinforces the reductionist fallacy at a more subtle level. This is most obvious in their discussion of intensity of preference, which is integral to their critique of majority rule. Strict majority rule, they claim, imputes to every voter equal intensity of preference, but there is no reason for "imputing to each individual . . . [this] . . . most restrictive utility function. . . . To the modern economist this approach to individual calculus seems anachronistic and sterile." Their defense of logrolling and vote trading also turns on this claim; it is just because of the presence of different intensities that these devices can produce superior results. "Applying the strict Pareto rules for determining whether one social situation represents an improvement over another, almost any system of voting that allows some such exchange to take place would be superior to that system which weights all preferences equally on each issue."[21]

But what is really being argued here? Note for one thing that this reasoning again ignores the resources problem. Thus it is entirely compatible with a system in which landowners require tenants to vote as directed or be thrown off the land. The tenant who complies when he otherwise would not have merely reveals a more intense preference to stay on the land than to vote the other way. In terms of the "strict Pareto rules" the outcome is superior. Once logrolling and vote trading are permitted on the grounds that they produce Pareto-superior results, it is hard to see any reason to limit the existence of a "free" market in votes. Even if we keep money and actual buying and selling of votes out of it, many will find counter-intuitive the notion that if you desire that the United States goes to war in Central America

more intensely than I desire that it does not, the world will be a
better place if *for that reason* a way could be found for the war to
be fought.[22]

In sum, Buchanan and Tullock's claim that unanimity rule
has unique properties that would make it the rule of choice,
absent decision making costs, at the constitutional stage, is analytically false, and romanticizes the ideal of unanimity in the
Pareto system in two different ways. It is analytically false because it rests on a misleading theory of action that takes no
account of omissions as actions, and it illicitly assumes that market actions that have resulted in a given status quo will correspond to the preferences of all relevant agents at any given
time. The defense of unanimity is romantic first in that it is
thought to imply that if we allow only those collective actions
that mimic what the market would produce, this will somehow
produce a neutrally scientific and efficient form of collective
action, geared to the preservation of private rights. We saw that
this relies on assumptions about intensity of preference that,
while obviously useful in the prediction of price-behavior in a
market economy, have no necessary place in other rules of
collective decision. We saw also that, through their evasion of
the resources problem, Buchanan and Tullock exhibit an indifference to distributive questions, hidden behind a guise of scien-
tistic neutralism that cannot without some as yet unsupplied
argument amount to a justification for unanimity rule. The
commitment to unanimity is romantic in a deeper sense in that
it relies on a benign model of competitive economies that we
have no good reason to believe are realistic. Just as unanimity as
a rule of collective decision can permit minorities to tyrannize
over majorities, the same can happen in the realm of private
action unless we make unwarranted assumptions about the ease
of organizing collective action privately, and the collateral benefits to third parties of self-interested private action.

A second sense of unanimity, which contributes to the reductionist fallacy in a different way, concerns its use in the construction of the choice problem. At the constitutional stage, where
future decision rules are chosen, the need for unanimity is
taken for granted.[23] This is a common move in contractarian
argument.[24] But the great difficulty with the contractarian ap-

proach, encapsulated in Rousseau's remark that Hobbes included in his account of natural man "a multitude of passions which are the product of [his] society,"[25] is that they assume what they need to establish. So for Hobbes a savage natural man makes political absolutism unavoidable, for Nozick a congenial but comparatively inefficient state of nature legitimates minimal government, and for Rawls risk-averse agents design a welfare principle to protect the interests of the most disadvantaged. For Buchanan and Tullock contractarian argument is doubly problematic. First, they do not escape the basic problem of theoretical arbitrariness: while operating at the constitutional stage, they assume the existence of institutions that obviously postdate the constitution—a regime of private property rights and a market economy. Indeed their whole analysis of rules in terms of their comparative external costs assumes the existence of a legal system, since an external cost is defined as a reduction in an individual's "net worth" that is "not specifically recognized by the *existing legal structure* to be an expropriation of a defensible human or property right. The damaged individual has no recourse; he can neither prevent the action from occuring nor can he claim compensation after it has occurred. . . . [I]t is the existence of such external costs that rationally explains *the origin* of either voluntarily organized, co-operative, contractural rearrangements or collective (governmental) activity."[26]

This clearly makes no sense. If an external cost is defined as a legal but harmful by-product of the actions of another, the concept cannot be invoked to evaluate the different rules that might be employed in the design of the legal system. The only way to avoid absurdity here would be to invoke a notion of natural property rights and externalities, which Buchanan and Tullock never do. Indeed they clearly view property rights as conventional.[27]

Their contractrarian method undermines Buchanan and Tullock's substantive argument in a different and more serious way, since it rests on assumptions about the primacy of politics and collective choice that are incompatible with their view of these as resulting from market failure. The problem is cast in terms of defining the conditions under which it is legitimate to depart from a regime of private action. So they speak of the "continuation of private action" as comparatively desirable and they defend unanimity because it allegedly requires everyone to agree prior to collective action, claiming that "the individual will not rationally choose to collectivize an activity" under other conditions.[28] Yet the contractarian ideal implies the theoretical primacy of collective action, for which it is sometimes criticized. "Competitive markets require stable property rights and the absence of force, fraud, transaction costs and externalities," as Jules Coleman has recently reminded us. This amounts to saying that "[a] scheme of secure property rights is a collective good for those who have it."[29] From the standpoint of contractarian theory this collective good and its scope have to be agreed on at the constitutional stage or later; certainly they cannot be agreed on prior to it. Far from a presumption against collective action, the burden of proof would seem from this standpoint to rest with those who advocate the creation of that particular collective good (assuming it is a good) of a competitive market system. The only way to be a contractarian and at the same time avoid commiting to the theoretical primacy of politics is also to commit to a theory of natural private rights, which Buchanan and Tullock are loath to do. Yet in the absence of such a theory, it is hard to discern a viable basis for their reification of legal rights that are both conventional and pre-contractual, and that can sustain their presumption against collective action.

III. The Constitutionalist Fallacy

Perhaps out of an awareness that unanimity as a decision rule has no special advantages for the preservation of individual rights, that it "distorts" preferences and, like any other decision rule, is manipulable through such devices as agenda control, democratic theorists have sought alternative bases for protecting minority rights from the potential devastations of majority rule. The argument can be made from several points of view; from a natural rights standpoint as embodied in the Declaration of Independence, from a utilitarian standpoint, where the argument is that the protection of certain individual rights from collective process best conduces to long-term human prosperity; or from a republican standpoint, where the separation of powers and concomitant limitations on majoritarian legislatures prevent corruption and promote political stability. The constitutionalist argument that concerns me here differs from all of these in that it purports to rest solely on findings about the defects of legislatures in the public choice literature of the past three decades, on the claim, that is, that enhanced judicial scrutiny is an appropriate democratic remedy for the analytical defects of majority rule.

Among others, Riker and Weingast have forcefully defended the view that ubiquitous voting cycles in legislatures warrant greater judicial scrutiny of their actions to protect individual rights. This is the view that Riker has characterised as "liberal" in opposition to "populist," arguing that "in the populist interpretation of voting, the opinions of the majority *must* be right and *must* be respected because the will of the people is the liberty of the people." In Riker's "liberal" view, by contrast, "there is no such magical identification. The outcome of voting is just a decision, and has no special moral character."[30]

Riker and Weingast recognize the powerful American constitutional tradition of courts protecting individual rights from the legislative process, but they argue that in recent decades an indefensible preference has been afforded civil over property rights. Since the New Deal, they argue, the Supreme Court has tended increasingly to view the economic rights of minorities as "no longer in need [of] protection above and beyond that provided by legislatures." They recognize that the tradition of judicial deference in matters of economic regulation is much older than the New Deal, traceable at least to the Court's proclamation in *Munn v. Illinois,* 94 U.S. 113, (1877), that even when legislative power in this area is abused "people should resort to the polls not the courts." Nonetheless, they argue that minimal scrutiny has given way to "complete and abject" abdication of judicial responsibility in the economic realm.[31] Decisions like *Nebbia v. New York* 291 U.S. 502 (1934), which held courts without authority to declare economic policy or to override the decisions of legislatures to adopt "whatever economic policy may be deemed reasonable to promote public welfare," affirmed a quite limited role for judicial scrutiny. This was reinforced by *United States v. Carolene Products Co.,* 304 U.S. 144

(1938), which sustained socioeconomic regulation so long as a state of facts, either known or reasonably inferrable, afforded support for the legislative judgment, and *Ferguson v. Skrupa,* 372 U.S. 726 (1963), which apparently abandoned even this requirement.[32] This is in stark contrast to both the strict scrutiny of the *Lochner* era and the increasing attention, which reached its zenith in the Warren Court, to legislative abuses of the civil rights of minorities. Indeed *Carolene Products* is usually taken to have set the terms of Riker and Weingast's problem. At the same time that the Court affirmed broad deference to legislative judgment in the area of economic regulation, Justice Stone penned his famous "footnote four"[33] which would later be be used to support greater judicial intervention in noneconomic affairs. Yet, in Riker and Weingast's view,

> neither the court nor legal scholarship has provided the theoretical underpinnings for the presumption of the adequacy of legislative judgment [in the economic sphere] and, indeed, neither has even asked whether legislative judgment really works. Fundamental questions remain unanswered: What protection is there against members of today's majority from providing private, redistributive benefits to themselves under the guise of public purposes and at the expense of some minority of owners and the efficiency of production? Why is the abridgement of a minority's economic rights less troubling than an abridgement of the same minorities' [sic] political rights?[34]

What, then, is the sense in which the legislative process can be said not to work in the economic realm? What, precisely, are the findings of social choice theory that render decisions of legislatures literally devoid of moral meaning, and at the same time tools for the illegitimate appropriation of minorities' economic assets? "Social choice theory," Riker and Weingast tell us, is concerned with "the way that tastes, wants, values etc. of individual members are amalgamated into a statement of the choices for a group." Beginning from Condorcet's insight that a fairly small degree of complexity among preferences and voters can produce perpetual cyclical majorities,[35] they argue that the very idea of representative government is deeply flawed. Although individual preferences may be rational and transitive, Arrow and others have proved their resulting social rankings may be fundamentally arbitrary, and strictly irrational in that they may not even be transitive.[36] Majority rule is thus an "unfair" method of preference aggregation that results in a "forced order."[37]

From this perspective, the problem with majority rule is not simply that it harms minorities. It is more serious. The result of any pairwise vote that produces a majority outcome does not even necessarily embody the will of the people in the restricted majoritarian sense. There may be members of a winning majority who would have voted differently had the alternatives been presented in a different order. Majority rule can "wander anywhere"; there is nothing in it that "inherently limits voting bodies from choosing undesirable policies."[38] This means that in any legislative body those who control the agenda and the order of voting can decisively influence the results. What appears to be majority rule may quite often be de facto minority rule.

Some disagreement exists in the public choice literature on the empirical likelihood of cycles,[39] but it is certain that they do occur.[40] This means, Riker and Weingast argue, that the "fundamental properties of majority rule" ensure a "fundamental arbitrariness to social choices" made under it.

> When there exists a modest diversity of preference (itself, the bare necessity for political controversy), there are too many majorities. The particular majority that forms on one occasion is subject to manipulation within the legislature, and people in the position to manipulate (e.g. committee leaders) are not subject to majority rule competition. Moreover, it should be apparent that if different interests (e.g., different committees) have control over the agenda in different areas, then there need be no logical relationship between the majority that forms to support one piece of legislation and the majority that forms for another.[41]

To the extent that there can be said to be a "view of Congress" at all, then, it is likely to be internally contradictory and easily

altered by strategically powerful committees, even minorities on
committees.

These problems are worsened by a second phenomenon that
has preoccupied public choice theorists in recent decades, strategic voting. Gibbard, Satterthwaite, and others have revealed a
wide variety of circumstances in which committee members can
manipulate outcomes by voting for something other than their
actual preferences if they know how others are likely to vote. It
is exceedingly difficult to trace this kind of strategic voting, since
it leaves no evidence, so that "even if an equilibrium of tastes
might legitimately be called the will of the people, we would be
forced, in our ignorance, to discount it entirely as a probable
product of strategic voting or agenda control."[42] Indeed, representation is strategic to the core. Political scientists have shown
that the legislator is "a placeholder opportunistically building
up an ad hoc majority for the next election." The effect of this
on legislation is that

> legislators do not mechanistically transmit majority opinion.
> Rather, they calculate the intensity of opinion, choosing
> their positions in such a way as to maximize the probability
> of successfully garnering citizens' votes. By and large, legis-
> lators build coalitions of minorities, each one of which is
> especially concerned with a particular set of issues. . . . One
> momentary majority of legislators finds that each one's elec-
> toral coalition would be strengthened by a particular regu-
> lation, often a small cartel. Another, possibly overlapping,
> later majority, also momentary, finds another regulation
> electorally helpful. Such legislation, of course, endures long
> after the electoral occasion. This has built up a cartelized
> society in which abridgements of property rights deter en-
> trepreneurship and restrain economic growth.[43]

The logical defects of majority rule, the problems presented
by strategic voting and opportunistic legislators, and their failure to represent anything that may confidently be termed majority opinion, combine to demolish the populist view of democratic government as embodying the will of the people.
Recognizing these defects, these proponents of the liberal or

Madisonian view argue that popular election can at most provide a popular veto on recent legislative action. Accordingly, majoritarian process cannot be expected to protect constitutional rights, and judicial process provides a needed "veto of another kind." Particularly in the area of property rights, where legislators typically operate as if the populist view legitimates their actions, the courts should scrutinize, and if necessary invalidate, legislation if it impinges on economic constitutional rights. Riker and Weingast explicitly deny that they are calling for a revival of the substantive due process of *Lochner,* which allowed judges to "substitute their own logic for that of the legislature." This, they note, "merely transfers the problem of unpredictability and insecurity of economic rights . . . to the judicial stage." Yet they conclude that "[w]hile we cannot fully explicate the rationale here, we do point out that judicial review, as developed in the seventeenth and eighteenth centuries, did render property rights more secure."[44]

Two major classes of difficulties confront Riker and Weingast's argument. First, if the claim is valid that the presence of cycles and strategic voting produces outcomes that are often, perhaps even typically, arbitrary with respect to the preferences of committee members, then they have proved too much. There is every reason to believe that courts are just as vulnerable to cycles in theory and in practice, not least because they also employ majority rule, and this has been shown in the public choice literature.[45] In fact the problems generated by strategic voting might as a matter of pure theory be expected to be worse in courts, where the numbers are sufficiently small and the votes of others sufficiently predictible to make it a more realistic option.[46] Furthermore, Riker and Weingast assume that the "constitutional rights" they defend but nowhere define have a special status that is somehow anterior to legislation. But the Constitution is, ultimately, one more piece of legislation, and Riker has himself documented the existence of some vote trading at the Constitutional Convention.[47] Certainly there is no a priori reason to suppose that there were not cyclical majorities and strategic voting there, or in the passing of the Bill of Rights and the other amendments.

Riker and Weingast operate with an implicit notion of certain preferred individual rights with a superior moral status, in need of protection from an interest group politics that generates encroachment on them from multiple origins. The "hodge podge of regulation" has "significantly encroached on property rights," creating a "cartelized society in which abridgements of property rights deter entrepreneurship and restrain economic growth."[48] Here we detect the same unwarranted assumptions about collective action as we did in our discussion of Buchanan and Tullock. Although failure to regulate (or, one must suppose, a collective decision to "deregulate" property rights) functions neutrally to the general benefit of society, decisions *to* regulate invariably benefit some well-organized pressure group at the expense of the general interest. Shepsle and Weingast have gone further, arguing that even in circumstances of demonstrable market failure the difficulties with collective action we have been discussing may warrant its rejection.[49] Whether they would go so far as to say that a court could strike down such legislation (which would be a literal return to the *Lochner* rule) is unclear. Yet to hold, as Riker and Weingast do, that there is a class of preferred rights that courts should enforce because their abridgement will "deter entrepreneurship and restrain economic growth" comes uncomfortably close to this position. In short, they appear to want it both ways: while regulatory economic policies enacted by legislatures are inherently suspect as the product of cyclical majorities and opportunistic legislators, collective judicial acts to enforce constitutional rights that may be vulnerable in the same ways—when enacted as well as during two centuries of continuing reinterpretation as to meaning and scope by the Court—somehow escape the problem.

If the argument regarding cyclical and strategic voting proves too much, undercutting the notion of a general or public interest so completely as to render all forms of majoritarian collective action literally meaningless, then it proves too little in restricting the problematical implications to majority rule. Arrow's impossibility theorem was a landmark in the public choice literature not because of his findings about majority rule. He showed more generally that there is no social welfare function that will prevent cycling if a few minimal conditions are assumed and preferences are sufficiently diverse.[50] A good deal of the voting theory literature since Arrow has been concerned with relaxing his assumptions or introducing constraints on the heterogeneity of preferences to save majority rule from the possibility of cycles.[51] But it is clear that if the findings Riker and Weingast invoke apply to majority rule, they certainly apply to some, perhaps all, other decision rules.[52] Since the possibility of cycling is partly a function of heterogeneity of preferences, not just of the properties of decision rules (except to the extent that any decision rule requires us actually to reach a decision at least for a time), it is likely that control of the agenda will confer decisive power, whatever the decision rule.[53] Sophisticated voting, too, plays no special role in majority rule. If I know the preferences of others and am willing to gamble on their strategic decisions with respect to my vote, the "honest" result that should be reached by any decision rule may be undermined, sometimes to the detriment of all concerned, as the game theorists have shown.

If Riker and Weingast's arguments reveal nothing special about majority rule, but instead are instances of more general findings that have been shown to undermine all known procedures of collective decision, their significance is cast in a different light. Were it possible somehow for society to "not undertake" collective action, as their comments about economic regulation by legislatures might be taken to imply, this might amount to a prima facie argument against all collective action.[54] But, as we saw when discussing Buchanan and Tullock, the creation and maintenance of a system of legal rights and rules that makes possible what they think of as unregulated private action is itself the provision of a public good, partly financed by implicit taxes on those who would prefer some alternative system. Once this is conceded, the question must inevitably arise: why have this rather than some alternative system? The problem of collective action is then seen to be inescapable.

Collective action is inevitable in a different sense, having to do with the ubiquitous presence of power relations in all known societies. Riker and Weingast limit their concern (as do Wolff and Buchanan and Tullock) to coercive acts performed by the state. If this turns out to be an implausibly narrow view of the problems of power and collective action, then the dimensions of social life along which we are bound to think of collective action as inevitable will necessarily expand.

These theoretical difficulties aside, what of the implications of Riker and Weingast's arguments in the actual world of American politics? Should we be persuaded that the actions of legislatures are wholly arbitrary and morally bankrupt as a result, necessitating stricter scrutiny on all fronts by the federal courts? Assuming away, for now, the problems of collective decision within courts, as well as the difficulty that the norms courts try to enforce can themselves be argued to be theoretically arbitrary, it seems clear that Riker and Weingast's proposals would encounter intractable difficulties in the real world of American constitutional law. Their practical argument turns on the different constitutional treatments of economic and political rights, but the Constitution treats these differently. Riker and Weingast indicate some awareness of these issues when they remark that "[i]t is one thing to argue that some rights are 'preferred' and should therefore receive greater scrutiny and wholly another to argue that some rights require and deserve no scrutiny."[55] But this is to wave misleadingly at the complexities of different tiers of judicial scrutiny.

To begin with, it is not obviously true that there is so radical a disjunction between the supreme Court's treatment of economic and civil rights as they assert. The cases Riker and Weingast cite deal explicitly with the institutional incapacity of courts to fashion economic policies, but they do not declare the courts to be without power to defend economic rights. We may not go all the way with Dworkin in holding that questions of "principle" are entirely separate from those of policy,[56] recognizing that policies always embody principles and that choices of principles invariably restrict the range of possible policies. But it will still be the case that a range of economic policies may be consistent with basic constitutional protections, so that the claim that the courts are incompetent to make economic policy but competent to protect economic rights is by no means vacuous. Certainly it has been the presumption behind a great deal of American constitutional law. In the realm of protecting economic rights, the courts have not been nearly so inactive as Riker and Weingast suggest, as has recently been shown by Martin Shapiro.[57]

More generally, the distinction between civil and property rights has become a good deal harder to draw in recent decades. Civil rights lawyers, in response to the strong protection afforded property rights in the *Lochner* era, invoked the language of Reich's "The New Property"[58] to argue with some success that what had traditionally been thought of in civil rights terms were in fact property rights.[59] Riker and Weingast offer no account of what is to count as a property right, and it is therefore difficult to evaluate their claim that property rights have received inferior protection.

With regard to the Court's alleged activism in the civil rights area, there are good reasons for thinking that this and its effects have been considerably exaggerated in much of the literature. Charles Black has usefully pointed out an important artificiality to much of the debate on the countermajoritarian problem since Bickel, in that the overwhelming majority of the activities of federal courts, even when engaged in judicial review, have nothing to do with the *Marbury v. Madison* problem of the authority of the Court to review the actions of Congress. Between 1937 and 1967 the Court annulled acts of Congress only twelve times. By far the greater part of federal judicial review is of the actions of state courts for federal constitutionality as provided for in Article VI, geared towards bringing the states into line with national law.[60] It is not because the actions of state or municipal institutions are acts of legislatures (when they are) that such actions are subject to review, but rather because they are the actions of subordinate institutions in the national federal structure; it is a Supremacy Clause issue. This has nothing to do with the countermajoritarian difficulty as Riker and Weingast conceive of it. Further, whether the constitutionality of state or federal law is involved, the typical case of federal judicial review[61] is not of the actions of a legislative branch at all, rather it is review of the actions of a federal or state official, a policeman, an investigator, a prison warden or a prosecutor. When we think of judicial activism in the civil rights area we are accustomed to think of the Court usurping legislative functions, but typically the problem is administrative action where the legislative branch of the national government has not spoken,[62] or actions of questionable legality because undertaken by parts of

legislative bodies rather than being the product of the full deliberations of lawmaking bodies as provided for in the Constitution.[63] Furthermore, much of the Court's alleged activism in the
civil rights area has been in furtherance of Congressional mandates such as the Civil Rights Act of 1964; it has had nothing to
do with protecting minority rights from the actions of a ram-
pant legislative branch.[64]

In the economic realm, too, the Court is bound to enforce
federal law, and its actions are limited by those provisions of the
Constitution explicitly conferring on Congress the power to
legislate in the national economic interest.[65] Riker and Weingast's position seems to require a return to *Lochner* not only for
the analytical reasons already noted, but also for historical ones.
The history they lamentingly describe is really the history of the
Supreme Court's retreat (to the extent that it has retreated)
from the doctrine of substantive due process. Tribe points out
that during the New Deal and afterwards the Court never entirely accepted the pluralist interest group theory of the political
process, remaining wedded to the notion that legislatures, "at
least in their regulatory capacity, must always act in furtherance
of public goals transcending the shifting summation of private
interests through the political process." But as a matter of institutional competence it retreated to the view that "even if the
public good or social justice could be defined apart from the
aggregation of political interests, and even if particular legislative restraints on liberty were profoundly unjust according to
some cognizable standard or principle, legislative choices among
conflicting values were beyond judicial competence to criticize
and hence beyond judicial authority to strike down."[66] It may
be that this "democratic relativism" was not entirely coherent
within its own terms, as Tribe, Smith and others have argued,[67]
since some set of substantive values is immanent in even the
most minimal standards of judicial scrutiny. But if this is so, it
cannot be argued that rights (property or any other) should be
defended by the Court against the actions of legislatures, however unrepresentative these latter might actually be, unless some
theory is supplied to explain which rights are desirable, and
why. This is the kind of task commentators such as Tribe and

Smith set for themselves. Whatever the difficulties confronting such enterprises, Riker and Weingast appear not even to notice that they are required. Instead they take it for granted that property rights should be protected by the Court because their abridgements "deter entrepreneurship and restrain economic growth."[68] For this wealth-maximizing theory of Constitutional scrutiny to be defended, an empirical theory would presumably have to be supplied establishing that it is in fact true. Riker and Weingast would then have to square the circle by arguing simultaneously that they are not violating Oliver Wendell Holmes's dictum in criticizing the *Lochner* rule, namely that "the Fourteenth Amendment does not enact Mr. Spencer's *Social Statics.*"[69]

Squaring this circle would require more than a theory of the deficiencies of majority rule. All that the latter can generate on its own in the way of justification for judicial scrutiny of Congressional action is footnote four justification for intervention in the specific circumstances where power is abused by corrupt incumbents to the point where the system of majority rule fails to operate (in the traditional sense of violating its own procedural rules, not the public choice sense of failing to produce "socially rational" outcomes), or some "discrete and insular minority" is systematically excluded from participation.[70] Such a rationale would not, however, generate a wealth-maximizing jurisprudence. Nor would it generate a utilitarian one geared to defend or maximize "equal concern and respect" as Ely would have us believe. The public choice theorists have taught us that to expect majority rule to produce that even in principle is to expect too much. One is bound to be likewise skeptical of the claims of such commentators as Beitz who note that the mere quantitative fairness of equal voting power will never ensure substantively democratic outcomes. In his view a truly democratic system of "qualitative fairness" requires a prior system of "just legislation," since mere equal voting power can never be guaranteed to produce fair outcomes. Lacking here the space to deal with this argument in detail, I simply note that the large number of competing theories of justice we have seen in recent years, none without serious difficulties that have been much commented upon in the journals, inevitably makes one skeptical that a theory of just legislation agreeable to all is around the corner.[71]

A footnote four justification, then, can at most legitimate intervention to make majority rule operate; it cannot posit some outcome that is alleged to be substantively democratic, and intervene on its basis. Nor does it result in a general defense of "economic" or of "political" rights. Only if they were the rights of dispossessed groups, excluded from participation in the political process, would they merit judicial protection from legislatures. These would include some "economic" and some "political" rights, but not, one suspects, those Riker and Weingast are most concerned to protect.[72] Indeed, a footnote four justification would be properly indifferent to the vulnerabilities of the wealthy, propertied, and powerful at the hands of majority rule, minorities though these latter well may be.

IV. The Instability Fallacy

Aside from their constitutional implications, what are the more general political ramifications of the public choice findings on the instability of majority rule? "Equilibrium," Ordeshook and Shepsle tell us, "is the pivotal concept of analytical political science."[73] Yet Condorcet, Arrow, Black, Plott, and their progeny established conclusively that equilibrium under majority rule can be predicted only in highly restricted circumstances. If there is some disagreement on the extent of political disequilibrium in the actual world,[74] and if theorists like Ordeshook continue to have faith that equilibrium might be redefined in ways that make it attainable,[75] equilibrium has yet to be achieved without the addition of substantial constraints on preferences, bias toward the status quo, or both.[76] For the moment one has to be persuaded by Riker that "politics is *the* dismal science because we have learned from it that there are no fundamental equilibria to predict. In the absence of such equilibria we cannot know much about the future at all, whether it is likely to be palatable or unpalatable, and in that sense our future is subject to the tricks and accidents of the way in which questions are posed and alternatives are offered and eliminated."[77]

Preoccupation with the relations between democratic procedures and stability is, of course, much older than the discipline of public choice, and different commentators have understood markedly different things by the term stability, and thought it desirable for different reasons. Pluralist theorists such as Dahl made the Hobbesian assumption that the alternative would be chaos. Indeed Dahl went so far as to argue that it would be desirable in principle to devise a voting system that took some account of intensity of preference, in part because this would engender political stability.[78] Although the public-choice theorists differ among themselves concerning the meaning of the term "equilibrium" (and hence of stability and instability),[79] they are united in approaching the problem from a quite different standpoint.

Far from assuming the alternative to government to be anarchical chaos, we have seen that the implicit counterfactual in this tradition is that private action is essentially benign, that collective action becomes necessary paradigmatically in circumstances of market failure, and that the problems then get generated because there is no rational way of organizing collective action. Stability, then, has nothing to do with social states. It is treated as a property of collective rationality and is desired for that reason. Thus, although Ordeshook concedes that governmental action is sometimes necessary to "break" what are really negative equilibria in the private sphere—such as prisoners' dilemma situations—the use of government in this way

> engender[s] new kinds of dilemmas. With a government's usual powers to expropriate wealth, interest groups form to lobby for particularlized private benefits. Economic efficiency becomes the new undersupplied public good, and, while all groups might agree jointly not to use the coercive powers of government for their particularized ends, none has any incentive unilaterally to choose another course. There is now, in fact, a growing belief that governments, in the grip of this dilemma, have grown too large and unwieldy, and that new constitutional rules such as spending limits are required to control the prisoners' dilemmas

among interest groups and constituencies that governments engender.[80]

The problem with instability in this public choice sense is that it makes possible, perhaps inevitable, constant cycles where new coalitions of interest groups form, that always have incentives to overturn an existing status quo for their individual benefit by adding taxes that directly or indirectly benefit them, to the overall detriment of society.

In a brilliant little essay, Nicholas Miller has shown that the traditional pluralist sense of political stability and the technical sense employed in the public choice literature contradict each other. Traditionally, a pluralist society was thought to be the polar opposite of a single-cleavage society (such as a feudal society). The early pluralists worked with a model of multiple cross-cutting cleavages; society was thought of as "ridden by a dozen oppositions along different lines running in every direction." One's allies in one context might become one's adversaries in another, so that society, as Ross put it, is "sown together by its inner conflicts."[81] Theorists treated this "pluralism of cleavages" as conducive to stability for four different but mutually reinforcing reasons. First, it was argued to moderate political preferences; the "cross-pressure" mechanisms that result from the fact that not all socialization forces operate in the same direction allegedly meant that political commitments are many-sided and less extreme. Second, pluralism was argued to moderate behavior because, in contrast to a polarized society in which "an individual or group has permanent friends" and "little incentive to behave moderately toward permanent enemies," future alliances are uncertain, and the possibility that a present opponent may become a future ally tends to moderate present behavior. Third, pluralism was thought to distribute political satisfaction more widely. No one wins all the time, making it simultaneously less likely that the same majority will systematically invade the rights of the same minority, and that any particular group will lose so often as to have no commitment to the system and nothing to lose but its proverbial chains. Finally, the very fact that pluralist politics invites political "strategems" of negotiation, coalition building and splitting, agenda manipulation, strategic voting, patronage and pork-barrel politics was thought to promote commitment to the system rather than extra-political action, since present losers have some realistic probability of becoming future winners.[82]

Yet these same factors undermine stability in the public choice sense of collective rationality. This can be seen from the theoretical strategies employed in the public choice literature to avoid cycles and produce stable equilibria. Exclusion conditions (which limit the admissible arrays of preferences such as Black's single-peakedness, Vickery's single-cavedness and Sen's value restriction), popularity conditions (postulating a high degree of consensus among voters, even where exclusion conditions are violated), and balance conditions (like Plott's condition requiring symmetry of disagreement) all share this in common: they attempt to combat the fact that as the number of preferences increases and becomes more heterogeneous, so does the likelihood of cycles. So they try to limit heterogeneity in a variety of ways, at the cost of undermining those factors that make for pluralist stability. Although pluralist theorists have not explicitly argued that cycling is desirable (they have tended to ignore it), "they have argued that certain preference patterns promote, and others threaten, political stability, and it turns out that the former typically entail, whereas the latter preclude, majority cycling"[83]

Miller distances himself from early pluralists such as Latham and Truman, who had argued, under the banner "for every group an interest and for every interest a group," that public policy is "actually the equilibrium reached in the group struggle at any given moment."[84] Differences in size and resources and the failure of some "potential groups" ever to organize effectively means, as Schattschneider and others have noted, that even where equilibrium among organized groups exists and determines public outcomes, it "merits no particular approbation as fair public policy."[85] Miller wants to rescue a version of pluralist theory that is not vulnerable in the ways that the early groups theories were vulnerable, and argue that pluralist stability in this new sense should be chosen over the public-choice stability qua rational social equilibrium. Miller argues not just that cyclical majority preference is an "otherwise undesirable

phenomenon that happens to come along with pluralistic preference patterns and that we must accept [it] as the unavoidable
cost of achieving the great benefit of political stability." Rather,
he goes further, arguing that the instability of the political process is itself desirable because it moderates attitudes and behavior, distributes political satisfaction more widely and engenders
political participation. He even toys with the notion that this
kind of instability may actually play a causal role in creating a
pluralist society.[86]

Miller's argument that stability in the public-choice sense is
undesirable is persuasive. Apart from the potential Stalinist implications that would attend any attempt to enforce institutional
limitations on preferences, we saw in our discussion of Riker
and Weingast that the problem of cycling is practically insurmountable. Any particular solution to it turns out also to be
vulnerable to cycling (as are courts and procedures for determining "constitutional" rights), or to be arbitrary. Ordeshook's
suggestion that there should be new constitutional constraints
on spending because of the problem of cycling under majority
rule can be shown to be similarly vulnerable. Just as we have no
way to increase public spending neutrally, we have no way to
cut it neutrally, as the Reagan tax cuts of the 1980s revealed all
too well. One cannot argue that there is no public good when
criticizing majority rule, and then wheel out the same idea to
limit its operation. When Ordeshook says that under majority
rule economic efficiency becomes an "undersupplied" public
good,[87] like Buchanan and Tullock before him, he is disguising
in neutral language a claim that by its nature cannot be neutral,
unless we implausibly solve the resources and externalities problems by definition. Given that the option of literally no government of any kind is unavailable, the inescapable fact is that
different amounts and kinds of taxation and spending will benefit different groups differently, and there is no theoretical
reason to expect—indeed there is every theoretical reason to
doubt—that any mode of taxing and spending can be said to be
neutral in that it benefits everyone, let alone that it benefits
everyone equally or proportionately.

Miller's argument that promoting public-choice stability undermines pluralist stability, by reducing incentives for the al-

ready dispossessed to participate, and by reinforcing (and perhaps even tending to create) small numbers of deep cleavages that are pervasive over time and space, is plausible so far as it goes. His picture of a pluralist culture is, however, too sanguine for our circumstances. First, his attempt to separate himself from the naive assumptions about power and resources of the early group pluralists is less than persuasive. Miller distinguishes their group pluralism from his own "pluralism as dispersed preferences," but this does not dispose of the problem that different individuals have vastly different resources for making their preferences effective, different amounts, that is, of social and economic power. Whether applied to individuals or to groups and organizations, the happy pluralist story can be true only if there are not radical inequalities in capacity to influence the political process, and Miller's tangential remarks about power fail to persuade that this is so.[88] Second, Miller contends that a stable (pluralist sense) majoritarian political process actually creates pluralism, on the grounds that "if an effective constitutional consensus prevails, members of society are free to pursue their own more particular preferences (for government outputs, rather than for forms of government), which are more likely to be pluralistically distributed."[89] This is implausible in the absence of a good deal of further argument that is not supplied. One does not have to go all the way with the Marxists to be skeptical of the claim that the existence of majority rule and competitive parties is sufficient to create a genuine social "pluralism of dispersed preferences," to the point where jettisoning the model of fundamental cleavages is warranted. For the pluralist case to be plausible we have to assume, as Miller more or less concedes,[90] and as the early pluralists certainly assumed, that the causal arrows run in the opposite direction, that we already have a society that is fundamentally pluralist.

This seems unwarranted for two reasons. First, we know that there are vast inequalities of wealth that inevitably bring with them unequal influence in the political process. Congress has attempted to reduce this by limiting political expenditures on behalf of candidates, but the Supreme Court held that such limitations are unconstitutional abridgements of the First

Amendment; Congress may limit only contributions to political parties and political action committees, not expenditures.[91] Even in countries such as Great Britain, where political expenditures and advertising are far more strictly regulated, it is common knowledge that the amount spent on behalf of Conservative Party candidates always greatly exceeds that spent on behalf of the Labour Party.

Second, a thoroughgoing pluralism of "dispersed preferences" has to come to terms with the problem of political elites (leaving aside, to make it an independent point, the relations in which they may stand to social and economic elites). Pluralists such as Dahl developed their theories partly in reaction to the elite theories of Michels and others, but if they argued that no "iron law of oligarchy" exists such that a single elite would find a way to get control of any political system however organized, they did acknowledge that in the world of mass politics and widespread political apathy, the most one could realistically hope for was a circulation of elites.[92] Cycling majorities may remove incumbents from power on a fairly regular basis,[93] but we should not delude ourselves that what is at work here is a "pluralism of dispersed preferences" where everyone gets her turn.

If the public-choice theorists have taught us that elected representatives seldom represent majorities, and that interest group politics benefits coalitions of minorities at best, we might welcome cyclical majorities for a different reason than Miller's. Since we remain unpersuaded by the public choice theorists' other claim—that there can be some morally and distributively neutral devices (whether courts, constitutional spending limits, or unanimity voting) for limiting interest group politics in the public interest—it follows that a degree of illegitimacy will invariably attach to incumbents. If politics is inevitable but political powerholders are invariably illegitimate in that they derive disproportionate benefits for themselves and minority constituents, we might welcome a system that makes incumbents perpetually vulnerable. We would do so not out of any belief that this reflects (let alone creates) a substantively democratic culture (whatever that might be), but simply because they should be gotten out. In the classic example from the public choice literature, if there is a hundred dollars in possible benefits to be distributed by majority rule, and three or more people voting on its allocation, whatever self-interested coalition forms to distribute it to its members (or their constituents), that coalition will be vulnerable to an alternative majority coalition that might form containing some present winners and some present losers.[94] Yet if no group can really claim legitimate title to the benefits, and, *pace* Buchanan and Tullock, Riker and Weingast and Ordeshook, "not having" the benefits is not an option because collective inaction turns out in particular cases always to amount to an implicit tax on some interest group or individual, then the perpetual vulnerability of current beneficiaries is desirable. Everyone should always be gotten out because the politics of distribution can never be neutral and the gains of present beneficiaries are therefore to some extent ill-gotten, but the paradoxical reality is that someone always has to be in.

V. Democracy and Political Power

It is remarkable that so little of the literature in democratic theory attends to the question of what politics is about. Yet any evaluation of majority rule as a decision-making mechanism must surely be parasitic on a view of politics, or we are without criteria to judge its success or failure. Every democratic theory operates, of course, with implicit assumptions and expectations about the nature of politics, and a little digging can usually bring them to light. We saw that the public choice theorists' explicit position is that the business of politics is preference amalgamation, although they often operate with implicit utilitarian commitments to policies they believe conducive to wealth maximization. Traditional pluralists such as Dahl and their latter-day progeny such as Miller see politics as about something quite different, the circulation of groups or elites through the political process to provide as much representation as it is realistic to expect in a post-Schumpeterian era, while maintaining social stability. Conventional Marxists see bourgeois politics in purely instrumental terms, to be employed tactically as a harbinger of a future of superabundance that will render it redundant. Communitarian democrats like Barber believe that politics can be, and can be experienced as, a joint enterprise of common interests without such extravagant assumptions about socio-economic transformation.[95] Utilitarians like Harsanyi employ end-state principles to argue that leaving things to political experts will produce more desirable outcomes than enhancing participation.[96]

My own view is that politics is fundamentally about the possession and dispossession of power, and that three inescapable truths about power must shape our theoretical argument. The first is that power relations are ubiquitous; this much we have learned from Foucault (some would say Plato). They are ubiquitous both in that they emerge in virtually every facet of social and economic life, and in that attempts to eradicate power relations invariably fail.[97] This is not to deny (as Foucault may have done) that some ways of managing power relations are preferable to others; it is only to say that there are no permanent, and no neutral, solutions to the struggles that drive political conflict.

A second truth about political power is that possession of it is inherently corrupting. I do not mean to suggest that all forms of power are corrupting. Power is sometimes simply an enabling condition for an individual without reference to anyone else; the empowerment that comes from conquering a neurosis may be unambiguously liberating. But that is not political power, for political power is inherently other-regarding, it is power over others.[98] Indeed, I propose to define political power in this way, because it avoids restricting political power to power exercised by or through state agencies. That limiting assumption, we saw, played a large part in driving both the reductionist and constitutionalist fallacies. Whenever power over others is exercised it is political on my view—though whether it is politicized (seen as political by the relevant agents) is another matter. Thus rape of a wife was always a political action, but it only became politicized when the common law presumption of its impossibility was displaced by statutes defining it as a crime.[99]

If power relations are ubiquitous and the possession of political power tends to corrupt, the third truth about power that we cannot afford to ignore is that lack of power in a world of ubiquitous power relations is demeaning and destructive for the powerless. Powerlessness is not a happy state. When we see those without power rebel they tend to arouse our sympathy, if not empathy, and when victims of power fail to rebel we find it deeply troubling. Consider the amazed consternation in public debate and scholarship alike at evidence of Jewish complicity in the Holocaust. We find such phenomena troubling just because they conflict with our sense that the downtrodden should fight back.

From the understanding that politics is fundamentally about power thus conceived, we are now in a position to sum up the defects behind the fallacies discussed in this chapter. The reductionist fallacy's central weakness is its failure to deal with the problem of resources, and we can now see that in so doing it ignores most of what politics is really about. For the sense of powerlessness that sometimes motivates political action, and at other times generates our intuition that political action is warranted, is exactly the lack of resources of individuals and groups to achieve goods and limit harms on their own. The constitutionalist fallacy also results largely from ignoring problems of power. Although the public-choice theorists here discussed are persuasive that we have no reason to expect majority rule to produce fair or just outcomes, this does not supply a rationale for what is often a utilitarian jurisprudence geared towards maximization of wealth. Rather, real differences in resources can legitimate judicial activism aimed only at weeding out manifest corruption of public officials and to protect the politically excluded in terms of footnote four, a jurisprudence of permanent sympathy for the underdog but no more. Some will find this an insufficiently robust basis for judicial activism, particularly if we disallow expansionist readings of footnote four such as Ely's, which attempted to incorporate much of the Warren Court's judicial action. I am not foreclosing the possibility that there might be grounds for judicial activism other than ensuring the actual operation of majority rule, though these cannot be derived from democratic theory alone. Whatever their additional premises, proponents of broad latitude for the Court in interpreting and enforcing constitutional values[100] must live with the risk that although it can give us the Warren Court, it can also give us *Lochner* and what we are likely to get from the Court in the next several decades. Gone is the time when we can live on a Bickelian act of faith that the Court will reflect public attitudes, even if it reflects changes in public attitudes more slowly than frequently reelected legislatures. Nor is it reasonable to believe in a secular trend toward the triumph of more enlightened views; our own circumstances belie this.

The stability fallacy ignores power in another way, since the public-choice theorists fail to see that their sense of stability is the very enemy of the democratic aspiration. Democracy is fundamentally an ideology of opposition, not government; it is about displacing entrenched elites, undermining the powerful, empowering the powerless. If the public-choice theorists have shown us that there is no way of translating this ideal into a fair system of government, of domesticating it, not only should we not be surprised, but this fact should make us welcome the perpetual instability of dominant coalitions. Although we do not share Miller's faith that *this* instability will create or promote a pluralist stability of equitably circulating interest groups—we know too much about the ubiquity of power and inequality to believe that—at least the dominant coalitions with their ill-gotten gains will from time to time be displaced. In saying this we should avoid the characteristic liberal trap of assuming that it is only the power of government that we need to fear, even to fear the most. Government is one major source of organized power, but there are many others. And it is just because politics is fundamentally about power, and only incidentally about governmental power, that democracy as an effective ideology of opposition or of disruption can be brought to bear in the many different dimensions of social life that are structured by power relations. Thus have we seen strong democratic rationales in recent years for the politicization of employment and family relations. No doubt the democratic ideal will, in the future, provide the impetus to politicize relations that we today take for granted as wholly without political significance.

Yet we are bound to conclude with a view more complex than that instability is always and everywhere desirable. There are too many moral ambiguities surrounding the power that, through politics, we seek to manipulate, control, escape, and possess. In a world of ubiquitous power relations, where the possession of power is frequently as corrupting as the lack of it is demeaning, it may be that although the democratic aspiration of empowering the powerless and undermining the powerful is indispensible, it remains inherently problematical as a philosophical ideal.

NOTES

1. John Hart Ely, *Democracy and Distrust: A Theory of Judicial Review* (Cambridge: Harvard University Press, 1980), 7–8; Bruce Ackerman, *Social Justice in the Liberal State* (New Haven: Yale University Press, 1980), 323; William H. Riker and Barry R. Weingast, "Constitutional Regulation of Legislative Choice: The Political Consequences of Judicial Deference to Legislatures," *Working Papers in Political Science*, no. P-86-11 (December 1986) (Stanford: The Hoover Institution), 25.

2. Mill, for example, argued for a second vote for the intellectual classes, in order to temper the influence of the new majorities on bastions of privilege and autonomy; and Tocqueville argued to the Ultras in the 1830s that they should accept the inevitable expansion of democracy so as to have some hope of influencing its future direction. John Stuart Mill, *Utilitarianism, On Liberty, and Considerations on Representative Government* (London: J. M. Dent & Sons, 1972), 276–92; Alexis de Tocqueville, *Democracy in America* (New York: Doubleday, 1969), 12–13ff.

3. See Louis Hartz, *The Liberal Tradition in America: An Interpretation of American Political Thought since the Revolution* (New York: Harcourt, Brace, Jovanovich, 1955), 35–86.

4. James Buchanan and Gordon Tullock, *The Calculus of Consent: Logical Foundations of Constitutional Democracy* (Michigan: Ann Arbor Paperbacks, 1962), 78, 96 (emphasis in original).

5. Ibid., 63–77.

6. Ibid., 77, 73, 73–74, 75, 75–76.

7. Ibid., 126.

8. This is not strictly true if vote trading is allowed. Under that assumption, and also assuming no decision-making costs, there is no optimal decision rule for the same reason as Coase showed that, in the absence of information costs, wealth effects, external effects, and other blockages to exchange such as free riding, no system of tort liability rules is more efficient than any other. Whatever the system, people will then make exchanges to produce Pareto-optimal results. R. H. Coase, "The Problem of Social Cost," *The Journal of Law and Economics* 3 (1960): 1–44. Assuming that a pure market in votes does not exist, however, and Buchanan and Tullock acknowledge that some con-

straints on it are inevitable, they maintain that unanimity would uniquely be chosen in the absence of decision-making costs. Buchanan and Tullock, *Calculus*, 270–74.

9. See Douglas W. Rae, "The Limits of Consensual Decision," *American Political Science Review*, 69 (4) (1975): 1270–94. See also James S. Fishkin, *Tyranny and Legitimacy: A Critique of Political Theories* (Baltimore: Johns Hopkins University Press, 1979), 69.

10. When the number of voters is odd the optimal decision rule is majority rule, *n* over two, plus one-half; when *n* is even, the optimal decision rule is either majority rule (*n* over two plus one), or majority rule minus one (simply *n* over two). Douglas W. Rae, "Decision-Rules and Individual Values in Constitutional Choice," *American Political Science Review*, 63 (1) (1969): 40–56.

11. Barry Nalebuff has pointed out to me that there are other ways of tackling the problem of bias toward the status quo. For instance, our decision rule might be to adopt the policy that commands the largest majority among all proposals, including the status quo, in pairwise comparisons. Note that this is empirically unrealistic (collective decisions are seldom presented in this form), however, and it ignores the organization costs of mobilizing to displace a status quo that will presumably be positive.

12. Robert Paul Wolff, *In Defense of Anarchism* (New York: Harper & Row, 1970), 27.

13. See Ian Shapiro, *The Evolution of Rights in Liberal Theory* (Cambridge: Cambridge University Press, 1986), 163–64.

14. Wolff, *In Defense of Anarchism*, 72, 76–78.

15. Robert Nozick, *Anarchy State and Utopia* (New York: Basic Books, 1974), 54–87; Shapiro, *Evolution*, 165–78.

16. Buchanan and Tullock, *Calculus*, 65–66 (emphasis added).

17. Ibid., 74, 82.

18. Ibid., 91.

19. For a fuller discussion of these tests see Shapiro, *Evolution*, 169–76.

20. Buchanan and Tullock, *Calculus*, 91.

21. Ibid., 126, 132–33 (emphasis deleted).

22. As Rawls has noted, those who have greater confidence and stronger feelings on an issue are no more likely to be right, and indeed they are often less sensitive to its complexities than are others. John Rawls, *A Theory of Justice* (Cambridge: Harvard University Press, 1971), 230–31, 361.

23. Buchanan and Tullock, *Calculus*, 77.

24. Thus Rae argues that because majority rule has unique proper-

ties that make it preferable to unanimity rule, it would probably be chosen by every individual under conditions of uncertainty. Rae, "Decision Rules," 40–56. And if we move backwards in the contractarian tradition to Locke, or forward to Rawls and Nozick, the problem is typically construed as devising a set of institutional rules or structures that did or would command unanimity for the basic societal charter. It merits attention that here we expect less from reality than from theory, since no historical constitution has ever commanded anything approaching full unanimity.

25. Jean-Jacques Rousseau, *The First and Second Discourses*, ed. R. D. Masters, trans. J. R. Masters (New York: St Martin's, 1964), 129.

26. Buchanan and Tullock, *Calculus*, 71 (emphasis added).

27. Thus human and property rights qualify for strong protection against majoritarian processes "after these have once been defined and generally accepted by the community. Property rights especially can never be defined once and for all." Ibid., 73.

28. Ibid., 74, 88, 93.

29. Jules Coleman, "Competition and Cooperation," *Ethics*, 98 (1) (October 1987): 82.

30. William H. Riker, *Liberalism Against Populism: A Confrontation between the Theory of Democracy and the Theory of Social Choice* (San Francisco: W. H. Freeman, 1982), 14.

31. Riker and Weingast, "Constitutional Regulation" 3–7, 26.

32. For a more complete analysis of these and related decisions, see Lawrence Tribe, *American Constitutional Law* (Mineola: N.Y.: Foundation Press, 1978), 450–55.

33. "There may be a narrower scope for operation of the presumption of constitutionality when legislation appears on its face to be within a specific prohibition of the Constitution, such as those of the first ten Amendments, which are deemed equally specific when held to be embraced within the Fourteenth. . . .

It is unnecessary to consider now whether legislation which restricts those political processes which can ordinarily be expected to bring about repeal of undesirable legislation, is to be subjected to more exacting judicial scrutiny under the general prohibitions of the Fourteenth Amendment than are most other types of legislation. . . .

Nor need we enquire whether similar considerations enter into the review of statutes directed at particular religious . . . or racial minorities . . . whether prejudice against discrete and insular minorities may be a special condition, which tends seriously to curtail the operation of those political processes ordinarily to be relied upon to protect minorities, and which may call for a correspondingly more searching judicial inquiry." (*United States v. Carolene Products Co.*, 304 U.S. 144, 152 n. 4, citations omitted).

34. Riker and Weingast, "Constitutional Regulation," 6.

35. Condorcet noticed that if there are at least three voters and at least three issues, certain rankings of those preferences can produce a potential for endless cycles of majority preference, making the order in which issues are voted on the key determinant of the outcome. For instance, if voter 1 prefers policy *a* to *b* and *b* to *c*, voter 2 prefers *b* to *c* and *c* to a, and voter 3 prefers *c* to *a* and *a* to *b*, there is no stable result. That is, there is a majority for *a* over *b* (voters 1 and 3), a majority for *b* over *c* (voters 1 and 2) and a majority for *c* over *a* (voters 2 and 3).

36. As in the example in the preceding footnote, where society prefers *a* to *b*, *b* to *c*, and *c* to *a*.

37. Riker and Weingast, "Constitutional Regulation," 8–10.

38. Ibid., 13.

39. Dennis C. Mueller, *Public Choice* (Cambridge: Cambridge University Press, 1979), 38–49; Riker, *Liberalism Against Populism*, 119–23, 186.

40. See Riker and Weingast, "Constitutional Regulation," 13–18 for some anecdotal examples.

41. Ibid., 19.

42. Ibid., 25.

43. Ibid., 22 (footnotes omitted).

44. Ibid., 23, 24, 26.

45. See Frank H. Easterbrook, "Ways of Criticizing the Court," *Harvard Law Review*, 95 (1982): 802–32. For an earlier argument, see Walter Murphy, *Elements of Judicial Strategy* (Chicago: University of Chicago Press, 1964), 37–122. For a more general argument that if voting really is as meaningless as Riker claims, this undermines his "liberalism" at least as much as it does the "populism" he attacks, see Jules Coleman, and John Ferejohn, "Democracy and Social Choice," *Ethics*, 97 (1) (1986): 11–22.

46. Of course this will not invariably be so, as when the preferences of judges are limited by precedent, as Lea Brilmayer has pointed out to me. But when precedents are ambiguous or conflicting in their applications, judicial decisions become vulnerable to problems of collective decision. There is also the fact that when a precedent was initially created it may have resulted from agenda manipulation in the presence of cyclical preferences, strategic voting, or some other theoretically arbitrary collective decision.

47. William H. Riker, "Vote-Trading at the Constitutional Conven-

tion," in William H. Riker, *The Art of Political Manipulation* (New Haven: Yale University Press, 1986), 89–102.

48. Riker and Weingast, "Constitutional Regulation," 22.

49. Kenneth A. Shepsle, and Barry R. Weingast, "Political Solutions to Market Problems," *American Political Science Review,* 78 (2) (1984): 417–34.

50. See Kenneth J. Arrow, *Social Choice and Individual Values,* 2d ed. (New Haven: Yale University Press, 1951, 1963), 51–60.

51. See ibid., 61–120 and Mueller, *Public Choice,* 184–226 for discussion.

52. There are some exceptions. For example Caplan and Nalebuff have shown that a "supermajority" rule of 64 percent will under certain conditions avoid cycles, although this requires some constraints on the diversity of preferences. Andrew Caplan and Barry Nalebuff, "On 64 Percent Majority Rule," unpublished paper, June, 1987.

53. For a useful summary account of the public choice findings on the significance of agenda control, see Mueller, *Public Choice,* 44–45, 57–58, 70–71, 83, 197–98, 211–12, 219–21, 224–25, 266–67.

54. For a useful discussion of the practical implications of conflating neutrality and inaction in the context of *Lochner,* see Cass Sunstein, "Lochner's Legacy," *Columbia Law Review* 87 (1987): 201–47.

55. Riker and Weingast "Constitutional Regulation," p. 26.

56. See Ronald Dworkin, *A Matter of Principle* (Cambridge: Harvard University Press, 1985), 81–89ff.

57. Martin Shapiro, "The Supreme Court's 'Return' to Economic Regulation," in *Studies in American Political Development,* vol. 1, ed, K. Orren and S. Skowronek (New Haven: Yale University Press, 1986), 91–141. Indeed, as I write this (June 1987), the Supreme Court handed down a six to three decision holding that the takings clause entitles property owners to compensation for changes in zoning regulations that deprive them of reasonable use of their land (not just invalidation of the new rules), *First English Evangelical Lutheran Church of Glendale v. County of Los Angeles,* 107 sct. p. 2378, heralded as a major victory for property owners and real estate developers.

58. C. A. Reich, "The New Property," *Yale Law Journal,* 73 (5) (1965): 733–87.

59. Thus, for example, in *Goldberg v. Kelly,* 397 U.S. 254, 261–2 (1969), the Supreme Court was persuaded that welfare recipients' benefits are statutory entitlements, and that due process therefore required that they could not be terminated by state officials without a hearing. It was just this assimilation of property rights with welfare benefits that outraged Justice Black in dissent, who argued that welfare

recipients' benefits should not be raised to the status of a property right, and so gain the due process protections property rights enjoy, 275.

60. Charles L. Black, Jr., *Structure and Relationship in Constitutional Law* (Baton Rouge: Louisiana State University Press, 1969), 67–76.

61. Excluding the review of interpretations of federal law by state courts, which clearly is of no interest to the issues at hand here, and which no one doubts are properly reviewable by federal courts. *Martin v. Hunter's Lessee* 1 Wheaton 304 (1816) upheld the power of Congress to direct the Supreme Court to hear writs of error of state court judgments denying federal claims under a jurisdictional statute that treated federal constitutional claims with other claims. Black, *Structure and Relationship*, 74.

62. As in *Miranda v. Arizona*, 384 U.S. 436 (1966).

63. As in *Barenblatt v. United States* 360 U.S. 109 (1959). Black, *Structure and Relationship*, 83, 88–91.

64. Indeed, there are scholars who tell us that even in the famed area of school desegregation since *Brown*, the role of the courts has been greatly exaggerated; the critical changes came about as a result of legislative action. David L. Horowitz, *The Courts and Social Policy* (Washington, D.C.: Brookings Institution, 1977), 255–98; Gerald N. Rosenberg, "The Courts, Congress and Civil Rights: Comparing Institutional Capabilities," paper presented at the annual meeting of the American Political Science Association, Washington, D.C., 1983. See also his *Hollow Hope* (Chicago, University of Chicago Press, forthcoming).

65. The Constitution gives Congress the power to tax (art. I, sec. 8 [1], sec. 10, [1,2]; borrow (art. I, sec. 8 [2]; regulate international and interstate commerce (art. I, sec. 8 [3], sec. 9 [5 and 6]), bankruptcy (art. I, sec. 8 [4], and money (art. I, sec. 8 [5]; prevent fraud (art. I, sec. 8 [6]; and issue patents and copyrights (art. I, sec. 8 [8]). The takings clause of the 5th Amendment requires only "just compensation," it does not otherwise limit the power of eminent domain, and Congress is explicitly authorized, in section 5 of the 14th Amendment to "enforce, by appropriate legislation," the requirement of Section 1 that no person be deprived of "life, liberty, or property, without due process of law."

66. Tribe, *American Constitutional Law*, 451, 452.

67. Ibid., 452–45; Rogers M. Smith, *Liberalism and American Constitutional Law* (Cambridge: Harvard University Press, 1985), 114–16. The term "democratic relativism" is Smith's.

68. Riker and Weingast, "Constitutional Regulation," 22.

69. *Lochner v. New York*, 198 U.S. 45, 75 (1905).

70. For powerful critique of even this narrow interpretation of footnote 4 see Lea Brilmayer, *"Carolene,* Conflicts and the Fate of the 'Insider-Outsider'," *University of Pennsylvania Law Review,* 134 (6) (July, 1986): 1291–1334.

71. Ely, *Democracy and Distrust,* 76–77, 82; Charles Beitz, "Equal Opportunity in Political Representation," in *Equal Opportunity,* ed. Norman E. Bowie (Boulder, Colorado: Westview Press, 1988), 155–74.

72. For a useful account of footnote four and its purposes, see Robert Cover, "The Origins of Judicial Activism in the Protection of Minorities," *Yale Law Journal,* 91 (7) (1982): 1287–1316. For a critical discussion of Ely's attempt to base an entire substantive jurisprudence on it, see Smith, *American Constitutional Law,* 90–91, 170.

73. Peter C. Ordeshook and Kenneth A. Shepsle, eds., *Political Equilibrium* (Boston: Kluwer-Nijhoff Publishing, 1982), xii.

74. See Mueller, *Public Choice,* 38–49; Gordon Tullock, "Why so much stability?" *Public Choice,* 37 (2) (1981): 189–205; Riker and Weingast, "Constitutional Regulation," 13–18; Coleman and Ferejohn, "Democracy and Social Choice," 23–25.

75. Peter C. Ordeshook, "Political Disequilibrium and Scientific Inquiry: A comment on William H. Riker's 'Implications from the Disequilibrium of Majority Rule for the Study of Institutions'," in Ordeshook and Shepsle, *Political Equilibrium,* 25–31.

76. Wolff, *In Defense of Anarchism;* and Mueller, *Public Choice.*

77. William H. Riker, "Implications from the Disequilibrium of Majority Rule," 19.

78. Robert A. Dahl, *A Preface to Democratic Theory* (Chicago: University of Chicago Press, 1956), 92–102.

79. Two of the most common definitions, as formulated by Ordeshook, are (1) in situations when people are essentially acting alone, "an equilibrium corresponds to an outcome in which, *ex post,* no one person has any incentive to change his or her decisions unilaterally and to do something else"; and (2) in "situations in which people can act in concert, with various subsets of people coordinating their actions to form 'coalitions,' an equilibrium corresponds to an outcome in which no coalition has the incentive or the means of unliaterally insuring an improvement in the welfare of all its members." Ordeshook, "Political Disequilibrium," 26.

80. Ordeshook, "Political Disequilibrium," 28–29.

81. E. A. Ross, *The Principles of Sociology* (New York: Century, 1920), 164–65.

82. Nicholas R. Miller, "Pluralism and Social Choice," *American Political Science Review,* 77 (3) (1983); 735, 736–38, 743.

83. Ibid., 739–40.

84. E. Latham, "The Group Basis of Politics: Notes for a Theory," *American Political Science Review*, 46 (2) (1952): 390.

85. Miller, "Pluralism," 735.

86. Ibid., 742, 736.

87. Ordeshook, "Political Disequilibrium," 28–29.

88. "I assume here that political power relations are simple, probably majoritarian—i.e., any majority coalition can bring about any outcome." Miller, "Pluralism," 735.

89. Ibid., 736.

90. Ibid.

91. *Buckley v. Valeo* 424 U.S. 1 (1976). See also *First National Bank of Boston v. Bellotti*, 435 U.S. 765 (1978), extending the *Buckley* protection of unlimited expenditures to corporations as well as individuals, and *Federal Election Commission v. NCPAC* 105 S.Ct 1459 (1985), holding it to be an unconstitutional limitation on political speech for Congress to limit expenditures of political action committees on behalf of candidates, as a condition for the receipt of public funds by those candidates during election campaigns.

92. Dahl, *A Preface to Democratic Theory*, 131ff.

93. Although, as Miller notes, the relations among changing preferences, voting and outcome are likely to be considerably more complex than this formulation suggests. Miller, "Pluralism," 743.

94. For further discussion of these kinds of examples, see Mueller, *Public Choice*, 38–49.

95. See Benjamin Barber, *Strong Democracy: Participatory Politics for a New Age* (Berkeley: University of California Press, 1984).

96. See John Harsanyi, "Democracy, Equality and Popular Consent," in *Power, Inequality and Democratic Politics: Essays in Honor of Robert Dahl*, ed. Ian Shapiro and Grant Reeher (Boulder, Colorado: Westview Press, 1988) 276–83. For criticism of this view see my "A comment on John Harsanyi's 'Democracy, Equality and Popular Consent'," in Shapiro and Reeher, eds., *Power, Inequality, and Democratic Politics*, 284–90.

97. For my account of why power relations are ineradicable in principle, see Ian Shapiro, "Gross Concepts in Political Argument," *Political Theory*, 17 (1) (1989), 51–76.

98. I take this understanding of the nature of political power to be behind MacIntyre's poignant observation that as Marxists approach power they tend to become Weberians. See Alisdair MacIntyre, *After Virtue*, 2d ed. (Notre Dame, University of Notre Dame Press, 1984), i–ix, 261–62.

99. For further discussion, see Shapiro, "Gross Concepts." On the

changing law of marital rape, see "To Have and to Hold: The Marital Rape Exemption and the Fourteenth Amendment," Note, *Harvard Law Review*, 99 (1986): 1255–73.

100. For a defense of the view that there are objective Constitutional values (against the conventionalist arguments of Stanley Fish and others) deriving from the "interpretive community" of federal judges, see Owen Fiss, "Objectivity and Interpretation," *Stanford Law Review*, 34 (1982): 739–63, and his "Conventionalism," *Southern California Law Review*, 58 (1) (1985); 177–97.

5

DEMOCRATIC THEORY AND
THE DEMOCRATIC AGENT

DIANA T. MEYERS

Democratic theories as opposed as those of James Buchanan and Benjamin Barber, not to mention the many shades of opinion in between, advocate liberty and equality—the two values that have assumed preeminence in modern democratic theory.[1] Despite the divergent interpretations of these values proffered by different theories, liberty and equality are seen as valuable from the personal as well as the social point of view. The rights that liberty and equality mandate shield individuals from the frustrations and humiliations of others' unwarranted interference or pretended superiority. Moreover, through the enfranchisement of every citizen, democratic theories capitalize on the distinctive contributions to society that individuals are capable of making. In the privacy that democracy accords individuals and in the role it invites them to play in political life, democracy pays homage to the dignity of human agents, as such.

In this chapter, I explore the conceptions of the self that underlie three types of democratic theory: public-choice theory, radical-participation theory, and majoritarian theory. My objec-

I am grateful to the editors of this volume for their helpful comments on earlier versions of this chapter.

tive is to develop an account of the democratic agent that renders democracy's characteristic respect for persons intelligible. I begin by arguing that both the individualistic self associated with public-choice theory and the social self associated with radical-participation theory lack a convincing account of individual integrity. Neither sufficiently anchors personal identity to account for the individual interests democratic institutions are designed to secure and the individual capabilities democratic institutions are designed to tap. I then furnish an alternative conception of the self—the self-defining agent—and I argue that this conception supports an explication of individual integrity that makes sense of the democratic view of the person.

My conclusions regarding the nature of the democratic agent seriously undermine the conceptions of consensus that public-choice theory and radical-participation theory respectively uphold. These two conceptions presuppose a self so adaptable to its political surroundings that individual integrity collapses into selfish or ignorant obstinacy. Consequently, neither of these theories is sensitive to the pain that compromised integrity brings, and neither adequately protects people from it.

In contrast, Ian Shapiro's chapter, "Four Fallacies Concerning Majorities, Minorities, and Democratic Politics," rejects consensus as the goal of democracy and treats majoritarian democracy as an ideology of opposition in the name of empowerment and empowerment through opposition. I am sympathetic to many of Shapiro's claims about democracy; for example, his stress on the ways in which majority rule facilitates realignments of power and on the inability of popular sovereignty to eliminate social conflict. But I have some reservations about Shapiro's view—reservations that arise from what strikes me as a pervasive skepticism, even cynicism, that seems to exclude ideals of justice and political participation from democratic theory.

Shapiro affirms that the only rights that deserve constitutional protection are those that are instrumental in democratic processes, and he denies that there is any such thing as just legislation. All political issues should be settled by majority rule, and no political decision should outlast the majority that enacted it. Although majoritarianism comports well with the self-defining agent's weak ties to some of its qualities, I believe that majoritarian theory does not attend to the full range of the democratic agent's capacities. Specifically, this view overlooks the ways in which faculties of self-definition inextricably bind democratic agents to some of their qualities. This process of identification makes democratic agents liable to compromised integrity and, I shall urge, justifies counter-majoritarian principles that safeguard people's integrity.

1. The Individualistic Self, the Social Self, and Consensus Democracy

Shapiro and I concur in rejecting two democratic theories — public choice theory and radical-participation theory. As Jane Mansbridge points out, both of these theories are concerned with political consensus.[2] But, because each conceives of consensus differently, they furnish discrepant accounts of the purpose of consensus and of the process of arriving at it.

For the public-choice theorist, the object of requiring consensus is to protect individuals when their interests conflict by arming each person with a veto. No action can be taken unless it is acceptable to everyone. Accordingly, political consensus occurs when government institutes Pareto optimal policies, that is, policies that make some people better-off without making anyone worse-off.[3] Disregarding information costs, on this view, unanimity is possible because no deprivation is beyond compensation, and popular sovereignty is analyzed in terms of the aggregation of individual interests. Since everyone can be bought off, in one way or another everyone's desires can be satisfied.

In contrast, radical-participation theory sees the search for consensus as a search for common interests that undergird policies expressing the collective will of the citizenry. Consensus is a product of social unity, and the process of arriving at consensus maintains solidarity within the group. Political consensus is the outcome of that ongoing social interaction through which common purposes are articulated and mutually acceptable ways of pursuing these purposes are discovered. Here, reciprocal understanding and care seconded by interdependence and shared culture engender unanimity, and the participants gain fulfillment by realizing their potential as social beings.

In order to make credible the democratic practices each of these views recommends, each must subscribe to a different conception of the democratic agent. Public-choice theory reduces the self to a desire-generator hooked up with an ancillary transaction device. Although some of the desires produced may bring greater satisfaction or frustration to the individual, all of them are qualitatively similar. Each is equally a product of the generator. None has any rational warrant apart from its amenability to satisfaction and its coherence with other desires, and none is crucial to the identity of the individual. Since all desires are accidental in this sense, they are interchangeable; hence, people can be expected to trade satisfactions freely. The rootlessness of the self renders the political consensus that public choice theory envisages as intelligible.

The proponent of radical participation must adopt a diametrically opposed view of the democratic agent. Whereas the public choice theorist sees the self as a self-sufficient, atomic entity spitting out contingent desires, the radical participation theorist maintains that the self is a social product and that its boundaries are porous. Society endows the developing individual with desires, and the self is indistinguishable from the constellation of desires it has absorbed. The self is a desire-sponge hooked up to a conversation device. It is no wonder, then, that the radical-participation theorist is optimistic about achieving political consensus through reflection on and discussion of shared experience. This interaction is itself a socialization process that is constitutive of the individuals who engage in it. Although radical-participation theory celebrates a form of political consensus that depends on the rootedness of the self, those roots are the homogenizing forces of socialization.

Michael Sandel develops a pair of conceptions of the self that parallel the individualistic desire-generator and the social desire-sponge, but that formulate these conceptions in subtle and revealing ways. To clarify the deficiencies of the view of the self underlying each kind of consensus theory, I shall examine Sandel's presentation of these conceptions in some detail.

Sandel dubs the individualistic conception of the self associated with public-choice theory the voluntarist self.[4] On this view, the agent is a will. As such, it lacks ends until it chooses them, and it chooses them solely on the basis of its preferences.[5] Sandel calls his alternative conception the cognitive self; it corresponds to the social desire-sponge of radical-participation theory.[6] On this view, the agent is a faculty of critical reflection and a plethora of socially given ends. Whereas the individualistic view makes the problem of identity formation a problem about how to acquire some ends (a matter of decision making), the social view makes it a problem about how to distinguish oneself from one's environment (a matter of understanding).[7] Moreover, the individualistic view establishes an unbridgeable gap between the self and its ends: each person *has* a conception of the good. This self is disembodied because the self does not embrace ends from within itself, that is, those have accumulated in the course of experience. In contrast, Sandel's view conflates the self with its ends, and each person *is* a conception of the good. As a result of social experience, the self is full of ends—it is "radically situated"—and adopts ends that it already contains.[8]

Sandel analyzes the agent along two dimensions: (1) its operational capability, that is will or critical reflection; and (2) its relation to social experience, that is disembodiment or radical situation. Moreover, he couples will with disembodiment and critical reflection with radical situation and treats these pairs as if they were the only possible combinations. As a result, Sandel offers two puzzling, almost paradoxical, conceptions of agency.

His construal of the voluntarist, disembodied self denies that any attributes are constitutive of the agent. Accordingly, the agent is fixed, though insubstantial; yet personality, which is generated by the agent's choices, is maximally malleable. Nevertheless, since Sandel denies that this agent has any rational basis for embracing this or that end, or, in other words, for changing his or her personality, the plasticity of personality is unavailing. The individualistic agent is so shallow that he or she is always in a position to make a deal. No blow to its adopted ends could impinge on the agent's identity. But the bargains entered into by this type of individual seem static and unfulfilling, for they involve nothing more than trading away those desires that others refuse to satisfy and substituting a set of desires to which others are more receptive. Such an individual manipulates his or her preferences for the sake of striking a bargain. Politically, then, this individualistic agent is oddly at the mercy of others' whims.

By contrast, the cognitive, radically situated self has nothing but constitutive qualities. Since social experience implants ends in the self, the self is maximally open to the vicissitudes of circumstance and, conversely, minimally under its own control. Although its powers of critical reflection endow this agent with a rational basis for change, the only kind of change he or she can execute consists of orchestrating given elements. Thus, this agent's cognitive powers also seem unavailing. Although the social self is capable of assessing the worth of different life directions, this individual's aspirations are limited to those options made available by a pre-existing social order. Again, self-fulfillment seems devoid of any progressive dimension. To be fulfilled is to insert oneself into a niche one can accept and thus to make the best of one's situation. Correlatively, politics is hobbled by the social origin of all ideas. Although democratic agents can collaborate with others to reorganize or redistribute culturally available options, they cannot hope to fashion a new social vision.

For Sandel, there is a trade-off. The agent may have control but lack depth, or the agent may have depth but lack control. Now, someone might object that these are caricatures of the conceptions of the democratic agent underlying public-choice theory and radical-participation theory. In one respect, I would concede this point. So far as I know, no one explicitly embraces either of these conceptions. In public-choice theory, James Buchanan's acknowledgment in his most recent volume of essays of the role social context plays in shaping fundamental human interests evidences ambivalence about the extremely individualistic conception of the self his theory requires.[9] Yet, he does not alter his model of democracy to reflect this concession to verisimilitude. For Buchanan, democratic politics remains a species of market bartering among independent traders transposed into a different institutional setting.[10] Likewise, the radical-participationist, Benjamin Barber, talks about achieving "creative consensus" while preserving individual autonomy.[11] Nevertheless, despite this commitment to finding ways to differentiate people without setting them irreconcilably at odds, Barber has much to say about how "strong democracy" will dissolve competing interests and little to say about how this democratic modality will protect individuals from pressures to disregard their interests and endorse popular initiatives.[12] In sum, neither camp has developed an explicit and cogent account of the democratic agent, and, while each has incorporated either an individualistic or a social element to soften its predominantly social or individualistic conception of the democratic agent, neither has modified its theory of democracy to bring it into line with this adjustment. Ultimately, collectivistic consensus is jeopardized once a measure of independence is attributed to individuals, and Pareto optimal consensus is jeopardized if people fervently hold some of their beliefs.

2. THE SELF-DEFINING AGENT

Democratic theory rests on two claims about the members of communities. First, these individuals have distinctive viewpoints. Not only do they have personal interests to advance, but the ideas they dream up often prove valuable to society. Second, these individuals can find common ground as a basis for cooperation. Despite their disparate viewpoints, they are not fundamentally and implacably in conflict with one another, and they are sufficiently pliable to tolerate collective policymaking covering a broad range of issues. A weakness that the individualistic self shares with the social self is that both ensure democracy's cooperative basis at the expense of democracy's respect for individual distinctness. To guarantee that mutual accommodation is possible, they loosen the bonds between individuals and their desires. People's desires are reduced to events that merely happen to them.

The individualistic self—the desire-generator or Sandel's voluntarist, disembodied self—models personal identity on the wardrobe of a shopper who lacks any interest in style or utility. If the wardrobe turned out to have any merits, they would be fortuitous, and the casual decision-procedures used to acquire the clothing would have no intrinsic or instrumental value. Yet, the social self—the desire-sponge or Sandel's cognitive, radically situated self—models personal identity on a wardrobe of uniforms supplied by institutional edict and accompanied by a rudimentary sewing kit that equips individuals to embroider their names on their outfits. Both conceptions fail to appreciate the complexity of the process of self-definition that gives rise to personal identity.

Lacking reasons for its choices, the individualistic self has no commitments that it would not cheerfully relinquish and no antipathies that would decisively preclude its appropriating any desire if the right compensation were offered. But people routinely distinguish crucial desires from relatively minor ones, not to mention abhorrent desires from acceptable ones. Few would mistake, say, a powerful impulse to take a winter vacation for the enduring importance of the personal goal of financing the college education of one's children or the moral aim of ameliorating the misery of the homeless. A person's identity includes core concerns as well as peripheral ones, and the contrast between the former and the latter cannot be analyzed in terms of the individualistic self's capricious or stubborn attachment to some qualities and relative indifference to others. Core qualities are not commensurable with peripheral ones.

Whereas the differentiation that typifies personal identity is beyond the powers of the individualistic self, the social self fails to account for the uniqueness of individuals. The social self is chained to convention, for it lacks imagination and resistance to social force. People are endowed with faculties that can combine to reinforce established reasons and courses of conduct, but that also can propel people in new directions. Alone or in concert with others, people sometimes conceive novel reasons (for example, the idea of comparable worth has not always been around), and they sometimes conceive innovative ways of putting novel or familiar reasons into practice (for example, elective single-parenthood is a recent phenomenon). Although no one is free of social influence, people process social experience differently, and the intensity and the persistence of the social pressure brought to bear upon one's desires provides only a partial explanation of one's convictions and commitments. A person's identity need not be a standardized social product.

Since people draw qualitative distinctions among their desires, the faculties that underwrite personal identity must enable people to sort their qualities along a spectrum. At one extreme, some qualities must be definitive of an individual's identity: a desire to complete a book manuscript or a principled commitment to freeing political prisoners might have this status. At the other extreme, some qualities must be such that the individual is determined to expunge them: a yearning for hot fudge sundaes or a tendency to despise racial minorities might have this status. I shall call the former vital qualities, and I shall call the latter disavowed qualities. Spread along the spectrum that the poles of vitalness and disavowedness demarcate are qualities that I shall call annexed qualities. In introducing this terminology, I mean to suggest that annexed qualities are not negligible inasmuch as they are tacitly or explicitly accepted components of the self, but also that they are secondary inasmuch as some of them can be sacrificed without violating the integrity of the individual. Moreover, it is important to note that annexation is a matter of degree. An annexed quality can be nearly vital; it can border on disavowal; or it can stand close to the middle. Its location on this scale is a measure of its importance to the individual.

Against the individualistic conception of the self that relies on unconstrained voluntarism and the social conception of the self that relies on socially molded cognition, and also against the expedient of simply synthesizing these conceptions, I would conjecture that nothing less than a repertory of coordinated skills is necessary to drive this process of self-definition.[13] Not only are people sometimes empowered to transform themselves in ways that break the chafing bonds of their social backgrounds, but people sometimes conceive life plans that sharply diverge from available social norms and that give vivid, accurate expression to their distinctive identities. Whereas critical reflection alone is insufficient to account for such innovation, volition alone is inadequate to account for the self-understanding that grounds such innovation. Furthermore, whether or not innovation of this kind figures in a person's life, volition and critical reflection must collaborate with other faculties to establish an identity with vital, annexed, and disavowed qualities.

The repertory I have in mind includes introspective skills that

enable people to discern their needs and desires and to interpret their feelings; imaginative skills that enable them to envisage alternative courses of action and to anticipate what it would
be like to carry them out; reasoning skills that enable them to
assess the merits of their plans in light of relevant facts, values,
and competing goals; communicative skills that enable them to
assimilate others' insights into their abilities and character, to
benefit from others' ideas about how they might proceed, and
to grasp the impact their conduct is likely to have on their
associates; and volitional skills that enable them to resist unwarranted social pressure and to maintain their resolve to follow
their own counsel. Exercising this repertory of skills enables
people to decipher what they really want from a moral or a
personal standpoint and enables them to act accordingly. Assuming that the self is an evolving collocation of traits, feelings,
desires, beliefs, emotional attachments, values, goals, principles,
and the like, I suggest that a self-defining self is such a collocation that evolves through the exercise of the repertory of skills I
have set forth.

This repertory of skills supports a two-tiered approach to
identity formation that makes sense of individual innovation, as
well as qualitative distinctions among individuals' desires. By
exercising these skills, people not only develop a self-portrait, a
composite understanding of what they are like and what they
do want, but they also form personal ideals that they seek to
measure up to and life plans that they endeavor to carry out.
Accordingly, self-definition is the incremental process of recognizing one's potentialities as well as one's limitations, coupled
with the gradual and halting process of bringing one's self and
one's conduct into line with one's personal ideals and one's life
plans, and one's personal ideals and one's life plans into line
with a realistic assessment of what one can accomplish. This
account exploits the reciprocity that can hold between self-portraits, on the one hand, and life plans and personal ideals, on
the other. In the ongoing process of self-reading coupled with
self-testing in action and self-challenging through aspiration,
people discover what they are capable of and what they are not,
what matters to them and what does not, what they value about
themselves and what they do not, what they can change and

what they cannot, what they should approve and what they
should not, and so on. In sum, self-defining agents are neither
complacent nor quixotic about themselves and their conduct.
They command a repertory of skills that enables them to accept
themselves and their circumstances insofar as doing so is compatible with their own standards, but those skills also allow them
to seek to improve themselves and their circumstances, insofar
as their standards call for improvement, and to pursue plans
gauged to their talents and opportunities as well as to their
liabilities.

The difference between self-defining people and others is not
the trajectories they follow, but rather the way in which they go
about making their choices and living their lives. Taking advantage of the full range of human faculties, these people have
both vital and disavowed qualities that are not susceptible to the
pull of transient moods or the eddying of social forces. Having
tested their self-portraits, personal ideals, and life plans in the
crucible of experience, as well as having subjected them to the
judgment of sensibility and reason, these people are not fickle.
But neither are they rigid. Attunement to their inner lives, lively
imagination, and confidence in their own competence ensure
that these people are capable of recognizing signs of discontent
and that they will take measures to cure it. They are capable,
then, of elevating annexed qualities to the vital category and of
demoting annexed qualities to the disavowed category. Self-
defining people grow. Moreover, if the self-defining individual
follows social convention, it is only after having made those
practices his or her own. If this individual invents an idiosyn-
cratic course, it is only because any other would be alien. Though
the self-defining agent does not conform for lack of alternatives,
such an individual does not rebel just to stand apart.

The random accumulation of qualities and the tenuous hold
on those qualities that called into doubt the identity of the
individualistic self as well as that of the social self have no place
in the life of the self-defining agent. The self-defining agent
encompasses many and varied qualities and is only weakly identified with some of them. Still, the self-defining agent has integrity: some courses of conduct would betray the individual's traits,

beliefs, affections, values, goals, and the like, and others would be beneath such a person.

Democratic theory advocates enfranchisement of every individual in order to respect the integrity of each individual without sacrificing the benefits of cooperation to be gained through collective decision making. These two aims are compatible provided that personal integrity does not require that every individual's unmediated desires always be satisfied. Of course, as public-choice theory maintains, trading off some goals in order to maximize fulfillment of others is sometimes perfectly legitimate, and, as radical-participation theory maintains, accommodating others' interests to the detriment of one's own need not compromise one's integrity. Not every choice makes faithfulness to one's self an issue. The self-defining agent has annexed qualities, and personal integrity is not jeopardized by choosing to forgo expression of any particular annexed quality. A person who is both a scuba diving enthusiast and an opera buff could choose to skip a pilgrimage to Bayreuth in order to go on a diving expedition in the Caribbean. Nor does one usually compromise one's integrity by giving expression to annexed qualities, although one can compromise one's integrity by becoming so obsessed with an annexed quality that vital qualities are haplessly neglected. When a patron of the arts cancels an order for a new limousine in order to support a fledgling dance company it is not objectionable unless this philanthropic activity consumes resources earmarked for more integral projects.

Yet, some choices bring questions of personal integrity to the fore. Cautioning against authorities empowered to force people to betray their convictions, teachers recount to school children the story of Galileo's recanting, at the bidding of the Catholic hierarchy, the scientific theory to which he had dedicated much of his life. A satisfactory account of the democratic agent, one that endows the individual with an identity that demands respect, must explain why this episode appalls us as much as it does.

For the individualistic self of public-choice theory, the trouble can only be that Galileo failed to obtain full compensation for what he gave up; he sold himself short to the priests. For the social self of radical-participation theory, the trouble must be that Galileo had not internalized the dogma that he publicly affirmed: he renounced his belief in the heliocentric universe before fully assimilating the papacy's point of view. Although the individualistic self's desires are self-generated and the social self's desires are socially conferred, neither of these explanations captures what is disturbing about this incident, for neither conception of the self sees any desires as integral to the self. The operational capabilities of the individualistic self and the social self are too limited to account for the distinction between vital, annexed, and disavowed qualities. Without such differentiation, however, personal integrity is trivialized. It is not surprising, then, that these conceptions of the self are associated with monochromatic democratic theories that make no sustained attempt to address the problem of personal integrity in the political arena.

The self-defining agent offers a more convincing explication of the gravity of compromised personal integrity. One betrays one's identity when one fails to express vital qualities or when one fails to suppress disavowed qualities. People's endorsement of the former and their scorning of the latter are not on a par with their relation to their annexed qualities. Their sense of who they are depends on their unity with vital qualities and their distance from disavowed ones. The clergy forced Galileo to detach himself from a vital belief and to embrace a disavowed one. What is horrifying about Galileo's denunciation of the heliocentric theory, then, is that he belied his very identity.

Still, annexed qualities are not extraneous to one's identity. Since much of the complexity and fascination of most personalities derives from annexed qualities, systematically silencing one's annexed qualities also compromises one's integrity. Accordingly, a democratic theory that respects the integrity of individuals must defer to people's vital and disavowed qualities and must provide a conduit for people's annexed qualities.

3. MAJORITARIANISM, COUNTER-MAJORITARIANISM, AND THE DEMOCRATIC AGENT

Consensus democracy seeks to do away with political losers. If consensus is achieved before political action is taken, no one ends up in the minority on any legislative question. Political minorities could be dissolved in this way if opinion on important questions were uniform within the community, as for example, in a hypothetical, Islamic country in which everyone is a devoted, fundamentalist Muslim, and persons holding other religious beliefs are expelled. Because few, if any, modern nation states are so uniform and only the most draconian measures could bring any existing nation state into such uniformity, cultural homogeneity is not a viable basis for consensus democracy. Alternatively, political minorities could be dissolved if collective decision making were confined to those issues over which consensus can be achieved with no risk of compromising individual integrity; for example, minor administrative problems that do not matter much to most people. Because this solution would unduly narrow the political sphere, I am convinced that the consensus stipulations of public-choice theory and radical-participation theory should be jettisoned. Instead, I propose to follow Ian Shapiro in the direction of a procedural, nonteleological democratic theory. But because I believe that democratic agents are more complex than Shapiro would allow, I shall maintain that people ought to have constitutionally guaranteed rights that are not limited to rights of political participation.

The taxonomy of the self's qualities presented in the preceding section meshes neatly with a system of majoritarian democracy curbed by countermajoritarian rights. In view of the fact that people can have personal commitments and moral beliefs that are peripheral, but not alien to their individual identities (that is, annexed qualities), I shall urge that majority rule provides an appropriate mechanism for handling a corresponding array of political issues. Yet, in view of the fact that people can have personal commitments and moral convictions that are integral to their individual identities (that is, vital qualities) as well as personal or moral positions that are anathema to them (that is, disavowed qualities), I shall argue that it is necessary to limit

majority rule to those issues that impinge neither upon this core
of individual identity nor upon these decisively excluded qualities. Constitutional rights enshrining such values as due process,
equal protection, privacy, and personal liberty place the needed
constraints on majoritarian legislation.

In a pluralistic society, the practice of majority rule makes it
unlikely that anyone will always be on the winning side. Majority
rule assumes that democratic agents are prepared to accept
compromises and to endure severe setbacks. Therefore, a society could not respect the integrity of its members if it allowed
questions centering on vital qualities to be decided by majority
rule. To be in a defeated minority when one's vital qualities are
at risk is to have one's integrity compromised. One's integrity is
safe, however, even if some of one's annexed values are sometimes undercut and some of one's annexed desires are sometimes frustrated. Since no particular annexed quality must be
given expression on pain of compromised integrity, people are
not justified in insisting on the sanctity of views based on these
qualities. Instead of attempting to impose what they believe to
be the correct solution or the just outcome, people can be satisfied with a fair-decision procedure that empowers everyone.

Issues decided properly by a simple majority vote include
those that concern competing interests that must be balanced
and regulated, such as pollution control and historical preservation; administrative provision for social goods, such as high-
ways and recreational parks; or policies that involve uncertainty
and hence controversy about justice, such as taxation and the
minimum wage. Because many reflective and decent people are
to be found on the various sides of these issues, and because
making concessions with regard to the annexed qualities to
which these issues pertain does not destroy anyone's integrity, it
would be unreasonable to adopt an intransigent stance on policy
questions of this kind. Sometimes opposing groups must recognize that their preferences are merely self-interested. For example, residents of Seattle want Boeing to get a pending defense contract because big government contracts are good for
the area's economy. Sometimes they must recognize that, although their positions are justified by appeals to principle, other
principled positions are tenable. For example, an opponent of

reverse discrimination might appreciate the force of arguments to the effect that not implementing this policy perpetuates the effects of past wrongs. Sometimes they must temper zealous proselytizing for their principles with respect for other people, if not for their views. An early advocate of racial desegregation might understand how cultural history can obstruct people's moral insight. In cases such as these, only a fanatic could refuse to accept delay, compromise, or even, in the first two types of case, outright defeat.

Still, it is a peculiar virtue of majority rule that when people find themselves in the minority, they need not relinquish their values and projects and wholeheartedly endorse total reversals or even disappointingly limited victories. Majoritarian institutions guarantee people the right to mount a counter-offensive and to seek reform or repeal of legislation they oppose. Minorities can remain faithful to their annexed qualities while accepting the verdict of the majority.

Neither radical-participation theory nor public-choice theory can accommodate unremitting contestation of public policy. Of course, consensus theories of democracy need not require that every consensus that is reached be permanent, but they cannot countenance disagreement with a policy in the immediate aftermath of its enactment. Minority discontent with a democratically reached decision would belie the social unity that consensus is supposed to reflect in radical-participation theory. Similarly, no democratic decision that promptly sparks minority protest could have met the standard of Pareto optimality that public-choice theory upholds. Ongoing minority agitation for change signals a breakdown of the participatory process, for example, residual dissatisfaction has not been heard and incorporated into social policy; or a miscalculation in the public choice solution, for example, some individuals are not satisfied with their compensation.[14] Because majority rule eschews substantive criteria applicable to legislative outcomes in favor of formal criteria of procedural propriety, it raises no barrier to spirited social rivalry. By providing an institutional setting in which people can peacefully dispute policies that affect their annexed qualities, majority rule respects people's integrity as agents while securing a mechanism that avoids social deadlock.[15]

All annexed qualities are contestable, but some are of considerable moment to people. Since people cannot sacrifice these qualities casually, they ought to be in a position to press claims based upon them. The course of public debate is unpredictable. Seemingly permanent arrangements, such as progressive taxation and Social Security, can suddenly come under attack and become candidates for repeal. In view of this uncertainty, no one can presume that legislative proposals will never impinge on his or her annexed qualities in ways that call for partisan action. Though different people will choose to invest their resources to a greater or lesser extent in political activity, political impotence threatens everyone's integrity as an agent. Just as methodically stifling one's annexed qualities damages one's integrity, so does passively submitting to the erosion of one's opportunities to express those qualities. To be deprived of political power is demeaning and destructive to the individual, for some annexed qualities are not readily fungible. It follows that the need to be in a position to vie politically to promote one's annexed qualities is a universal vital need—one that is inextricable from everyone's identity as a person.

Political minorities are inevitable. It is fitting, then, that the vital need to have political prerogatives at one's disposal should be shielded from the vagaries of majority rule. Accordingly, I agree with Ian Shapiro that those rights that are necessary to the democratic process, including the right to vote in free elections, the right to run for public office, the right to freedom of expression, and the right to assemble, ought to be constitutionally protected.

Here, I am implicitly taking issue with radical participation theory's characteristic contention that political engagement is a duty, not merely a right. As Benjamin Barber maintains, "civic activity . . . stands in lexical priority to all social activities in strong democracy." [16] And elsewhere, "Citizenship is not necessarily the highest or the best identity that an individual may assume, but it is the moral identity par excellence." [17] For Barber, democratic participation results in "human self-realization through mutual transformation," and the goal of "creative consensus" cannot be attained without "citizens' active and perennial participation in the transformation of social conflict through

the creation of common consciousness and political judgment."[18] Human fulfillment is impossible without democracy,
and democracy is impossible without universal political participation.

Yet, there are grounds for doubting that political institutions
should oblige everyone to join actively in political life, for there
is little reason to believe that politics is an activity that all people
necessarily find inextricable from their identities. Indeed, the
social self at the core of radical-participation theory cannot easily support the claim that political engagement is a duty. Because all desires are socially constructed and socially transform-
able, on this view, the desire for a political voice is as subject to
the vicissitudes of cultural history as any other desire. Accordingly, if there is a universal duty to join in the political process,
it cannot rest on a universal, vital desire to do so. Moreover,
there is a venerable tradition that stakes salvation on aloofness
from quotidian politics.[19] Thus, for some people, political participation is a disavowed quality. These people could not participate in politics without compromising their integrity.

Still, the case against obligatory political participation should
not rely on the assumption that politics is necessarily a nasty
world of petty rivalries, distasteful alliances, and strident con-
frontations.[20] More to the point is the thought that, since people
are different, some temperaments are drawn to politics more
than others are, and, since individuals are differently situated,
some individuals are more likely to be adversely affected by
political decisions than others. It is not surprising, then, that
many people do not regard political participation as indispensable to their fulfillment. Furthermore, the commitment to individual freedom that lies at the foundation of democratic theory
calls the duty of political participation into question. It is dubious that one could consistently maintain that people should
feel free to pursue whatever morally permissible occupation
most attracts them regardless of whether it is socially optimific
and also that, because it is socially optimific, people are obliged
to invest a substantial amount of their time in political participation regardless of their inclinations. No doubt, people have a
duty to keep abreast of serious injustices in social policy and to
oppose them, but routine politics is largely concerned with is-

sues that have little or no bearing on justice. Accordingly, it is
hard to see why people who find politics tedious, if not repellent
—people who do not gain fulfillment through political participation—should nonetheless devote themselves to this enterprise.

Political participation should be accorded no preeminent status. People should be free to opt out of politics. But people
must also have the option of becoming involved. It is the need
to have this option available rather than the need to exercise
this option that is vital. Though indifference to public policy
bearing on one's annexed qualities in the short-run can be imprudent in the long-run, majoritarian principles—the open
democratic agenda coupled with tolerance for dissent—secure
the possibility of working for reform when one perceives the
urgency of doing so.

Now, it is necessary to inquire whether people have any other
vital qualities that warrant constitutional guarantees. For example, there seem to be matters of justice that no longer allow
for reasonable and conscientious controversy: equal pay for
equal work and racial desegregation of schools, restaurants,
buses, and similar facilities are cases in point. Should people be
willing to accept reversal on these issues because a simple majority has had a craven or malevolent change of heart? In addition,
there seem to be nonpolitical rights that free people to pursue
projects and to realize values that are integral to their personal
identities. Should observant Jews be willing to accept a ban on
Passover ceremonies? Should Bernardo Bertolucci be satisfied
with screening a sanitized version of *Last Tango in Paris*? It is my
contention that the answers to these questions should be no,
and that this response reflects the intuition that the vital moral
and personal qualities of democratic agents ought to be shel-
tered from majoritarian politics.

We have seen that people are capable of distinguishing their
core personal projects from ancillary ones and their ancillary
personal projects from alien ones. Thus, they can commit themselves to distinctive discretionary values or projects that are
inextricable from their personal identities, and they can discern
which nonmoral values and projects would undermine their
personal identities. There is a presumption, then, that people

care deeply about some of their projects and values. If they are prevented from carrying out these components of their life plans, they are forced to sacrifice their integrity. Likewise, a presumption exists that people profoundly despise some possible projects and values. If they are compelled to pursue any of these, they are again forced to sacrifice their integrity. Moreover, I have stressed that the self is dynamic, that it is an evolving collocation of qualities. Annexed qualities may be disavowed; disavowed qualities may disappear; annexed qualities may become vital; vital qualities may become annexed; and novel qualities may appear. The course of this development is unpredictable. Still, the vital qualities people may come to embrace are no less important than the ones they presently embrace, and the disavowed qualities they may come to exclude are no less repugnant than the ones they now exclude. Democracies that needlessly restrict this developmental process do their members a grave disservice. Yet, it is by no means a foregone conclusion that any individual will be able to persuade the other members of a consensus or a majoritarian democracy that recognizes no personal liberties that they should tolerate, let alone support, a radical departure from established convention.

Civil rights, including equal opportunity, freedom to travel, freedom of expression, freedom of worship, freedom from arbitrary arrest and seizure, and privacy, carve out a sphere of activity in which people are authorized to live as they see fit. Welfare rights, which secure such goods as adequate housing, education, and employment, provide people with a minimum level of wherewithal to carry out their plans. Though some people will avail themselves of these diverse rights less than others, it is reasonable to assume that everyone will have some need for these rights, if only a need for the broad-minded, compassionate social climate that these rights foster. Without these guarantees, the range of options that people can realistically regard as feasible will be sharply curtailed. Furthermore, denial of these guarantees casts suspicion on unorthodox beliefs, values, goals, and practices and puts pressure on individuals to dismiss them out of hand. As a result, there will be projects that are worthy of consideration that people will nonetheless ignore. Vital potentialities will remain latent, and vital qualities will be self-censored for lack of a congenial environment. To permit a majority of one's fellows to dictate the direction of one's life in this way would compromise one's integrity. Thus, it is a mistake to think, as Ian Shapiro does, that all constitutional rights other than those that contribute to democracy merely enshrine the interests of the powerful and strengthen their position. They legitimize the interests of every self-defining agent.

In addition to vital personal beliefs, values, projects, and the like, people have vital moral principles and goals. That democratic agents have vital moral qualities entails that they can arrive at moral views justified in such a fashion that these individuals need not tolerate opposition. The democratic agent, then, must compass the capacity for rational reflection on normative matters leading to incontrovertible conviction. As John Rawls observes, each person has a sense of justice coupled with the capacity to articulate and to modify the contents of this inchoate sense and, on this basis, to evaluate practices and institutions.[21] Though Rawls depicts the process of moral reflection as a solitary intellectual exercise, for most people a corresponding social process sustains moral reflection. The inception of new principles of justice or social goals precipitates a period of public debate often accompanied by legislative experimentation. Whereas the moral visionaries who lead great social movements are evidently capable of committing themselves unequivocally to innovative principles or goals in advance of this social inquiry, most people need to see how such proposals work in practice before they can become convinced of their rectitude. This initial reservation of judgment eventually leads to one of three outcomes: (1) the decisive rejection of the innovative principles or goals along with the decisive reaffirmation of the traditional practices or perhaps a modified version thereof; (2) the decisive affirmation of the innovative principles or goals along with the decisive rejection of the traditional practices; or (3) the permanent contestation of these contrary principles or goals.

The democratic agent's capacity for moral reflection and conviction suggests two conclusions about democratic institutions. The first concerns the nature of popular participation. Though in contemporary democracies citizen activism is commonly organized into a battle royal between antagonistic interest groups, people are capable of responding to social issues in a less dogmatic, more probing manner that the political system rarely taps directly. Though much has been written about the apathy and self-interest of democratic agents, their moral perspective has largely been ignored. Only radical participation theory has sought to devise procedures that would release this potential.[22] Yet, it appears that in fact American democratic institutions have been structured to accommodate it. Specifically, the constitutional amendment mechanism makes it possible to formalize progressive moral insight in a way that is minimally vulnerable to transitory shifts in public opinion, and in litigation the constitutional provisions for due process and equal protection can be invoked to reinforce settled principles of justice should they come under meretricious attack.

The second conclusion suggested by the democratic agent's capacity for moral reflection concerns the need for countermajoritarian devices. Some policies comport with principles that are dictated by any morally sensitive person's sense of justice, while other policies conflict with any principles that could plausibly be advanced as being dictated by anyone's sense of justice. Having a sense of justice and being a self-defining agent entails decrying certain policies and supporting others. Many issues that raise questions of justice are never finally settled, and they remain within the purview of majoritarian procedures. Others finally are settled. Though people do not all follow the same schedule of moral enlightenment—some progress faster than others—there comes a time, after alternative practices have been tried and their relative merits have been debated, when reasonable disagreement ceases. Arguably, in American society racism is among the issues that have been subjected to this thorough public and personal scrutiny, and I take it for granted that no thoughtful and decent person today could approve of bringing back slavery or permitting discrimination on grounds of race. Thus, annexed principles and goals can become vital, and people can only suppress the latter at the expense of their integrity. By contrast, previously accepted principles or goals can become disavowed, and, once this happens, people can only support them at the expense of their integrity. At this point, vigorous democratic rivalry and fluid policy development rightly yield to settled conviction, for people cannot live in and contribute to societies that abrogate such elementary requirements of justice, especially societies that also repress dissent, without betraying their moral nature. For this reason, it is appropriate that constitutional guarantees such as due process and equal protection should be deployed in defense of well-tested policies and practices.

Because democratic agents are equipped with a complicated repertory of skills that enables them to be self-defining individuals, not all of their concerns can be relegated to the level of personal preferences or internalized social norms. More than malleable packages of self-generated or socially given qualities, democratic agents identify with many of their beliefs, values, and plans. As an expression of this identification, their striving to advance their interests through majoritarian politics evidences their dignity as agents. Depriving them of a voice in public policy is an insult to their integrity. Still, since some of their personal and moral commitments are not expendable, majority rule must be constrained. As a complement to majority rule, countermajoritarian principles instituting basic human rights and codifying established principles of justice belong in democratic theory. Indeed, it is the democratic agent's powers of moral insight coupled with the historic failure of many societies to make provision for individual integrity that ultimately legitimate one disorderly form of opposition that has been central to modern democratic theory, namely, rebellion in the name of justice.

NOTES

1. For an overview of the role of liberty and equality in democratic theory, see J. Roland Pennock, *Democratic Political Theory* (Princeton: Princeton University Press, 1979), 16–58.

2. Jane Mansbridge, *Beyond Adversary Democracy* (New York: Basic Books, 1980), 252–55.

3. For an illuminating example of what public-choice theory has in mind, see James M. Buchanan's discussion of how the Social Security

system might be dismantled in compliance with the requirement of Pareto optimality in *Liberty, Market and State: Political Economy in the 1980s* (New York: New York University Press, 1986), 178–85.

4. Michael J. Sandel, *Liberalism and the Limits of Justice* (Cambridge: Cambridge University Press, 1982), 58.

5. Ibid., 58, 159.

6. Ibid., 58.

7. Ibid., 152.

8. Ibid., 21, 62.

9. Buchanan, *Liberty, Market, and State,* 83.

10. As Buchanan states, "Politics is a 'market in interests or values'." (Ibid., 49).

11. Benjamin Barber, *Strong Democracy* (Los Angeles: University of California Press, 1984), 224, 232.

12. Barber recommends forestalling "mob rule by developing internal checks rather than by developing a system of external limits [such as constitutional rights] on government" (ibid., 160). Moreover, he sanguinely assures his readers that "the fragmentation and pluralism of most contemporary liberal societies would seem to leave ample room for a safe infusion of communitarian values" (ibid., 243).

13. For detailed exposition and defense of this conception, see Diana T. Meyers, "Personal Autonomy and the Paradox of Feminine Socialization," *Journal of Philosophy,* 84 (11) (November, 1987): 619–28 and Diana T. Meyers, *Self, Society, and Personal Choice,* (New York: Columbia University Press, 1989.).

14. In this connection, it is worth noting that Jane Mansbridge makes a persuasive case against using consensus both to achieve group unity and to protect individual interests through the veto power. When a practice of decision by mutual agreement is adopted for the former purpose, using it for the latter purpose becomes delegitimized. Dissenters are stigmatized as opponents of the common good; deals are seen as suspect; and minorities are "suppressed in the interests of a 'managed' or coercive unanimity." (*Beyond Adversary Democracy,* 264–65) Thus, a system combining the two forms of consensus theory does not seem to be a tenable alternative to majority rule.

15. For discussion of the role of majority rule in ironing out social discord and facilitating social choice, see Elaine Spitz, *Majority Rule* (Chatham, NJ: Chatham House Publishers, 1984), 201–211.

16. Barber, *Strong Democracy,* 229.

17. Ibid., 224.

18. Ibid., 215 and 225.

19. For a discussion of a version of this view stemming from Ameri-

can transcendentalism, see George Kateb, "Democratic Individuality and the Claims of Politics," *Political Theory*, 12 (3) (August, 1984): 354–55.

20. For an argument that focuses on the deplorable aspects of politics as a basis for rejecting obligatory political participation, see Hilliard Aronovitch, "Pluralism, Participation, and Tyranny," *Revue de L'Université d'Ottawa/University of Ottawa Quarterly*, 56 (2) (April–June, 1986): 138–39.

21. John Rawls, *A Theory of Justice* (Cambridge: Harvard University Press, 1971), 46–47. For an alternative account of moral autonomy, see Diana T. Meyers, "The Socialized Individual and Individual Autonomy: An Intersection between Philosophy and Psychology," in *Women and Moral Theory*, ed. Eva Feder Kittay and Diana T. Meyers (Totowa, NJ: Rowman and Littlefield, 1987), 139–53.

22. Benjamin Barber, *Strong Democracy*, 267–307; Joshua Cohen and Joel Rogers, *On Democracy: Toward a Transformation of American Society* (New York: Penguin Books, 1983), 161–83; Carol Pateman, *Participation and Democratic Theory* (Cambridge: Cambridge University Press, 1970), 67–84 and 109–111.

6

POLITICAL EQUALITY

THOMAS CHRISTIANO

INTRODUCTION

Philosophical thinking about democracy has not come very far in spelling out the standards that legitimate democratic institutions should meet. Political philosophers and theorists have not got beyond general justifications of democracy and some vague outlines of what the ideal they use in justifying democracy might entail when it comes to defining standards for institutions.[1] Elsewhere I have worked out a justification of political equality in terms of a conception of egalitarian justice that requires equality in the distribution of resources. I have shown how that notion of equality ought to apply in circumstances of conflict over certain goods. Those goods are what I call collective properties of society, which are defined as properties that affect all or most people in some way, good or bad. I have argued that these goods ought to be chosen by means of collective decision-making procedures and that the resources for determining the outcome of these procedures ought to be distributed equally.[2] Here I elaborate on what the idea of political equality involves.

The question is, what is a coherent and plausible conception of political equality that will fit within the constraints imposed by the argument for political equality? In particular, what are the relations between procedural and political equality? My main conclusion is that procedural equality has a far less significant role to play in an egalitarian theory of democracy than is usually thought.

This is so even when we try to insulate the political process from disparities of wealth in society. It is necessary to have a collective decision-making procedure that is insulated from the distribution of economic resources since open exchanges between the economic and the political realms would likely lead to neglect of collective interests.

The first difficulty in constructing a notion of procedural equality is that those criteria associated with it allow for indeterminacies in outcome. In order to get determinate outcomes, we will either have to violate one of the conditions of procedural equality or we shall have to expand the concept of political equality to include resources that are not procedural. A second difficulty arises when we consider that to be fully egalitarian a procedure must be global in the sense that it settles all relevant issues as a package. This is because an egalitarian theory requires comparisons between complete life prospects. Since this procedure cannot work in our world and furthermore, since the outcomes of partial procedures, when added up, are not the same as the outcome of a global procedure, we have another serious difficulty for procedural equality.

Social-choice theorists have analysed the properties of procedures and it is from them that we can learn the most. Two points stand out: we have philosophized relatively little about the implications of social-choice theory for political philosophy. There has been some argument about the defensibility of Arrow's axioms, and many attempts to relax the axioms to avoid the impossibility result. More importantly, however, philosophical discussion has concentrated almost exclusively on the idea that the purpose of democratic procedures is to reveal the popular or general will.[3] In social-choice theory, this is called the collective or social preference. Explanations of this concept have not evolved much since Rousseau's writings. If this is what social-choice theorists have in mind in their mathematical analysis of procedures, then we can say that their work has been unhelpful at best. The very idea that the notion of a common will can be defined in terms of a function operating on an unlimited domain of individual preferences is without merit. And yet such a function is ostensibly what social-choice theorists and political philosophers who have concerned themselves with social-choice theory have been trying to define. Though this standard view of the normative implications of social-choice theory does not get us very far, we ought to use the insights of social-choice theory supplemented by game theory into the structure and operation of voting procedures in order to analyze the problems in the idea of procedural equality.

POLITICAL EQUALITY AND MAJORITY RULE

The basic principle of political equality is that in collective decision making designed for the purpose of deciding upon collective properties of society, all the relevant means to securing desired ends ought to be distributed equally. Voting power is the first important candidate for inclusion among these means, so I start with an analysis of procedural equality in voting.

Procedural equality gives each participant one vote per issue and the decision is made by determining which alternative wins a majority of votes cast. At least this would be the method for the simplest procedures and decision problems, namely, two alternatives that the group must decide between, and one need only vote for one's first preference. An example of this kind of procedure is provided by Brian Barry.[4] Imagine five individuals in a train compartment, some of whom smoke and some of whom do not. Some of them prefer that no one smoke while others are willing to permit it. The decision to be made is framed as a decision between allowing anyone or no one to smoke. Each person gets one vote. If at least three vote in favor of smoking then the decision is to permit smoking and if at least three vote against then the decision is to prohibit it.

What is it about this procedure that makes it egalitarian? In a clear sense it is not egalitarian: some people end up getting what they want and the others do not. That is, the outcome can be described as inegalitarian. But this outcome does not show us the nature of the procedure because it is compatible with egalitarian outcomes if everyone is in agreement. Nevertheless, the procedure can produce inegalitarian outcomes. Hence, we cannot look at outcomes alone to determine whether the procedure is egalitarian.

Anonymity and Neutrality

In social choice theory, in the functional relation between preferences of voters and outcomes of the procedure, majority rule can be shown to be egalitarian. Majority rule has three properties that qualify it as an egalitarian procedure. It is a one person-one vote system and it is anonymous and neutral. To say that majority rule is anonymous means that the decisions that the method produces will not change as long as the number of votes for and against remains the same. It does not matter who has voted for or who against. This requirement would be violated by a plural voting system. If A's vote were counted twice and the votes of B, C, D, and E were each counted once, then it would make a difference who voted for what since the votes of A and B would produce a tie whereas those of B and C would not. (This property of anonymity is also called symmetry or undifferentiatedness by some.)

Neutrality is a property of voting procedures that are not biased in favor of any of the alternatives. An alternative is more favored if it takes less votes to get it passed than the others. Hence, most kinds of unanimity rule are non-neutral since they favor the status quo. Only one vote for the status quo is necessary to assure its victory over competing alternatives, while every vote for some alternative to the status quo is necessary to get that alternative.

A simple majority procedure decides between only two alternatives when the outcome is victory for either one or a tie. It is easily shown that simple majority decision satisfies the two egalitarian conditions as well as two other conditions, positive responsiveness and decisiveness. Positive responsiveness assures that a vote for an alternative that is already tied with or defeating its opponent secures victory for that alternative. Decisiveness implies that the procedure will always produce an outcome. Indeed, Kenneth May has shown that simple majority decision is the only decision procedure that has these properties.[5]

It is clear why anonymity is egalitarian. It simply specifies that the decision procedure itself does not give any more weight to one person's vote than to anyone else's. As far as the procedure is concerned, each vote has an equal effect on the outcome. Neutrality is also egalitarian.[6] It does not mean that all individuals are treated equally rather that all alternatives are so treated. But this condition is tied to individuals insofar as they introduce the alternatives for consideration. The neutral decision procedure does not give any better chances of one measure passing than any other and therefore, indirectly, it does not give any person an advantage in getting a measure he prefers passed. Non-neutral procedures favor some outcomes over others. For example, special majority rules (e.g. those requiring two thirds of voters or all voters to vote in favor) will favor the decision that retains what is already in place over the alternative that challenges it. This is because a non-neutral procedure requires a way of determining which alternative is to be tested by the special majority and which alternative will be the default choice. Without a default rule, the special majority procedure will not select an outcome every time. For example, if a procedure requires that an alternative get two thirds of the vote in order to win, there may be many cases in which a majority of less than two thirds will vote for one alternative and more than one third will vote for the other. In these cases, the procedure will not select an outcome. It is not decisive. Whatever default rule we choose will put one of the alternatives at a disadvantage and therefore put one or some of the participants at a disadvantage in selecting an outcome. Therefore, non-neutral procedures violate the principle of procedural equality.

An objection can be raised to this reasoning. One could argue that no particular or nameable individual is disadvantaged by this feature of a voting procedure. All individuals are faced with the difficulty of displacing the status quo (or whatever the default choice is) in the case of special majority procedures. Some simply happen to prefer the status quo, but this has nothing to do with the nature of the procedure, The procedure is compatible with everyone preferring the status quo and with no one preferring it as well as with only some preferring it. Those who prefer the status quo are advantaged by that but they are no more in an advantaged position than those who prefer a position that the majority happens to prefer in a majoritarian procedure. This objection states, in effect, that if a condition is not the same as anonymity, then it is not an egalitarian condition. And since neutrality is independent of anonymity,[7] it is not an egalitarian condition.

Perhaps this objection could be raised against some proponents of neutrality. The problem with neutrality is as follows. Neutrality seems to be an important condition, because it makes a great difference to the outcomes of a procedure whether it is neutral or not. Special majority rules make it more difficult to pass certain measures than others, while ordinary majority procedures gives the measures equal opportunities to pass. The objection is, however, that inequality in opportunities among measures to be passed is not in itself a cause for concern. Who cares about equality among the measures themselves? Reason does not require equal treatment of measures. Hence, it seems that if neutrality (or non-neutrality) is intrinsically valuable (like anonymity) as a condition of equality it must be valuable in a way that is understandable in terms of the equal treatment of individuals. Neutrality may be instrumentally valuable if one wants to increase the rate of change in legislation. Non-neutral procedures such as special majority rules where the default choice is the status quo are usually selected to slow the process of change. Hence, neutrality and non-neutrality are important properties of decision-making procedures because of their potential effects on the group using the procedure. Is it also a necessary condition for egalitarian procedures?

The claim that neutrality has intrinsic value from an egalitarian standpoint has two possible interpretations. It may be an equality condition for individuals qua voters. That is, non-neutrality might somehow give some voters an advantage over others.[8] But this condition would not be distinct from anonymity. Or it might be that neutrality would be a condition of equality for individuals qua initiators of legislation. This interpretation is the more plausible for neutrality. This accounts for the fact that neutrality is an egalitarian condition since individuals participate in a decision procedure in two different ways: as voters and as initiators. Insofar as a procedure is biased in favor of a particular piece of legislation at a particular point in time, it is biased in favor of that person who favors it and against those who would offer alternatives.

Whether anonymity and neutrality are sufficient to make a decision procedure egalitarian is still a question. First, I would like to consider two difficulties with these conditions: indeterminacy and composition.

Indeterminacy

One trouble with majority rule is that it does not easily move from handling decision problems with only two alternatives to problems with three or more. Majority rule satisfies two important egalitarian conditions on voting procedures. It does this while also being decisive and positively responsive to individual preferences. But these conditions all hold for majority rule only in cases of dichotomous choice. In the face of more than two choices, majority rule can fail to be decisive.

Consider the following case. Suppose we have three alternatives, x, y, and z, as well as five ($n = 5$) voters A, B, C, D, and E. And further suppose that A and B support x while C supports y and D and E vote for z. The rule that the alternative that gathers $n/2 + k$ votes wins will not tell us who the winner is. It is not decisive for issues that have more than two alternatives. To stick with majority rule, we could try to alleviate this problem by devising a voting method that pairs each of the alternatives against each other and determines which one can defeat all the others in pairwise voting. At each stage of the voting only two alternatives will be pitted against each other and so we will be able to use simple majority decision at each point. In our example we should expand our knowledge of each person's preferences to see how they rank all the alternatives. Suppose that A and B agree to the ordering xyz (where xyz means x is prefered to y and y is prefered to z), while C orders the alternatives yzx, and D and E agree on zyx. If we see how each alternative fares against each other we will find that y defeats x with the votes of C, D, and E and y beats z with the votes of A, B, and C, while z defeats x with the votes of C, D, and E. Hence pairwise voting between all the alternatives makes y the winner because it can defeat both of its rivals. In this case, y is called the Condorcet winner. We shall have to think about the significance of a Condorcet winner but now I would like to inquire further into some of the properties of majoritarian decision rules.

Since y can beat each of its rivals in pairwise majority voting, any procedure that consists of pairwise voting either in sequence or simultaneously will produce y as the outcome. These are called binary procedures. They fail, however, in the presence of so-called cyclic preferences. Suppose A and B agree on the order xyz, C's preference is yzx, and D and E each have the ranking zxy. Here, not only is there no majority winner when all the alternatives are voted on together, but no alternative can defeat each of its alternatives in pairwise voting either. X defeats y with the votes of A, B, D, and E; y defeats z because of the votes of A, B, and C; and z defeats x thanks to C, D, and E. Each alternative is defeated by some other alternative in the pairwise voting. Figure 6.1 illustrates these preference orders. Majority rule, even in its extended form, is indeterminate in this case.

We can get a determinate outcome in pairwise voting over any number of alternatives by means of the amendment procedure. This is characterized by first pitting two alternatives against each other and then pitting the winner of that contest against the third alternative. Here the determinate outcome is the alternative that remains after all others have been sequentially eliminated. The trouble is that the outcome could depend on the order in which the alternatives were pitted against each other. In fact, someone who could determine the order would do best, if the preferences were of a cyclical sort, always to bring his favored alternative in last. The alternative of the three cyclic preferences that is pitted against the victor of the first contest will always win.[9] It is easy to see how this is true. If we assume that the participants have the preferences described above, if we want x to win then all we have to do is have x compete against

FIGURE 6.1. *Cyclical preferences.*

	A	B	C	D	E
1	x	x	y	z	z
2	y	y	z	x	x
3	z	z	x	y	y

the winner of the contest between *y* and *z*. And this can be done for all three alternatives.

The difficulty with the amendment procedure is that it violates our egalitarian condition of neutrality since it makes the outcome depend on the order in which the alternatives are presented. The procedure is biased in favor of the alternative that is introduced last. It buys decisiveness at the price of equality. Again, this may not always be a defect; the amendment procedure is frequently used in legislative committees because of its non-neutral character. They use the amendment procedure and always introduce the status quo alternative last. In the absence of an alternative that can beat all others in pairwise voting, the status quo will usually win.[10] Nevertheless, we lack a complete specification of the notion of equality in decision-making procedures.[11] We lack a notion of procedural equality that is able to give us a solution to the problem of equal division in certain circumstances.[12]

Composition

Another difficulty with procedural equality is the problem of composition. If we think that a procedure is egalitarian and we apply that procedure to two separate issues we may get a result that is quite different from using the same procedure to decide on the two issues in combination. Consider the following array of preferences for the issues *w* against *x* and *y* against *z* for our five voters *A, B, C, D, E*. Let *w* and *x* stand for the no smoking-smoking issue and *y* and *z* may stand for no radio playing-radio playing. *A, B, D,* and *E* prefer *w* to *x* while *C* ranks *x* over *w*. *C, D,* and *E* prefer *y* to *z* while *A* and *B* want *z*. If we were to treat these preferences in separate procedures, *w* would defeat *x* and *y* would beat *z*. Our egalitarian procedure would produce *w* and *y*. Now consider how the orderings look when the preferences over the two issues are combined (fig. 6.2). Here the voting procedure that combines the two issues into one with four alternatives, *wz, xz, wy,* and *xy*, produces cycles that include all four alternatives.[13] Here, *wz* is preferred by a majority to *xz*, which is preferred to *wy*, which in turn is prefered to *wz*. There is another as well: *xy* is preferred to *xz*, which is also preferred to *wy*, which in turn defeats *xy*. In any event no alternative defeats all

FIGURE 6.2. *Voting with complementary preferences.*

	A	B	C	D	E
1	wz	wz	xy	wy	wy
2	xz	xz	xz	wz	xy
3	wy	wy	wy	xy	wz
4	xy	xy	wz	xz	xz

the others, hence we have the same situation as the problem described in the previous section. But it is interesting that *wy*, which would have been the choice had the issues been decided separately, now loses to *xz*. Not only is the outcome of this procedure indeterminate, it also defeats the separately chosen outcomes.

Obviously, this is because new information is being allowed to determine the outcome. This can be shown by the fact that none of the voters' second and third rankings could have been predicted on the basis of the results of the earlier procedures. We have no reason, on the basis of the earlier separate decisions alone, to believe that *A, B,* and *C* would have ranked *xz* over *wy*. Nor do we have any reason to believe that *D* and *E* would split on the ranking of *wz* and *xy*. Furthermore, had either one of *A, B,* or *C* preferred *wy* over *xz, wy* would have been the winner on our extended majority rule. Or even if just two of them had been indifferent between *wy* and *xz, wy* would have been the winner. In order to explain the peculiar result above, either *A* or *B* think that the issue of radio playing is more important to them (they would rather hear the radio play even if it means putting up with smoking than not hear the radio and not allow smoking), or there is some kind of complementarity between the issues (smoking and radio playing combined just are better than no smoking and no radio playing).

The problem of combining and separating issues becomes even more serious when the preferences over the alternatives are non-separable.[14] Nonseparable preferences are preferences over alternatives such that if one of the preferences is not satisfied then the other preference ordering will change. To take another example from Barry's paper, we would not want to vote for buying some piece of land unless there is going to be money to build something on the land. Similarly, certain preferences may depend on other preferences not being fulfilled, as with the case where I may want to have pollution control or the construction of a public monument but not both, because together they would be too expensive.[15] Obviously, most of politics is concerned with nonseparable preferences and so those problems concerning procedures with nonseparable preferences are serious for a theory of political equality. Figure 6.3 is a variation on our previous example. If the issues *w-x*, and *y-z* are decided in combination, then the result will be a victory for *wy* since *wy* is the Condorcet winner. Now suppose that the issues are decided separately. Suppose that at one time *t*, the issue *w-x* is decided and only later at *t'* is *y-z* decided. The majority winners of the separate procedures would be *x* and *z*. If, on the other hand, at *t* the voters had voted on *y-z* and at *t'* they had voted on *w-x*, then the outcome would have been the same as in the combined procedure.[16] Furthermore, if the issues are voted on simultaneously with no vote trading, the outcome will be *x* and *y*.

The difference appears to be that the voters are able to take more information into account when they vote in the combined than in the separate procedures. Their votes can express a more subtle appreciation of the alternatives available.

Why are these results disturbing for someone who wishes to defend egalitarian procedures? The reason is that an egalitarian wants to defend the combined over the separate procedures. The reason for thinking that the combined is superior to the

FIGURE 6.3. *Voting with nonseparable preferences.*

	A	B	C	D	E
1	wy	wy	xy	xz	xz
2	xz	xz	wy	wy	wy
3	xy	xy	xz	wz	wz
4	wz	wz	wz	xy	xy

separate procedures is because it gets closer to the realization of the idea that equality is to be among persons and hence that an egalitarian regime requires equality of persons in terms of their total life prospects. Insofar as the combined procedure takes more issues into account, it is closer to taking whole lives into account. But this reasoning leads us to require that an egalitarian procedure take all issues into account in a single shot. It requires that an egalitarian procedure not only combine different issues, but that it must be a global procedure and combine all issues that will come up in the lives of the participants. The argument can be stated as follows: political equality is a kind of equal control over whole life prospects (concerning collective properties of the society); political equality is to be interpreted in terms of procedural equality; therefore procedural equality must be a kind of equal control over whole life prospects. Partial procedures, that is procedures that are concerned with marginal changes in the collective properties of society, do not guarantee individually equal control over whole life prospects, that much is obvious. The question is whether partial procedures will, when taken collectively, constitute equal control over whole life prospects. Now it appears from the examples that a collection of partial procedures will not always produce the same results as a global procedure would were it to be applied to all the issues, even when the global procedure gives a Condorcet winner. This difference in result in itself gives us reason to believe that the collection of partial procedures is not sufficient for political equality. Insofar as the global procedure has a Condorcet winner that is the majority winner of an egalitarian procedure on a global level, those procedures that defeat the Condorcet winner on the same issues must be inegalitarian. It is the explanation for the difference that shows further that the collection of partial procedures does not amount to equality of control over whole life prospects. The explanation above is that the collection of partial procedures neglects certain important elements of whole life prospects—the way issues are inseparably connected in individuals' preference orderings. It neglects the importance of the complementarity of preferences. Insofar as that complementarity is an important element of the total life prospects of an individual the collection of partial procedures must neglect an important element of the total life prospects of an individual in a way that a global procedure does not.

The global procedure, however, is unworkable even approximately in political life. We cannot know what issues are going to come up and what a person will prefer in various circumstances. And our examples show that the results of a global procedure can differ significantly from the combined results of the marginal procedures since they take more into account. If a global procedure is unworkable and the more partial do not give the same results as a global procedure, then we appear to have a serious gap in our conception of procedural equality because a truly egalitarian procedure is impossible and its outcomes cannot be assured by the less egalitarian procedures.

Agendas

Situations like the preceding, in which the outcome turns on how the issues are presented, suggest that political equality cannot be adequately characterized in terms of the voting procedure itself. There may still be a way the proceduralist might save the notion of procedural equality. We have a procedural mechanism at our disposal: a procedure for determining agendas. One might argue that political equality must include some egalitarian procedure for deciding how the issues are to be combined and ordered as well as which issues are to be up for a vote. This would determine how issues were to be combined into larger issues. It would also determine how alternatives were to be ordered in a voting procedure like the one I described above as the amendment procedure. There the order is a crucial determinant of what the outcome is going to be in many circumstances. If one selects one order and there is no Condorcet winner, then the last alternative may often be the winner, again assuming that voters vote sincerely. Finally, the issues that come up will obviously have an impact on what the collective decision procedure selects. Some individuals or groups might end up having little or no impact on collective decision making insofar as they are rarely or never able to place issues or alternatives on the agenda.

Hence, we might devise an egalitarian procedure for determining agendas since the agenda and its formation are so significant for determining the outcome of collective decision making. Though the outcomes of the agenda setting procedure would be inegalitarian the procedure itself would be egalitarian. Here we run into a serious objection to this resolution of the indeterminacy problem. Once we require a procedure to decide on the way another procedure is to operate, we appear to face a problem of infinite regress. That is, it is hard to see how we are going to come up with a procedure that satisfies the very constraints that we have outlined for the lower order procedures, and that does not have the very same difficulties those lower order procedures have. In order to solve those problems, we would have to have recourse to an even higher order procedure and so on. This is especially so since the set of alternatives does not diminish in size as we move to higher order procedures. For example, if we wish to determine the order in which the three alternatives in an issue are to appear in the amendment procedure, we will have three possible alternatives in the higher order procedure. This will make the problems in the higher order procedure as intractable as in the lower. If we could solve the problem for the higher order procedure, then we would not need to have recourse to it since the very same solution would apply to the lower. When the problem is one of ordering alternatives and voters are aware that certain specific orders may mean victory or defeat for their preferred alternative, choosing over orders is tantamount to choosing over alternatives.[17]

Two objections arise to the idea that agenda formation procedures can solve the problems of composition. First, a problem similar to the one above exists for determining the combination or separation of issues on an agenda. As was noted above, a procedure will give different outcomes depending on whether the issues are combined or separated. This follows because various complementarities might exist between the preferences for the alternatives. Some issues are of greater importance than others to the voters and some combinations of alternatives are preferred to combinations of others. In addition, the preferences of voters may be nonseparable. The determination of the agenda in these cases is an important part of the determination of the outcome. But here too we will have a problem with an indeterminacy, since some agendas are associated with a victory for some alternatives while others are conducive to victory for others.

The second objection is that the problem of global versus partial procedures is not resolvable by means of an egalitarian mechanism for setting agendas. The problem is due to the necessary limitations on those who must determine the agenda. Only persons with perfect information concerning the future and alternative futures could adequately determine what an agenda for a global procedure would be. Otherwise the procedure must be a partial one and hence, will be geared to the wrong level of comparisons, that is of marginal changes, and not whole lives. But to suppose even the possibility of perfect information about alternatives among participants would be to enter into a fantasyland. Thus the agenda procedure is not going to get us beyond the problem of composition that we analyzed in the last section.

This problem of agendas suggests that there cannot be such a complete concept of procedural equality. The possibility cannot be ruled out that in some circumstances, given the problems of indeterminacy and composition, that a procedure will give greater opportunity to some voters to determine the outcome. And also, given the fact that procedures are of necessity geared towards marginal changes whereas our conception of equality requires a more global equality, procedural equality is incapable of giving us an appropriate interpretation of political equality. It seems, therefore, that we have reached an impasse. Perhaps we ought to look at some extraprocedural features of voting processes.[18]

EQUALITY WITHOUT VOTING ON THE BASIS OF PREFERENCES

The foregoing proceeded on the assumption that the purpose of voting is to express preferences. That is, individuals vote in a way that is in accordance with their preferences regardless of the outcome of the vote. If they were asked to vote once on one issue, we assumed that they would vote for the alternative that is highest on their preference schedule. And for every vote they cast, they would always vote for the alternative they prefer. Indeed, this constraint on voting has great normative significance in social-choice theory. Most social-choice theorists have seen it as one of their main goals production of a voting mechanism that would get individuals to vote in accordance with their preferences over the alternatives. Their view is that votes expressing the sincere preferences have some fundamental importance.

On the other hand, most voting procedures encourage strategic manipulation under certain circumstances.[19] That is, if one votes in a way that does not put one's first preference among alternatives first, second preference second and so on, one can achieve an outcome that is better than if one votes in a way that does. For example, a plurality voting rule where each person casts a vote for a single alternative among three will encourage one to vote for one's second preference if one's first preference does not have many supporters. If one's first preference is not likely to win and one's last choice will win if one does not vote for one's second choice, then one will have an incentive to vote for one's second choice. Here, voters are voting only indirectly according to their preferences. Their first preference is not revealed by their vote. The vote is being cast in order to determine the outcome and in order to do that one must assess the alternatives in accordance with one's preferences and must determine how others are voting. This is called strategic voting. In many cases of voting one will vote for one's first preference, because that will be the best way of making it the outcome of the procedure. But if one is voting strategically, it is the outcome of the procedure that one is concerned with foremost and not whether one's vote is for one's first preference. When one votes for one's first preference over outcomes, this is usually called "sincere" voting. I shall call it "straightforward" voting so as to avoid the suggestion of insincerity in the notion of strategic voting.[20]

These kinds of manipulations will occur in cases of indeterminacy (for individual strategic voting) and complementarity or varying importance of issues (for vote trading). These are the circumstances under which majoritarian procedures are subject to strategic manipulation. If we know that one of the alternatives in a single procedure is a Condorcet winner, there is no reason for us to engage in strategic voting unless we can produce a cycle by allowing our vote for that winner to understate our preference. Furthermore when there is no complementarity of preferences among issues there is no incentive to trade votes. Let us look at each kind of manipulation respectively.

Suppose that C in the combined voting procedure (fig. 6.3) was aware that the distribution of the preferences would lead to an indeterminate outcome with wz and wy as the main contenders (since they each defeat two of the three alternatives while xy and xz will both probably lose since they each defeat only one alternative). C might choose to switch votes for one in which wy is placed ahead of xz. In this way, C could assure that wy would win and since C prefers wy to wz, it might well be reasonable for C to vote for wy over xz rather than risk a victory for wz, which is last on C's preference ordering.

Another example of manipulation of a special kind of majoritarian scheme can be seen with the amendment procedure when there are three voters A, B, and C, and three alternatives x, y and z, where A prefers x to y and y to z, B prefers y to x and x to z and C prefers z to x and x to y. Then x is the Condorcet winner (fig. 6.4). Let us suppose that the order of voting is x against z and then the winner against y. One would think that the outcome would be x, because x is a Condorcet winner. The situation is such, however, that B has available a strategy that can produce his preferred outcome y. B could vote for z, his least preferred alternative, in the first vote and this would make z the winner on the first round. Then when y comes up against z, y will win.[21]

It should be clear that C and B would not have got what they wanted had the other voters been aware of (1) the other's pref-

FIGURE 6.4. *Manipulation of majority rule.*

	Voter's Preferences		
	A	B	C
1	x	y	z
2	y	x	x
3	z	z	y

erences, (2) other voters' attempts to manipulate the outcome, (3) the fact that C and B were the only manipulators, and (4) the absence of possibilities for coalitions to develop.

If for example, in our first case (fig. 6.3), A and B had been aware of C's strategy they might have joined in a coalition to defeat wy by both placing xy in front of wy, thus producing another cycle. In our second case (fig. 6.4), C, whose second choice, x, stands to lose if z does defeat x and whose first choice z will lose either way, will have an incentive to vote against z (first preference) in favor of x (second preference) if she knows that B is planning to vote for z and A will vote straightforwardly.

The crucial elements that are affecting the outcomes here are information and the ability to manipulate individually as well as collectively. The amount of information required for our participants in our simple example includes information on everyone's preference orderings, on who is willing to vote strategically, and on what competence they have at this, as well as on what coalitions are likely to form. Furthermore, each person must be able to manipulate and form coalitions. Virtually any contested alternative can be defeated, depending on the level and distribution of this information and these abilities.

That the nature of the voting procedure may not matter as much as other considerations as long as certain constraints are imposed becomes more evident when we consider the fact that voting procedures are not used just once. Generally I have been discussing voting procedures as if they were used to decide all relevant conflicts in one single event. But, as noted in the section on the problem of composition, this way of thinking of voting procedures is extremely unrealistic. The information required of participants to determine what issues would be relevant over a long period of time as well as what their views on these issues will be is far greater than any person could acquire. In general, procedures are used to make piecemeal decisions about marginal aspects of social life. The decisions can also be revised over time given new information. And even the collection of such partial procedures may not produce the same outcome as a procedure that decided all the relevant issues at once.

But this feature of the use of procedures introduces another kind of manipulation that I described before as vote trading.

Insofar as voting procedures are concerned with piecemeal changes in the society and those piecemeal changes are, most of the time, complementary in value for individuals, or at least some issues that individuals find important are more important than other issues, individuals will attempt to trade votes on issues for other individuals' votes on other issues. Hence, an individual's vote on an issue will not be independent of their preferences over other alternatives when the procedures are concerned with piecemeal changes. This is not true for the global procedure I discussed earlier. Such a procedure would not give any incentive to individuals to compromise and make trades because all issues would be combined into the one global procedure. With partial procedures we get vote trading and with global procedures no vote trading. Of course there can still be strategic manipulation in a global procedure both of an individual and a collective kind.

The extent to which people can succesfully trade votes so as to get outcomes that they desire also depends on their ability to form coalitions as well as on their information about others' preferences and voting strategies. People with more information will be in a better position to get the outcomes they want. This is illustrated in figure 6.5. These are the preference schedules over the combination of issues w-x and y-z. As we can see, if the issues were to be decided separately and everyone voted according to their preferences, C, D, and E would ensure the victory of x and A, B, and E would make up a majority for z. If there were a combined procedure, xz would also be the Condorcet winner. To return to the separate procedures, let us suppose that A and C were aware of the preference orders of the others and knew that they would vote straightforwardly. A and C would

FIGURE 6.5. *Vote trading.*

	A	B	C	D	E
1	wz	wz	xy	xy	xz
2	wy	xz	wy	xz	wz
3	xz	wy	xz	wy	xy
4	xy	xy	wz	wz	wy

then have an incentive to trade votes on the issue. Since w-x is a more significant issue for A and y-z is more important to C, A could give up voting for z and vote for y in return for C's vote for w over x. They together would then be able to get the outcomes w and y.[22]

Obviously, these outcomes also could be upset. If B and D were aware of everyone's preference orderings and of the manipulations of A and C and were also aware of the passivity of E, they might also agree to trade votes. B would be willing to sacrifice w for the sake of getting z with the help of D, who votes for z if B would vote for x. Thus, the outcomes of the trading would be that x would win and z would win. Other manipulations are possible in these circumstances. E could attempt to stop A from trading with C by offering to vote for w in return for A not trading. This would at least secure the outcome z for E and that is the most important alternative on her preference orderings.

The situation here is already very complex and it is hard to say what outcome would actually be brought about. This would become even more complicated once we introduce more issues to be decided separately. The point here is the same as for manipulation in individual procedures. The importance of information and coalition building abilities is highlighted, and outcomes will depend heavily on their distribution.

FROM PROCEDURAL TO POLITICAL EQUALITY

Where has this argument taken us? I started by looking for a conception of political equality by attempting to define a procedure that treated everyone equally. Two criteria for procedural equality were proposed and argued for, but two serious difficulties were encountered. First, our criteria did not sufficiently determine the outcomes of collective decision making. Many outcomes might be produced by a procedure that satisfied these criteria, but to produce a single outcome some other procedural restrictions are necessary. Insofar as these further restrictions on the procedures are either illegitimate or have the effect of undermining equality, they proved not to be acceptable. We also considered supplementing decision-making procedures with agenda-setting procedures and found that this would not help us since the same problems arise for the latter. For these reasons, I conclude that procedural equality cannot give us a complete conception of equality in the determination of the outcomes of collective decision making. Either we must give up on a comprehensive ideal of political equality or we must look beyond purely procedural criteria for equality.

Furthermore, it is procedures that are majoritarian and deal with more than two alternatives that are capable of being indeterminate when voters choose strictly according to their preferences. It is these situations in which procedures are also subject to manipulation. Hence, the outcomes may not be determined in a completely egalitarian way since the outcomes will not be determined exclusively by the preferences and the egalitarian procedure. This is because the outcome, in cases that would be indeterminate with straightforward voting, would be determined in part by manipulations of the voters.

Let us turn our attention to the very idea of a procedure as a method by means of which outcomes are derived from preferences. This is a common way of thinking about democratic procedure.[23] At this point we need to reconsider this approach. First, it is impossible to have a method that can derive decisions directly from the unadulterated preferences of the participants. Second, it is not at all clear why it should be desirable. The first claim is demonstrated by the virtually universal manipulability of voting procedures. But even if one could develop "incentive compatible" methods of voting that had the effect of tricking individuals into revealing their preferences this would not be much to look forward to.

The usual reason for developing incentive compatible procedures is belief in an aggregative conception of procedures. This conception states that the purpose of a collective decision procedure is to take a set of individual preferences and transform them into a social preference. The use of the procedure must guarantee that we have an outcome of a certain sort. This is because the aim of the procedure will be to produce an outcome that reflects either the common will of the individual participants or a maximum of welfare for those individuals. This is the justification on such an account of using such a procedure.

But one necessary condition for a procedure to produce such outcomes is that it be incentive compatible. That is, only if the procedure aggregates over the true preferences of individuals can the procedure guarantee that the outcome reflects the common will or a utilitarian solution. If individuals misrepresent their preferences by voting strategically, the outcome will not be an aggregation from their preferences and, social-choice theorists argue, the outcome will have no meaning and will be simply arbitrary.[24] That is, the results will not necessarily be the common will or greatest good. Much of social-choice theory seems to be concerned with finding a social welfare function that will always produce one of these. I shall only briefly argue that social welfare functions would not be well suited to produce either kind of outcome even if it were possible to develop incentive compatible procedures. This undermines the point of seeking incentive compatible methods and suggests that we ought to develop another conception of collective decision procedures where these may not be necessary.

That the social preference should reflect in some way the common will seems misconceived from the start. The basis for the idea that collective decisions should be made on the consensus of common will is that everyone should benefit from the decision or the decision should in some way proceed from or at least be in accord with the will of each and every person. In order to do this one must find out the common will of all the individuals.[25] Needless to say, this expresses the ideal that social life should be based in some way on a principle of unanimity. It is not, however, a procedural principle; it is the idea that there are areas of common agreement among the individuals in the society if there is to be any society at all. The question for those who adopt such a principle will always be, What is the best method for discovering this area of agreement?[26] Clearly, this approach is inimical to that of the social-choice theorists since the latter are concerned with defining a function that satisfies certain properties, among which is that the function can operate on a relatively large if not unlimited domain of preferences. Social-choice theory starts from the assumption of a high degree of disagreement among participants. The assumption behind the idea of a common will is quite different. It is simply that in a society the preferences of individuals bear a certain relation of similarity to each other and that the point of a procedure is to discover this area of similarity. The idea behind social-choice theory is that it should be possible to construct a notion of social preference no matter how much difference there is.

A utilitarian approach to social preference wherein the social preference is a kind of maximum of welfare is equally misguided. This is because the domain of preferences over which the collective decision function is defined does not and cannot distinguish between self-regarding and other-regarding preferences, which distinction is crucial for any utilitarian notion of maximum welfare. It is not to my benefit to have my desire satisfied that another be treated fairly, certainly not in the way that it is to my benefit that my desire for ice cream be fulfilled. Satisfying the former preference will not in itself contribute to my welfare. The social choice procedures do not take into account intensity of preference, at least in particular procedures. It is only when procedures are manipulated and individuals vote strategically and trade votes that intensity of preference can be expressed. No conception of social preference that ignores these two points can guarantee or define utilitarian outcomes. Both the common will and the utilitarian approaches are instrumentalist with regard to procedures. They evaluate procedures in terms of whether they produce the right outcome that is specified independent of the procedure. Hence, the idea that there is some normative significance to the social preference should be rejected. This is independent of the Arrow Impossibility results.

But if no special significance attaches to the idea of a social preference then there is no reason to get people to vote straightforwardly in a system of voting. Furthermore the whole idea of defining a procedure as a "mapping from the preference orderings of the collective to the outcome"[27] seems to be pointless since we cannot have such an object and there is no reason to desire it. Finally, this definition would not be true of incentive compatible procedures. Collective decision procedures do not take us from the preferences of the collective to outcomes. One has to participate in a collective decision procedure to have any influence on the outcome. The fact that not everyone participates does not imply that there was no procedure. Further, even with an incentive compatible procedure, it is possible for someone to make a mistake when he votes. The procedure will still produce an outcome even if the vote did not express the person's preference. What, then, is a collective-decision procedure? It is a set of rules that operates (like a function) on a domain of actions (usually called "voting for x") to produce a decision that is binding on the collectivity.[28] The purpose of the procedure is to permit various members of the group to play a part in determining what decisions are to be made regarding some issue.

I call this the distributive conception of procedures. What the procedure does is assign the participants resources for determining the outcome. The general name for these resources is "voting power." Each individual may use the voting power they are assigned by the procedure to try to affect the outcome. These uses of voting power are what the procedure operates on to produce the outcomes. The distribution of voting power is defined by the particular properties of the procedure. This is what makes voting power a procedural resource; it is a resource the distribution of which is defined by the properties of the procedure.

I define egalitarian-decision procedure as a procedure wherein the distribution of procedural resources is equal. Majority rule is an egalitarian procedure because the distribution of voting power is determined by the principles of one person-one vote, anonymity, and neutrality. These properties of majority rule ensure an equal distribution of voting power. Inegalitarian methods of decision making such as monarchy and oligarchy can be described as methods that do not satisfy the anonymity property. If the king votes for x, then x is chosen regardless of what anyone else wants. Or if a majority of oligarchs votes for x then that is the choice. All the resources for decision making are given to one or a few.

Once majority rule is understood as a procedure in which resources for determining the collectively binding decision are equally distributed we can see why it might be thought desirable. Insofar as we subscribe to a principle of equality of resources and we recognize that such a principle of distribution should be applied to the properties of society that must be chosen by means of a collective-decision procedure, we should assign individuals equal resources to determine what those properties are to be. Majority rule is an egalitarian procedure for collective decision. It satisfies the basic principle of justice that we started with.

But what is missing in majority rule? Even when we have distributed the procedural resources equally, as in a majority rule procedure, we will frequently get indeterminate outcomes if we simply assume that individuals vote straightforwardly. There are two choices for resolving this issue. Either we relax the egalitarian features of the procedure, as with the amendment procedure, or we think of individuals as voting strategically. Let us suppose that we wish to preserve political equality. From the previous section we can see that knowing the situation they are in, individuals will vote strategically to produce an outcome more to their liking. They will do this on the basis of information, which is a crucial resource for individuals in determining outcomes. Information can be distributed in certain ways and the outcome may well depend on how it is distributed. Finally, information is not a procedural resource. Its distribution is not defined by the properties of any procedure. Indeed, this resource can be distributed unequally at the same time that procedural resources are equally distributed.

When a person votes he is participating in a collective decision-making procedure. This action takes place in a larger context. People are trying to discover information about alternatives, others' preferences, and strategies as well as building coalitions to trade votes. All of these activities and the procedure make up the collective decision making *process*. Furthermore, a collective decision-making process is egalitarian when all the resources relevant to determining the outcome are equally distributed. The process must be egalitarian, not merely the collective decision-making procedure that is a part of it.

Why is this so? First of all, collective decisions that are brought about as a result of a procedurally equal but inegalitarian process are no more nor less subject to criticisms from an egalitarian standpoint than a procedurally unequal method of making decisions. They simply involve different resources. Why should an inequality in the distribution of the nonprocedural resources be any less arbitrary for an egalitarian process than an inequality in procedural resources?

Would individuals complain if we were, on a systematic basis, to allot less votes to one person or group of persons than others but give them much more information and means for building coalitions than the others so that they were effectively able to secure the outcomes they desired? It should certainly be possible to compensate a person with nonprocedural resources if he or she lacked procedural resources.

The implications of the distributive conception of procedures on the issue of problems of composition are clear. Consider the following argument of Allen Buchanan's: "Vote bargaining undermines the ideal of equal control that animates the insistence on democratic control over allocation and distribution, because it is equivalent to giving some individuals more votes than others on a given issue by giving them fewer votes on other issues."[29] Buchanan assumes here what ought not to be assumed, that is, that equality of control over a decision-making process entails equality of control over each and every decision. This is a simple mistake. It is of the same order as a view of economic equality that would require that for individuals to be economically equal overall, they must have the same quantity of resources as everyone else for each possible object of consumption. That is, if objects of economic value such as money, land, and capital had to be distributed equally overall it would be a mistake to think that each item had to be distributed equally, that is, that everyone got equal quantities of all the items. This distribution may be compatible with overall equality but it is not required by it. All that is required is that each person's total bundle be equal, which equality may be defined as an envy free distribution of resources. Hence it is no violation of the principle of political equality that individuals have more power regarding some decisions and others have more power regarding other decisions as long as these differences are compatible with an overall equality. From this it should be clear that vote bargaining is quite consistent with political equality.[30]

But political equality is not only consistent with vote bargaining, it requires it. As I have shown in the section on composition, if procedures are to be insulated from each other in the way Buchanan proposes, the collection of partial procedures will not adequately implement equality over complete life pros-' pects. We come much closer to an egalitarian conception of the collective decision process if we permit individuals to trade on the resources they have between procedures. This is because vote trading makes it possible for them to use their procedural resources in ways that reflect the complementarity of their preferences and the varying importance that different issues have for them. And any egalitarian scheme that neglects the complementarity of preferences and differences of intensity, especially to the point that it will defeat Condorcet choices, is unable to give individuals equality over essential elements of total life prospects. Hence, insofar as a society must use partial procedures for collective decision making, it must also allow vote trading to take place.[31]

This endorsement of vote trading introduces another difficulty with the purely procedural approach to political equality. For as I show in the section on manipulation, one's success or failure at vote trading in achieving the ends one wants to achieve will depend greatly on the distribution of nonprocedural resources such as information and resources for building coalitions. The examples I considered illustrate that a maldistribution of these resources could enable some to achieve their ends at the expense of others just as much as a maldistribution of procedural resources might help those who have the procedural resources to achieve their ends at the expense of others. This is not a result of the indeterminacy of egalitarian procedures but the result of political equality being a relation between individuals who are using many procedures. Again, our notion of a collective decision process will come in handy. It can be used to describe the use of procedural and nonprocedural resources on one issue; it also differs from a collective decision procedure in that a process will encompass the application of procedures to many issues.

A collective decision process will be inegalitarian if the procedures that are used are egalitarian when the resources that are used for vote bargaining are unequally distributed. Now it is amply clear that equality of resources in the collective decision-making process is what the ideal of political equality amounts to rather than a mere equality in procedural resources.

Hence, our conception of political equality is not procedural. That is, political equality cannot be defined as a method or set of rules for deciding on outcomes on the basis of choices over these outcomes. Nonprocedural resources are an important part of the process and in an egalitarian conception must be part of the bundle of resources that are equally distributed. On the other hand, this conception of political equality is not outcome oriented. It does not require equal satisfaction of desires for individuals either with respect to collective properties or with respect to states of the society as a whole. Such a demand would conflict with the arguments for resourcism and against equality of welfare that I have presented elsewhere.[32] Nor does it impose any particular standard on the outcomes of democratic decision making.

This conception of political equality departs from most other normative conceptions in that it involves a conception of the political process as a competitive process in which individuals compete to procure the outcomes of collective decision making they prefer. It is quite distinct from the other usual conceptions of political equality, such as the demand that each person's interests are equally weighted in the process of decision making or the conception that regards political equality as part of an adequate notion of social preference. Insofar as the preferences of individuals conflict, the resources for procuring their ends ought to be divided equally so that each has equal opportunity either to get what they want or to strike a compromise with others.

NOTES

1. An exception to this is the considerable attention paid to the idea of collective preference or general will by social choice theorists and some philosophers. Most of this work has been negative. See William Riker, *Liberalism Versus Populism: A Confrontation Between the Theory of Democracy and the Theory of Social Choice* (San Francisco: W. H. Freeman

and Company, 1982) for a good discussion of this kind of issue. See Jules Coleman and John Ferejohn, "Democracy and Social Choice," *Ethics,* 97 (1986): 6–25; and Joshua Cohen, "An Epistemic Conception of Democracy," *Ethics,* 97 (1986): 26–38 for more philosophically sophisticated discussions of Riker's arguments. For other good sources of philosophical discussion of social choice, see Brian Barry and Russell Hardin, eds., *Rational Man and Irrational Society?* (Beverly Hills: Sage, 1982) and Jon Elster, ed., *Foundations of Social Choice Theory* (Cambridge: Cambridge University Press, 1986).

2. See Thomas Christiano, *Democracy and Equality,* Ph.D. Dissertation, University of Illinois, Chicago, 1988, Chs. 2 and 3.

3. See note 1 for some of the recent literature.

4. Brian Barry, "Is Democracy Special?," in *Philosophy, Politics and Society,* 5th series, eds. Peter Laslett and James Fishkin (New Haven: Yale University Press, 1979), 155–96.

5. Kenneth O. May, "A Set of Independent, Necessary, and Sufficient Conditions for Simple Majority Decision," In *Rational Man and Irrational Society?,* ed. Brian Barry and Russell Hardin (Beverly Hills: Sage, 1982), 297–304.

6. This idea is suggested by William Nelson, *On Justifying Democracy* (Boston: Routledge & Kegan Paul, 1980), 25.

7. See May, "A Set of Conditions," 302.

8. Neal Reimer, "The Case for Bare Majority Rule," *Ethics* 62 (1951): 16–32 states that special majority rules give greater weight to the voters of the minority and thereby violate equality.

9. See Robin Farquharson, *The Theory of Voting* (New Haven: Yale University Press, 1969) 62. For more generalized advice on how to win with the amendment procedure when there is no Condorcet winner see Bo Bjurulf and Richard Niemi "Order-of-Voting Effects," in *Power, Voting, and Voting Power,* ed. Manfred J. Holler (Wurzburg: Physica-Verlag, 1982) 153–77.

10. William Riker, *Liberalism versus Populism,* 69–70. Of course this assumes that everyone is voting sincerely. If everyone is voting just so as to get the best outcome and they know how everyone else is voting, the last alternative introduced will not win. See Farquharson, *The Theory of Voting,* and Bjurulf and Niemi, "Order-of-Voting Effects."

11. In the case described previously, we were unable to suggest how the notion of equality was to apply given the set of preferences. It might be objected that we need not devise a notion of procedural equality that is able successfully to handle any conceivable set of preferences. The example I have adduced, it might be argued, requires a relatively unusual set of preferences and that a theory of politics in

general and political equality in particular does not have to handle any kind of situation. I do not think that the objection to unlimited domain when trying to come up with the social preference will apply in this context. The former objection is conceptual, whereas the objection in this context is not. That is, it does seem odd to think that one could have a notion of social preference that would be able to tell us the social preference of a group of people who could not agree on anything. On the other hand it is quite reasonable to try to develop a notion of political equality that could handle disagreements like this since they certainly occur. These kinds of disagreements are at the basis of the cyclic preferences that we have been discussing. See note 19 for some discussions of domain restrictions.

12. It might be claimed here that there are methods that satisfy the neutrality and anonymity requirements but do not produce the indeterminacy problem. Two methods are the Borda method, and the modified Borda. These proceed on the basis of information about the relative positions in the preference scales of the participants as well as pairwise comparisons in order to produce outcomes. Thus, in figure 6.1, each alternative would win a number of points depending on its position in the orderings of the individuals. If we assign three points to first place, two to second place, and one to third, x would have $(3 + 3 + 1 + 2 + 2 =)$ 11 points, y would have 9 points, and z would get 10 points. The winner would be x, the alternative with the most points.

There are reasons for not using the Borda method as a method of voting. It seems to rely on some illicit assumptions about the comparisons between rankings of alternatives. The fact that the method gives three votes to one's first choice out of three and two to one's second choice and only one to one's last choice suggests that the differences in valuation between one's first and second choice and one's second and third choices are the same. Indeed, the Borda count requires that one make an assumption about the relative differences between one's preferences in order to produce a determinate result. Consider this array of preferences in figure 6.6. Here, if we assign three points to the first

FIGURE 6.6. *Point voting.*

	A	B	C	D	E
1	x	x	x	z	z
2	z	z	z	y	y
3	y	y	y	x	x

place choice, two to the second, and one to the third, then *z* will win with twelve points while *x* will have eleven points and *y* seven. If we assign five points to the first place choice and two points to the second place choice and one to the last choice, then *x* will win with seventeen and *z* will end up with sixteen. Hence, the determination of the outcome must depend on the relative assignment of points. The Borda count cannot be neutral with respect to the differences in intensities.

It is hard to see the justification for making such intrapersonal comparisons. Suppose, for example, that *A* and *B* were almost indifferent between *x* and the other alternatives while *D* and *E* ranked *z* far above the other alternatives. If one were to take intrapersonal and interpersonal comparisons seriously, *z* should be the winner and the Borda method would give us the wrong outcome. Though there should be a way in which individuals can express varying intensities of interest in different alternatives, this rigid and externally imposed way is inappropriate. Any procedure that determines independently of the voter what the possible comparisons between the alternatives are in such a crude way is unacceptable.

13. See Nicholas R. Miller, "Logrolling, Vote Trading, and the Paradox of Voting: A Game Theoretical Overview," *Public Choice* 30 (1977): 51–75. See also Barry, "Is Democracy Special?," 163–64 for a discussion of this example.

14. See E. M. Uslaner, "Manipulation of the Agenda by Strategic Voting: Separable and Nonseparable Preferences," in *Power, Voting, and Voting Power,* ed. Manfred, J. Holler (Wurzburg: Physica-Verlag, 1982), 135–52, for some startling results of separating and combining issues in the same procedure.

15. Barry, "Is Democracy Special?," 164.

16. This example is adapted from Miller, "Logrolling," 70.

17. This is not exclusively a difficulty for egalitarian theories. For a version of this problem in relation to notions of efficiency, see Russell Hardin, "Rational Choice Theories," in *Idioms of Inquiry,* ed. Terence Ball (Albany: State University of New York Press, 1987), 67–91.

18. The indeterminacy problem in political equality seems to arise from the possibility of certain kinds of preference orderings. That is, procedures that satisfy anonymity and neutrality are not decisive in certain circumstances because the preferences of the voters take the procedure into a cycle. Those procedures that are determinate and produce outcomes do not, on the other hand, fully satisfy neutrality. If the domain of preferences could be restricted in some way, then there would be a way to characterize certain procedures as fully egalitarian. For two different ways of restricting the domain of preferences, see

Duncan Black, *The Theory of Committees and Elections*, 2d ed. (Cambridge: Cambridge University Press, 1963), 19; and Amartya Sen, *Collective Choice and Social Welfare* (San Francisco: Holden Day, 1970), 168. I think that restrictions on the domain of preferences may be reasonable when one is elaborating a principle of collective preference, because the idea of a collective preference becomes senseless if there is no agreement at all among participants. When the subject is political equality, however, there need be no restriction on the kinds of conflicts between preferences that are resolvable by a politically egalitarian procedure, hence, there can be no justification for restricting the domain of preferences.

19. Allan Gibbard, "Manipulation of Voting Schemes: A General Result," *Rational Man and Irrational Society?*, 355–66. Gibbard's result is that all non-chance, non-dictatorial voting schemes that apply to more than two alternatives and do not admit of ties are manipulable.

20. See Farquharson, *The Theory of Voting*, and Gibbard, "Manipulation of Voting Schemes." In most discussions, the words "strategic" and "sincere" do not refer at all to attitudes but only to actions. One may determine how one ought to vote by seeing how others are voting and vote straightforwardly because this is the best way of ensuring the best outcome.

21. See Michael Dummett and Robin Farquharson, "Stability in Voting," *Econometrica* (1961) 29, 1: 33–43.

22. This example is adapted from Riker, *Liberalism versus Populism*, 159.

23. For this kind of definition of democratic procedures see Barry "Is Democracy Special?," 156, as well as Robert Dahl, "Procedural Democracy," in *Philosophy, Politics and Society*, ed. Peter Laslett and James Fishkin, 5th series (New Haven: Yale University Press, 1979), 97–133. This sort of conception of democratic procedures is standard among those social choice theorists who think that social choice theory is directly applicable to democracy; see Riker, *Liberalism versus Populism*, 22, as well as critics of his, Jules Coleman and John Ferejohn, "Democracy and Social Choice," 7. See also Robert Dahl, *A Preface to Democratic Theory* (Chicago: University of Chicago Press, 1956), chap. 3; Jane Mansbridge, *Beyond Adversary Democracy* (Chicago: University of Chicago Press, 1983); Peter Jones, "Political Equality and Majority Rule," in *The Nature of Political Theory*, ed. David Miller and Larry Siedentop (Oxford: Oxford University Press, 1983), 155–82; and also Peter Singer, *Democracy and Disobedience* (Oxford: Oxford University Press, 1973).

24. This is the conclusion of William Riker in *Liberalism Versus Populism*.

25. See Jean-Jacques Rousseau, *The Social Contract and Discourses,* trans. G. D. H. Cole (London: J. M. Dent and Sons, 1973), 200; and Brian Barry, "The Public Interest," *Proceedings of the Aristotelian Society* 38 (1964): 9–14.

26. See Rousseau, *The Social Contract,* 276–79; and Cohen, "Epistemic Conception," 34.

27. Coleman and Ferejohn, "Democracy and Social Choice," 7.

28. This is more in accord with the game theoretic account of procedures; see Gibbard, "Manipulation of Voting Schemes."

29. Allen Buchanan, *Ethics, Efficiency and the Market* (Totowa, New Jersey: Rowman & Allanheld, 1985), 31.

30. Of course it may be necessary to restrict trades in some ways so as to preserve equality from the cumulative effects of many persons acting in an uncoordinated way. For an egalitarian justification of these restrictions in the economic sphere see G. A. Cohen, "Robert Nozick and Wilt Chamberlain: How Patterns Preserve Liberty," *Erkenntnis* 11 (1979): 5–23.

31. Unfortunately, even these tentative solutions cannot give us a complete answer to the problem of global versus marginal political equality. This is because the information requirements that exist for adequately making decisions that take whole lives into consideration are too great for any person to meet. But from the point of view of equality, it is clearly an improvement to extend equality past the restrictions imposed by a decision-making procedure that insulates every decision from every other.

32. See Thomas Christiano, *Democracy and Equality,* chap. 2.

7

PUBLIC CHOICE
VERSUS DEMOCRACY

RUSSELL HARDIN

Public-choice theory offers two main classes of findings. First, aggregation from individual to collective preferences may not be well defined. Even though every individual may have a clear preference ranking of all alternatives before us, we may not be able to convert these individual rankings into a collective ranking. Second, individual motives for action may not fit collective preferences for outcomes even when the latter are well defined. We may all agree, for example, that we would all be better off if we would all pay extra for better pollution control equipment on our cars, but no individual has an interest in making the extra expenditure. Not only are we damned if we don't agree on what to do, we may also be damned if we do.

The first class of findings casts doubt on the conceptual coherence of majoritarian democracy. The second class has commonly been thought to yield a consensual justification for the coercive power of the state if, of course, the state is democratic. Just because our individual motivations work against our collective interests, we should choose to coerce ourselves to act in our

This paper has benefited from critical commentaries by John W. Chapman, Thomas Christiano, Robert E. Lane, and Alan Wertheimer.

collective interests. This consensual argument for coercion is, however, as logically flawed as the notion of majoritarian democracy. All that we may rightly conclude from the misfit of individual and collective interests is that we would benefit from having some central determination of our actions. We cannot conclude which of several possible determinations we should make.

The disconcerting implication of public-choice theory is that majoritarian democracy is both conceptually and motivationally flawed. Perhaps the actual practice of democracy may sensibly be viewed as a compromise to live within the constraints of these perverse conclusions. That practice is not an altogether happy compromise because it is not particularly majoritarian.

After a brief historical account of the recognition of the discoveries of public-choice theory, I address their bearing on democratic theory and practice. I then examine one possible empirical escape from the negative implications by way of the communitarian claim that we do not face the assumptions or conclusions of the theory's account of democracy. Finally, I consider an alternative solution to the difficulties of democratic theory, namely, that institutional devices can achieve what democratic choice may not. Throughout, my concern is majoritarian democracy, that is, procedures based on majority rule. This is the form in which we face the following problems because we have come to accept merely majority rule rather than to require broad consensus to make democracy workable. In modern political thought, the core of the notion of democracy is its etymological core—rule by the people—, which translates most naturally as majority rule if there are divisions of opinion.

1. Two Problems

Public-choice theory's first class of results is associated with Condorcet's problem of cyclic majorities and Kenneth Arrow's General Possibility Theorem, which is more aptly known as Arrow's Impossibility Theorem.[1] According to this theorem, there is no general rule for aggregating to a social choice from individual preferences that can meet certain apparently acceptable criteria. This theorem is essentially normative and conceptual. It says that collective preference cannot be defined as a logical analog of individual preference as that is commonly understood in economics. I will refer to this as the problem of social choice or, in its specific variants, as Condorcet's or Arrow's problem.

The second class of results is associated with Anthony Downs's analysis of voting, Mancur Olson's account of the logic of collective action, and the game theorist's Prisoner's Dilemma.[2] I will refer to this as the collective action or prisoner's dilemma problem. It is essentially an explanatory problem of motivation. It arises in contexts in which a common goal can be achieved only through individual contributions of effort or resources. For example, we may reduce pollution if each of us contributes by driving more expensively equipped cars. It may be in my interest not to cooperate in achieving our common purpose if I can get away with it even though it is in my interest for all of us to cooperate. How then do we get ourselves to cooperate? If we face no contrary sanction or inducement, we may all choose not to cooperate and so fail to achieve our goal.

Both of these problems are relevant to the general issues of organizing political societies. And they are a perverse and demoralizing pair. Arrow's theorem says we cannot generally stipulate a rule for acceptably aggregating to a collective preference from individual preferences. The conclusion of the standard prisoner's dilemma analysis is that, even where we find an acceptable rule for aggregating, we may still have motivational difficulties in implementing the collective preference.

The two problems are not only a perverse but a natural pair. Arrow's theorem is strictly about what state of affairs we want to attain. It does not deal with how to get there once we know what we want. Arrow never reaches the motivational concerns of how to implement a collective or aggregate preference once it is defined. In a sense, he need not reach such concerns for the simple reason that he shows we cannot in general define a determinate aggregate preference merely as a function of individual preferences. His proof involves logical assumptions that are far more complete in their possibilities than our real world may be. Although no general aggregation rule would fit all possible worlds, there might be one that fits ours. In that case,

we would want to know how to implement our collective preference. The logic of collective action says that, for an important
class of seemingly quite consensual issues, implementation may
be fouled by narrow self-interest. Arrow's theorem is not concerned with how to enforce a collective preference. The usual
prisoner's dilemma analysis and Olson's theory are fundamentally about enforcement.

2. Historical Background

Public-choice theory is an extension of neoclassical economics in
that it is based, both normatively and explanatorily, on the
assumptions of individual choice or preference. In early efforts
to understand productivity, these assumptions worked wonders
by replacing notions of intrinsic value with an understanding of
relations of supply and demand. When the simple theory of
incentives was systematically applied to economic life, the results
were generally counterintuitive and sanguine. The main result
was expressed in Mandeville's law that private vices beget public
virtues. Or, more explicitly, narrowly self-interested behavior in
production and exchange leads to collective benefits in the form
of a general increase in wealth. According to a contemporary
variant on Mandeville, greed makes America strong and pros-
perous.

Not everything can be handled by incentives for personal
benefit in free exchange. Public-choice theory arose mainly to
deal with what remains for the public to do, to deal with what
cannot be or is not done through the market.[3] This residual is
large and important. Hence, the problem of public choice is also
large and important, as is the scope of government. The results
of economic analysis of this residual are often counterintuitive
but not at all sanguine.

The problem of gaining compliance with government policies
has been recognized in political philosophy from Plato forward.
It is, of course, central for Hobbes. With slightly tendentious or
generous reading one can presume that many have seen the
logic of collective action or the prisoner's dilemma. For example, Glaucon (in Plato's *Republic*) and Hobbes think social

order depends on threatening individuals to get them not to transgress against others. This sanctioning is mutually beneficial if it means that virtually none of us transgresses or can transgress.[4] Ideally, for any one of us, it might be best if all others are intimidated into orderliness while we free ride on the general order and the wealth that it generates.

Most of the earlier treatments of motivating beneficial collective action focused on the negative issue that provoked Glaucon and Hobbes: to prevent harm by securing mutual abstinence. The more common modern focus, exemplified by Hume and Rousseau, has been on the possibility of securing cooperation for creative purposes.[5] This may owe some inspiration to economic thought, culminating in Adam Smith, and some to the development of contract law and doctrine, both of which treat cooperation and exchange as productive. In this sanguine variant of government's intervention to resolve a collective action problem, we might agree on mutual coercion to get all to contribute to a state of affairs that we all prefer to the status quo. Alas, although we might successfully use the state to prod us into mutually beneficial collective action, we might not agree on what collective actions to prod ourselves into.

The other class of issues in public-choice theory, the impossibility of finding a rule for aggregating diverse preferences into a single collective preference, has been noticed in limited ways in many contexts. Its general importance has only recently been widely recognized. The special problem is that, when we face a choice among three or more mutually exclusive policies, we may form a majority in favor of policy A over B, another majority for B over C, and yet another majority for C over A. No policy is preferred by majorities over all others. Condorcet saw cyclic majorities as an aspect of complex choices. C. L. Dodgson (Lewis Carroll), with his wonderful sense of the perversities of daily life, saw it in elections at his Christ Church College.[6] Generalization of the problem and appreciation of its potentially pervasive importance begins with the work of Duncan Black and Kenneth Arrow. Black saw the problem as inherent in committee choice and Arrow proved quite generally that there can be no acceptable universal rule to convert any collection of individual preferences into a collective preference ordering.

On his own account of his theorem, Arrow writes that he hit upon the general impossibility in the course of trying to show how individual preference orderings could be aggregated into a national ordering so that, in the analysis of international relations, one could treat nations as though they were individuals with standard game-theoretic utility functions.[7] In essence, Arrow was asking whether a state can be conceived as a unitary actor with its preferences derived in an acceptable way from those of its citizens. His answer was "no."

The history of our two issues has some irony. The first clear recognition of the trouble with aggregating individual into collective preferences came from Condorcet soon after sanguine views of the creative possibilities of the state in such thinkers as Hume and Smith[8] and of Rousseau's vision of a general will. As though in proof of the implications of his discovery, Condorcet died in the sanguinary aftermath of the French Revolution.

3. Social-Choice Problems

Although Condorcet's cyclic majorities are commonly associated with Arrow's theorem, as though the latter were merely a generalization of the former, the two are in fact quite different problems. The possibility of cyclic majorities arises when we vote on a specific issue that has three or more resolutions. This is a kind of choice that we may often face in political life at any level on which we decide by majority vote. Indeed, we can face this quandary no matter what our majority must be. For example, if we need a super-majority of 99 percent in favor to select a winner, we can have a cyclic majority with a hundred voters and a hundred possible positions on our issue.

Arrow's theorem is far more general in a powerful way that makes it unrealistic in direct application to our daily lives. Arrow supposes that we face a choice over whole states of affairs that are fully determined in every way that matters to us. We do not merely choose a president or decide on a law. We choose a total world in which everything is settled: all presidents, all laws. Once we have made this single social choice, nothing remains for us to choose collectively. Arrow was forced to conceive of the matter in this way because he wished to assume nothing more than purely ordinal preferences on the part of all individuals and in our final collective choice.

Why does this ambition push us into considering choices over whole states of affairs, states that are fully determined? Take any ordinary claim that I prefer A to *not-A*. There are few, if any, As of which we can believe that anyone would prefer A to *not-A* no matter what. In principle, we can almost always conceive a package, say of $A+B$, such that I would prefer *(not-A + not-B)* to *(A + B)*. If so, then it is not true that I prefer A to *not-A tout court*. Hence, in principle I cannot make ordinal choices over mere aspects of my state of affairs. I can make ordinal choices only over whole states of affairs.[9]

A certain lunacy lurks in thinking of our social-choice problem as a once-and-for-all choice over whole states of affairs. But for the moment, the only escape from that lunacy seems to be an alternative that almost all social theorists reject outright or one that any democratic theorist must reject. One alternative that might be compelling if it were conceptually sensible is to suppose we can make cardinal, interpersonally comparable evaluations of aspects of states of affairs. Then we could make a social choice by simply adding the evaluations of each of us together for all possible choices and selecting the choice that produces the largest sum. Of course, to say that I can make a cardinal evaluation of a particular aspect of my state of affairs is to assert that my evaluation of that aspect is not affected by other aspects. But that violates the principle stated above. This alternative is not cogent.

Another alternative is to suppose that we, or I, or someone simply knows a principle by which to evaluate aspects of our state of affairs that is not directly derivative from the preferences or interests of all of us. Candidate principles include various religious dogmas, naturalistic claims from what happens to be the apparent preference in a given community, and various intuited principles that one or another theorist approves. With the possible exception of the communitarian alternative, none of these is consistent with democratic principles. I will therefore not consider noncommunitarian principles further. I will leave the communitarian alternative for later.

In his theorem, Arrow supposes that our choice rule must meet several apparently appealing conditions. If our concern with the theorem is its relevance to our understanding of the possibilities of democracy, two assumptions in the theorem are in clear tension. First, our choice rule must be general in the very strong sense that it must apply successfully to any set of individual preferences. For example, it must be able to handle even a case in which the set of individual preferences is a cyclic majority. This is the condition of universal domain, or U. Second, the rule must be subject to the following Pareto principle: if no one prefers state of affairs x to state y and at least one of us prefers y to x, then the social choice must rank y above x. In particular, of course, if all of us prefer y to x, then our social choice must rank y above x. Suppose all of us prefer y to every other state of affairs. Then, as is true of any specific set of preferences, our set of individual preferences clearly violates condition U. But it does so in such a way that our society may have no difficulty at all in making a social choice that no one could object to on democratic principles.

Hence, Arrow's Impossibility Theorem does not rule out the possibility that we could reach a democratic social choice. It merely rules out the logical possibility that every society, no matter how lacking in agreement, can follow one single aggregation rule for the social ordering of all its alternative whole states of affairs. This is a logically strong conclusion, but it may fail to be empirically relevant. In this respect, it is like the Condorcet analysis of cyclic majorities: that analysis can be troubling, but it may not always be, because sometimes we may not have cyclic majority preferences.

What are we finally to make of Arrow's Impossibility Theorem? It is mitigated by other impossibilities. We cannot even get to Arrow's problem in general because we cannot know enough to give rank orderings over all whole states of affairs. The individual preference information that must be fed into an Arrovian social-choice mechanism or procedure is impossible. We might even suppose that the description of whole states of affairs in the real world, in which there are births and deaths that continually change the society of those choosing, makes little sense. And we may realistically suppose of many aspects of our social order that all or almost all prefer *A* to *not-A* in any plausible circumstances. And we typically need to make only a first choice without concern for the further ranking of all other alternatives. For these reasons, and perhaps others, we might actively prefer, and think it better, to make our social choices piecemeal. At most we decide a few things at one time and then decide other things later. And at that later time we might reconsider some of what seemingly has already been decided.

Unfortunately, this pragmatic response to Arrow's Impossibility Theorem is only a negative, not a positive, answer. It does not suggest how we may normatively determine what would be a best or a most democratic procedure for deciding what to decide now and what later, what to reconsider and what to leave decided, whom to include in the decision procedure and whom to leave out. Arrow's initial concern was to find a social-choice procedure that would meet a particular kind of normative justification, namely that the procedure was a rule for aggregating to a social choice from nothing but individual preferences subject to several constraints that, prima facie, seemed likely to be generally acceptable. His discovery is that there can be no such rule. We may rightly claim that his conditions and the general form of what he counted as a social choice (a complete ordering over all states of affairs) are unrealistic and therefore not compelling for our actual social choices. But we cannot thereby normatively rescue any social choice rule or mechanism. We need positive arguments in defense of a particular rule.

We have positive arguments for many social-choice procedures, but none is as tight and complete as the considerations Arrow raises. And no social-choice procedure seems fully acceptable even for a particular one of many contemporary complex national societies. Indeed, most social choice procedures that are analyzed by philosophers and others are not even sufficiently well defined for us to know how they work or whether they would work in plausible circumstances. We know that some societies seem to struggle through from one social choice to another. But success seems to turn on nondemocratic, coercive, and deceptive moves too much of the time for us to feel normatively at ease with it. Not only may minorities get trampled, but so may majorities. Within a democratic shell even the seemingly most democratic of modern governments may often be undemocratic.

Hence, although the conditions and form of Arrow's theorem are not ideally suitable for evaluation of social-choice procedures and possibilities, we must still be troubled by the negative implications of that theorem. More realistic assumptions will not block the conclusion that public-choice procedures are normatively incoherent if they are to translate individual into collective choices, as majoritarian democracy is supposed to do.

4. COLLECTIVE-ACTION PROBLEMS

If many of us would benefit from completion of a project that no one of us could afford to undertake alone, we may confront the perversities of the logic of collective action. If we depend on voluntary contributions to our collective interest in this project, I may wish to take a free ride on the efforts of others. My own contribution, whether an equal share or otherwise, might benefit me less than it would cost me, even though, if all of us contribute, all of us benefit more than our own contributions. Alas, we may all try to free ride and may therefore all fail to benefit from the project.

One resolution of this problem is to vote to have our government force us to contribute, usually through taxes. As Hume stated,

Political society easily remedies [such] inconveniences. Magistrates find an immediate interest in the interest of any considerable part of their subjects. They need consult no body but themselves to form any scheme for the promoting of that interest. . . . Thus bridges are built; harbours open'd; ramparts rais'd; canals form'd; fleets equip'd; and armies disciplin'd; every where, by the care of government, . . . one of the finest and most subtle inventions imaginable.[10]

Hume's is a lovely vision. Once we have government, we can resolve our collective-action problems. Moreover, we can move from this vision to a justification for coercion, in the collection of taxes and other ways, to provide collective benefits. Mild coercion might well be sanctioned by our own democratic preferences. Is this conclusion compelling? Unfortunately, it is far too quick. It faces at least two obstacles. First, few instances of collective provision are likely to be uniquely preferred, so that we may wonder about the justice of coercing those whose preferences are overridden. Second, despite the fineness and subtlety of the invention of government for the provision of collective benefits, our control of government is subject to problems of the logic of collective action even when there is strong popular agreement on particular collective provisions.

With reference to the first obstacle, suppose we have before us two mutually exclusive collective provisions. They could be mutually exclusive for various reasons. For example, either of them may be in essence an opportunity cost of the other. When provision q has been arranged, the additional marginal benefits of providing p may no longer outweigh p's costs. We may collectively benefit from dredging a harbor somewhere, but if we dredge the one in your community, dredging the one in mine will no longer be an attractive option. Or one collective provision may logically preclude another, as one system of property rights, s, might preclude another, t, or as the constitutional arrangements that promote the interests of Federalists might undermine those of Antifederalists.

Unfortunately for Hume, some of us may strongly prefer p and t to q and s and may consider ourselves losers when q and s are provided. Government may indeed overcome a collective-action problem, but it may overcome the wrong one for many of us. Is it now justified in its coercion of those of us who lost? Perhaps, but it is not justified by a simple claim that we mutually benefit, because we could also have mutually benefited from the alternative resolutions.[11] We can often get a utilitarian justification for sticking to a policy choice once it has been in place awhile.[12] But we cannot always get a prior democratic or consensual justification for the choice when it is made from a menu of variously preferred alternatives.

As to the second obstacle, recall Downs's analysis of voting in major elections. His most widely cited proposition is that two-party elections tend to produce candidates whose positions mirror those of the median voter. It may be stodgy to say so, but that would not be a bad or undemocratic result. The more discouraging result of Downs's analysis is the analog of the logic of collective action that is faced by ordinary citizens. Most of us much of the time, perhaps most of the time, cannot justify any special effort to understand the value of electing one candidate rather than another. Egregious failure of leadership on a major policy issue may lead to rejection at re-election time, as Herbert Hoover learned in 1932, because it will take us no effort to relate failure to the candidate. But most voters cannot be expected to know enough to cast votes in ways that would properly constrain most elected officials. To some extent this is merely a reflection of the difficulty of making good causal predictions no matter how well informed one might be. For example, many Americans who voted for peace in 1964 got Lyndon Johnson's Vietnam War; many who voted for a balanced budget in 1980 got Ronald Reagan's record deficits. But many voters would misstate even the clearly predictable policies of their candidates.

We have a tremendous body of empirical work on what voters know and what motivates their choices in elections. Some of that work is reassuring for our concern with democratic control of government. But some is demoralizing. Early views that voters are virtually stupid have given way over the past couple of decades to more complex views that voters, in deciding on candidates, do what sensible people do when making any decisions that affect their interests: given the costs of acquiring information, they take short cuts and use proxy measures of many things. Even on the most favorable accounts of voter sophistication and the quality of voter decisions, however, one cannot make strong claims that the outcome of democratic voting procedures is a coherent mapping of citizen preferences onto policies. This conclusion is not theoretically surprising because, in at least broad outline, it seems clearly to follow from the Downsian analysis of the incentives voters face.

5. THE COMMUNITARIAN ALTERNATIVE

Consider a political community in which Arrow's condition of universal domain is violated by widespread agreement on major issues. By Arrow's general principles, we may suppose the community can succeed in following the simple choice procedure of majority rule. We can do so because we will typically have overwhelming majorities in favor of one choice over any other that we may face. Suppose also that we do not face perverse interactive effects. If we think we prefer A to $not\text{-}A$ and B to $not\text{-}B$, then we will not find ourselves also preferring $(not-A + not-B)$ to $(A + B)$. Hence, we can make our social choices piecemeal without needing to make a single choice over all possible whole states of affairs, and we can make then consensually.

Under these suppositions it would seem that we escape at least the conceptual flaws of democracy. Wouldn't majoritarian democracy therefore work perfectly well for us? Surely the answer could be yes. With such agreement on our major political issues, we should even be able to overcome some of the motivational problem of the logic of collective action by creating political devices for the mild coercion necessary to get us to abide by our collective decisions. Recent communitarian moral and political theory seems to be based on these assumptions and, hence, to meet the objections of public choice theory. I think this conclusion is correct as a matter of pure possibility. This is to say that, by sufficiently balking the implications of Arrow's condition of universal domain and by not falling to the inherent logic of the interaction of the value of every aspect of our state of affairs with the value of every other aspect, we may be fortunate enough to make majority rule at least conceptually coherent. Moreover, it seems plausible that societies have existed in which these problems of public choice theory have not dominated social choice. For example, many small societies studied by anthropologists may meet these conditions.

It is hard to read the communitarian literature without thinking that much more is being assumed than merely the possibility of such a factual state of consensus. In particular, many communitarians seem to be driven by a more profound and determinate notion of the sources of consensus. The presumed fact of consensus is put as a constitutive point: individuals in a society get their values from the society. Unfortunately, despite a "common" source for our values in a given society, general consensus on major issues does not follow, as must be obvious for anyone living in a modern society. Alasdair MacIntyre seems to take conflict over values in our society as a criticism of the society, although he rather perversely supposes that the Athens that has given us a rich record of deep and occasionally violent conflict over values was exempt from this criticism.[13]

Irrespective of whether our dissensus is ground for moral criticism, it is ground for doubting the conceptual coherence of democracy in our condition. The communitarian alternative is not one we can simply adopt. We either do or do not find ourselves in it. If we had found ourselves in communitarian consensus, neither public choice theory nor much of historical political theory might ever have arisen. Jane Mansbridge notes that in "the early seventeenth century, both citizens and their representatives believed that a nation-state could make most decisions on the basis of a common good." That belief has since been so thoroughly shattered that, she says, "majority rule, once an incomplete substitute for full consensus, is now almost synonymous with democracy itself."[14] It seems likely that it is not our era but rather the era of belief in a common good that is the odd exception in the long history of the effort to understand politics. In any sense that would serve the analyses of the communitarians, we are not a community.

6. THE COMPROMISES OF DEMOCRACY

There is a third, emerging body of work in public choice in addition to work on the problems of social choice and collective action. This attends to the way institutions work. It is almost exclusively positive rather than normative. But it may have normative implications. Its central problem is how things manage to get publicly decided and implemented despite the impossibilities of Arrow and Condorcet and the motivational conundrums of Downs and Olson. For example, how does a legislative body such as Congress regularly succeed in adopting policies by apparently majority votes despite the supposed frequency of Condorcet cycles? Institutional public choice theorists argue that it may do so through the use of devices that mask cyclic majorities or that give someone or some group authority or power to force majority votes.

Well recognized antimajoritarian devices include deference to the status quo and giving some person or group power to manipulate the order of voting on issues. Votes in legislative bodies may be restricted to simple yes or no votes on particular issues, so that each measure is compared to the status quo rather than to alternative measures. If there is a cyclic majority over two alternatives and the status quo, the cycle can only show up in a future year when a measure that lost to the status quo this year defeats one that has since become the new status quo. In the meantime, we seem to be quite decisive. Alas, any historical bias in who benefits from the status quo may be further maintained by this device for handling cyclic majorities.[15]

We can break the status quo by giving decisive control over legislative voting to specific individuals or groups to contrive determinate outcomes. In the United States Congress, small committees often have extraordinary control over the content of legislation. Almost no congressional committee bill could be safe from amendments that would make it inferior to the status quo in the view of the committee members. Committees get the last word when legislation goes to conference committee to work out House and Senate differences. In conference, committee members have an ex post veto that guarantees that they do no worse than the status quo.[16] Committee control of legislation introduces strong bias if special interests tend to dominate committees that oversee their issues, as they commonly do. Hence, instead of a bias for the status quo, we have biased change. Moreover, this device may not only overcome the status quo domination of cyclic majorities, it may also overcome clear majority preferences that are not cyclic.

The bent here is not unlike part of the bent in the communitarian literature. It simply asserts facts of the matter that run against the demands of democratic theory and that allow us to make political choices. Unlike the communitarians, however, institutional public choice theorists seek to show how we make choices in non-majoritarian, even antimajoritarian ways. This is not a happy ploy for the democratic theorist. Recognition of the problems of public choice theory, however, should alert us to look for points in the system at which nonmajoritarian resolutions may be inherently biased. We may sometimes suppose such resolutions are unobjectionable, but we cannot easily reach this conclusion from merely democratic principles.

If there is a first constitutional lesson to be drawn from public choice theory, it is that there is no universally workable way for aggregating individual interests, preferences, or values into collective decisions. A positive implication of this finding is that no government of a complex society is likely to be coherently democratic. If we wish to explain political outcomes in such a society, we will require more than merely a rule for converting individual into collective views.

A normative implication of this lesson is that political theory cannot be grounded exclusively in democratic procedural values. If we wish to justify particular practices for adopting and implementing policies, we must have recourse to extra-democratic values. For example, we often call on such values as the protection of individuals in various respects and on such utilitarian values as the value of stable expectations or the value of making decisive choices so that we may get on with life. Or we call on psychological values not directly related to particular outcomes, such as the sense of satisfaction citizens may get from apparently fair procedures. Even though we might discover general consensus on any of these values in the abstract, they would not evoke general consensus in application in particular policy choices when, for example, we still must choose one or another policy before getting on with life.

We finally still face something vaguely like Arrow's problem. The terms and conditions of Arrow's theorem may not seem properly to fit the problems of political choice in actual societies. But they clearly challenge any effort to reach a sound conception of majoritarian democracy, without which we may not be able to make normative assessments of democratic procedures and institutions, and without which we have no coherent argument for justifying our social order in democratic terms. Moreover, in the face of the motivational problems of the logic of collective action we cannot give democratic justification of state coercion in our common political enterprise.

Where does public-choice theory leave us? Against the trend of results in the early incentive analysis of markets and production, it leaves us understanding less than what we might earlier have thought we knew. It does so by clarifying issues to reveal their apparent intractability. In the end, lack of agreement is the modal problem of democracy. Because of it we must have some kind of aggregation principle. But, after four decades of public choice theory, we have little ground to expect to justify any particular principle. Indeed, the more we understand the nature of the task, the more we seem to find it incoherent.

This is not to say that the democratic, majoritarian urge is wrong. At base it seems to have genuine appeal, both moral and practical. But it is nevertheless conceptually incoherent and, when defined in simple terms, practically infeasible. The application of economic reasoning and the assumption of self-interested economic motivation has done wonders for explicating many aspects of production and the wealth of nations. But, in keeping with the seemingly destructive tenor of findings in many areas of inquiry in this century, their recent application to democratic theory has largely helped to expose flaws—grievous foundational flaws—in democratic thought and practice.

Against the conceptual and motivational flaws of majoritarian democracy, one might argue, as Churchill did, that democracy is the worst form of government, except for all the other forms. This cannot be a comfortable a priori claim, however, if the very notion of majority rule is conceptually incoherent. If government is inherently nonmajoritarian, how are we to assess the degree to which it is democratic? If Churchill's judgment is merely an empirical assertion about the good that various forms of government do for us, it is clouded by still other conceptual problems. We might easily judge some actual governments worse than others and even some general forms of government worse than certain others. But we cannot easily present coherent principles to ground our judgments and our vision.

NOTES

1. Kenneth J. Arrow, *Social Change and Individual Values*, 2d ed. (New York: Wiley, 1963). See also relevant readings in Brian Barry and Russell Hardin, *Rational Man and Irrational Society?* (Beverly Hills: Sage, 1982). Despite voluminous work over the past two decades, the best textbook treatment is still Amartya K. Sen, *Collective Choice and Social Welfare* (San Francisco: Holden-Day, 1970; reprinted, Amsterdam: North-Holland, 1979).

2. Anthony Downs, *An Economic Theory of Democracy* (New York: Harper, 1957); Mancur Olson Jr., *The Logic of Collective Action* (Cambridge: Harvard University Press, 1965); Anatol Rapoport and Albert M. Chammah, *Prisoner's Dilemma* (Ann Arbor: University of Michigan Press, 1965); Russell Hardin, *Collective Action* (Baltimore: Johns Hopkins University Press, 1982). See also the readings in Barry and Hardin, *Rational Man* for more general information.

3. Geoffrey Brennan and James M. Buchanan write that, before the rise of public choice theory, economists ignored the difficulties of institutional implementation of policies and were satisfied merely to determine what was, in the abstract, the normatively best policy (*The Reason of Rules: Constitutional Political Economy* [Cambridge: Cambridge University Press, 1985], 83).

4. Hobbes was also concerned with the origins of the state—indeed, one may say this is the principal focus of his *Leviathan*. This problem is often related in contemporary writing to the prisoner's dilemma. I think this analogy is mistaken, that the rational creation of a state is more nearly a problem of coordination. For example, on Hobbes's account the state arises by coordination on a particular ruler.

5. Even before Hobbes, this was a sometime focus, as in Robert Bellarmine, *De Laicis* (New York: Fordham University Press, 1928, trans. Kathleen E. Murphy; Latin original from 1586–1593), 48.

6. For an account of Condorcet and Dodgson, see Duncan Black, *The Theory of Committees and Elections*, 2d ed. (Cambridge: Cambridge University Press, 1963), 156–238. Pliny the Younger saw a hint of the difficulties of social choice when there are more than two possible choices in a vote of the Roman Senate over three possible verdicts for freedmen accused of murdering their master. The freedmen could be acquitted and released, convicted and banished, or convicted and executed. Social-choice theorists might readily suppose that the result would be the median of these positions, or conviction and banishment.

Pliny's discussion of the case is reprinted in Robin Farquharson, *Theory of Voting* (New Haven: Yale University Press, 1969), 57–60; see also William H. Riker, *The Art of Political Manipulation* (New Haven: Yale University Press, 1986), 78–88.

7. Kenneth J. Arrow, *Social Choice and Justice*, vol. 1, *Collected Papers* (Cambridge: Harvard University Press, 1983), 3–4.

8. Smith is commonly supposed to represent the view that the state is destructive in its interventions, as when it grants monopolies and other favors that stand in the way of greater productivity. Those hostile to the growth of the state in our time have successfully captured Smith as their predecessor. But it was also Smith's view that the state can work miracles of collective action that are beyond the reach of individuals. Proponents of many state initiatives can therefore persuasively claim support from his writings.

9. See further, Russell Hardin, "Rational Choice Theories," *Idioms of Inquiry: Critique and Renewal in Political Science*, ed. Terence Ball (Albany: State University of New York Press, 1987), 67–91, esp. 78–80; and Barry and Hardin, *Rational Man*, 224.

10. David Hume, *A Treatise of Human Nature*, ed. L. A. Selby-Bigge and P. H. Nidditch, 2d ed. (Oxford: Clarendon Press, 1978: originally published 1739–1740), book 3, pt 2, sec. 7, 538–39.

11. Russell Hardin, "Political Obligation," *The Good Polity: Normative Analysis of the State*, ed. Alan Hamlin and Philip Pettit (Oxford: Basil Blackwell, 1989), 103–19.

12. Russell Hardin, "Does Might Make Right?" *Authority Revisited*, ed. J. Roland Pennock and John W. Chapman, NOMOS 29 (New York: N.Y. University Press, 1987), 201–17.

13. Alasdair MacIntyre, *After Virtue* (Notre Dame: University of Notre Dame Press, 1981).

14. Jane J. Mansbridge, "Living with Conflict: Representation in the Theory of Adversary Democracy," *Ethics* 91 (April 1981): 466–76. For evidence of the adversarial temper of democratic thought, see other articles in the "Symposium on the Theory and Practice of Representation" in that issue of *Ethics*. See also Mark Kishlansky, "The Emergence of Adversary Politics in the Long Parliament," *Journal of Modern History* 49 (1977): 617–40.

15. Despite the status quo rule, we might see cyclic majorities working their way through the legislative amendment process. The late Senator James B. Allen of Alabama was reputedly able to use cyclic majorities to wreck many legislative measures that seemed otherwise sure to defeat the status quo. Through his sophisticated reading of fellow senators he contrived amendments, each of which was favored

by a majority, to produce a newly amended bill that would be voted down, leaving the status quo intact.

16. For an example of such an effort, see Kenneth A. Shepsle and Barry R. Weingast, "Institutional Foundations of Committee Power," *American Political Science Review* 81 (March 1987): 85–104. Shepsle and Weingast explain how committees in the House of Representatives succeed in controlling the content of their bills against amendments on the floor of the House. This is hardly a democratic result, but it may be quite stabilizing.

PART III

CULTURAL PLURALISM AND GROUP RIGHTS

8

PLURALISM AND EQUALITY: THE STATUS OF MINORITY VALUES IN A DEMOCRACY

ROBERT L. SIMON

In his book, *Justice, Equal Opportunity, and the Family*, James Fishkin claims, "I should not be able to enter a hospital ward of healthy newborn babies and, on the basis of class, race, sex, or other arbitrary characteristics predict the eventual position in society of these children."[1] In a similar vein, Onora O'Neill maintains that "Substantively equal opportunity is achieved when the success rate of certain major social groups—such as the two sexes, various ethnic groups and perhaps various age groups—are equalized."[2]

It is not difficult to reconstruct the reasoning that might have led Fishkin and O'Neill to these views. If we can predict the eventual position in society of children based on class, race, sex, religious affiliation, ethnicity, or other accidents of birth, it would

I am grateful to Hamilton College for award of a Faculty Fellowship that supported my work on this chapter. An earlier version was read to the meeting of the American Society for Political and Legal Philosophy in Chicago in September, 1987. I am grateful to Jules Coleman and Joseph Carens for their helpful and provocative comments at that meeting, and regret that I was not able to incorporate some of their suggestions into my contribution.

suggest that they did not have equal starts in life. Lacking equal starts, differences in outcome would be morally suspect. That is, they would be the result of accidents of birth, of what in effect is a morally arbitrary lottery that distributes more or less favorable starting points in a purely fortuitous and undeserved manner.

Although this line of reasoning seems to me to express important constituents of an important strand of contemporary liberal egalitarian thought, it raises a problem concerning the value of pluralism in a democracy. Respect for a plurality of religions, cultural and ethnic traditions, and ways of life is widely regarded as a desirable feature of the liberal democratic state. Even those who doubt the intrinsic value of pluralism would hesitate before forcing assimilation on diverse groups.

The existence of diverse social groups has the implication just mentioned; namely, that we will not all begin our lives from the same starting points and as a consequence may end up at different positions.[3] Does the existence of diverse cultural, religious, and ethnic groups raise problems for important liberal assumptions about equality? For example, is O'Neill correct when she claims that "Only a society whose various social groups have lost their diversity . . . could remain a substantively equal opportunity society over a long period."[4] More generally, how does the issue of pluralism versus assimilation fit in with recent discussions of equality and social justice in the liberal tradition? Although such a broad question cannot be exhaustively explored here, even a preliminary overview may prove helpful. This discussion would not only continue the exploration of possible internal tensions in the liberal commitment to equality raised recently by Barry, Fishkin, and Sher, but also might raise interesting philosophical questions about the value of pluralism in a liberal democratic state.[5]

I. PLURALISM AND LIBERAL VALUES

The terms "pluralism" and "assimilationism" have a variety of meanings and uses, both in ordinary discourse and in the literature of various academic disciplines. As used here, however, pluralism refers to a normative principle, or family of principles, about the moral standing or value of diverse groups in society. Distinctions can be made among pluralist principles according to the kind of diversity with which those principles are concerned and the moral stance they take towards that diversity. Pluralistic principles can refer to religious, ethnic, cultural, or sexual diversity. In addition, different principles may express different moral attitudes towards the kind of diversity at issue. For example, diversity may be seen as permissible, desirable, or obligatory. The claim that religious diversity within a society is permissible is one kind of pluralistic principle, while the claim that it is also desirable is quite another.

Assimilationism can best be understood as the denial of particular pluralistic claims. In its strongest form, which will be of major interest here, assimilationism would be the denial of even minimal pluralistic claims. For example, a proponent of the strongest form of normative ethnic assimilationism would deny that ethnic diversity is even permissible within society. Richard Wasserstrom, considers (and sometimes seems to endorse) this view of sex differences when he argues that in the sexually equal society, we should pay no more attention to one another's sex than we presently do to one another's eye color.[6] Although assimilationism, strictly speaking, is best reserved for reference to the denial of even minimal pluralistic claims, it often is applied more loosely, and its meaning made clear by the context in which it appears. Fortunately, complexities of definition need not unduly concern us, since "assimilationism" will be used only in the strong sense unless otherwise indicated.

What is the relation between pluralism and other values to which proponents of liberal democracy adhere? In particular, what are the implications for pluralism, of the lottery argument and the underlying conception of equality of opportunity considered earlier? According to the lottery argument, if differences in initial environments in effect are merely the morally arbitrary results of a natural lottery, then differences in result that flow from them are morally arbitrary as well. As Rawls maintains, "No one deserves his greater natural capacity nor merits a more favorable starting place in society."[7] Lottery arguments, by emphasizing our lack of responsibility for our possession of traits that underlie merit or desert, lead to the conclusion that since the possession of such traits is an accident of birth, bestowed as if by a lottery, it would be morally arbitrary to make them the fundamental basis for distribution of social benefits and burdens.

Presumably, cultural, ethnic, religious, and other group differences in initial position are among the morally arbitrary factors that might fortuitously affect outcomes. They too would be covered by what we might call the lottery principle (LP) which can be roughly stated as follows:

> (LP) If X does better than Y with respect to some desirable good A because X possesses Z and Y does not, and neither X nor Y are responsible for who possesses Z and who does not, then X and Y did not have equal opportunity to attain A and the difference in outcome with respect to $X, Y,$ and A is (at least presumptively) unjust.[8]

LP implies that if differences in outcome are due to advantages conferred by, say, different socialization that takes place in different cultural groups, such disadvantages are (at least presumptively) unjust. Proponents of assimilation may base their case on social justice by viewing the diversity of groups as a barrier to equal opportunity.[9]

Endorsement of assimilation, however, does not follow from acceptance of LP alone. Rawls's theory of justice, for example, defends a social structure in which diversity can flourish without violation of LP. Let us consider whether LP and pluralism are compatible within the framework of Rawls's theory.

II. The Rawlsian Solution

In *A Theory of Justice,* Rawls briefly considers and then rejects the proposal that we avoid the presumptive injustice cited in LP either by handicapping the most favored so as to make competition equal or by making everyone as similar as possible. Instead, he proposes that we agree to "regard the distribution of natural talents as a common asset and to share in the distribution of the benefit whatever it turns out to be."[10] This suggestion can be extended to include pooling of social, religious, and cultural differences. We are to view all initial advantages, presumably including those arising from social and cultural differences, as purely fortuitous results of a lottery. This does not imply the absurdity that such advantageous traits as physical attractiveness or high motivation literally are to be appropriated and redistributed. Rather, those who do better than others as the result of possessing such traits are to be taxed to provide compensating benefits to the less favored.

The resulting social system is claimed to be just and fair. An individual's fate is not inequitably affected by arbitrary accidents of birth; these do affect outcomes, but only when compensating benefits are provided for the disadvantaged. Pluralism of groups is not only permitted but also is encouraged, as Rawls recognizes the value of social unions, so long as the basic social structure includes an acceptable compensatory mechanism.

Further consideration reveals that the idea of talent pooling is open to serious moral question. Several lines of argument expressed in the recent literature strongly suggest that LP and the idea of talent pooling morally impoverish the individual by reducing virtually all personal characteristics to resources to be employed for a greater social benefit; a fatal result for a theory designed to promote respect for persons in the first place.[11]

Here I wish to extend the existing critique by considering specifically the idea of pooling of initial assets, particularly the cultural and social resources of groups, and examining some of the internal problems to which such an idea leads. What exactly does it mean to regard our initial assets as part of a common pool? One version, which I will call the strong version (SV), goes beyond Rawls's actual account by viewing what we think of as individual assets as owned in common by all. SV is worth examining because it does capture what might be meant if the idea of pooling is pushed to an extreme.

> (SV) Initial assets are owned in common by all persons to promote their common benefit. Therefore, such assets may be used only in ways that most efficiently promote the common benefit.

A major problem with SV, as others also have argued, is that it nationalizes the individual.[12] Just as Rawls criticizes utilitarians for not taking differences between individuals seriously, so SV is open to the very same charge.

More important for our purposes, SV reduces the cultural and social assets of groups to resources for promotion of the benefit of the less favored. Pluralism, if valued at all, is valued only because pluralistic diversity promotes the welfare of the disadvantaged, not because diversity is regarded as desirable in itself or because it is felt that groups (or their individual members) have rights to pursue their own traditions, beliefs, or cultural norms. SV even implies that if by changing their traditions, religious beliefs, or cultural imperatives, groups could produce more for the less favored, then they have a duty to do so and act wrongly if they do not. This duty cannot be limited by claims to group or individual autonomy. As we have seen, autonomy does not extend to control over the accidental distributions of the lottery.

It is doubtful if the strong version of talent pooling will have many advocates. Perhaps the idea of pooling of initial assets would be more attractive if presented as a weakened version (WV).

(WV) Initial individual assets may be used in any way agents see fit (barring harm to others) so long as the basic social structure is arranged so that those who benefit provide appropriate compensating benefits to the less favored.

Unlike SV, WV allows individuals and groups to follow whatever paths they choose, thereby protecting individual liberty, so long as the success of the more favored yields appropriate compensation for the less advantaged. WV, but not SV, recognizes a purported distinction between group ownership of assets contingently possessed by individuals and restrictions limiting individuals rights to profit from the use of their own assets.

There are, however, difficulties with WV. For one thing, critics of Rawls might challenge the distinction between group ownership of assets, postulated by SV but allegedly not by WV, and restrictions on the right to profit from use of such assets, as stipulated in WV. In the view of critics, such restrictions if pushed far enough are not significantly different from communal ownership. Thus, if "profits" from the use of assets are held to include even the differential praise and respect generated by their use, the freedom to exercise our talents or to respond favorably or unfavorably to the exercise of talents of others might justifiably be limited if no compensatory social mechanism were in place. Such a restriction on the exercise of talent might differ only nominally from communal ownership, at least in the eyes of opponents of WV.

Contrary to the critics, however, intuitions may differ on this point. Fortunately, we need not pursue the point further here. Instead, let us consider whether WV really avoids the implications of the lottery principle. What proponents of WV may fail to realize is that the kind of "theft" at issue (uncompensated profit from initial assets) cannot be avoided in any sufficiently pluralistic society, even where the compensation mechanism is in place.

Even under WV, where an individual winds up will depend greatly upon the result of what the Rawlsian would regard as lotteries. Differences in innate capacities and in socialization will affect outcomes. Even though compensation will be provided for the less favored, compensating benefits will not have equal value to all people precisely because of differences traceable to socialization by families and groups. For example, the availability of medical care will have less value to a Jehovah's Witness than to others, just as the growth of high-tech communications will benefit a fan of ESPN while threatening the way of life of the Amish. Similarly, the amount of compensation one will have to pay also will depend on contingencies. Those who are willing to trade off salary for leisure and time with family, for example, will pay less by way of compensating benefits even though they may be at least as satisfied with their lot as those who make the opposite trade off.[13] Accordingly, if it is unjust to profit from the lottery without providing appropriate compensation, this injustice will occur even under WV. This is because the degree to which people will benefit from compensation or be required to provide it to others will depend upon the initial distribution of innate capacities and favorable environments. In particular, diversity among major social groups insures that similar distributions of basic or primary goods will have different value across group lines. The lottery will affect the significance of each person's share of goods—even primary goods—in a society that satisfies WV as well as in one that does not.[14]

A Rawlsian might object that social justice requires only that persons receive a fair share of primary goods, not that similar shares of primary goods have similar value to each shareholder. Justice regulates only the shares redistributed by the basic structure of society and not the significance assigned to them.

I doubt, however, if this sort of reply will get the Rawlsian off the hook. After all, a major reason for not allowing an unregulated sociogenetic lottery to determine outcomes surely is that it seems unjust to allow what is purely fortuitous significantly to disadvantage some relative to others with respect to their chances to lead a satisfactory life. But then, why isn't it also unjust for equally fortuitous factors significantly to disadvantage some relative to others in their chances to benefit from the basic structural organization of society? If the first is morally arbitrary, why isn't the second? If there is a difference, it is at best far from clear what it is.

Perhaps more importantly, considerations of group diversity raise related difficulties for Rawls's use of the notion of primary goods. According to the "thin" theory of the good, primary goods are those things it is rational for every person to want (and to want more of them rather than less) because they are means to secure the benefits of a broad range of life plans. The goods distributed by the basic structure, as required by WV, are primary goods because these are presumably neutral between different life plans or "thick" theories of the good.

If different packages of primary goods are valued differently along group lines, however, then primary goods may not be so neutral after all. At the very least, different packages of primary goods, expressing different weightings of specific goods, may be more attractive to certain groups than others. If so, questions of justice arise concerning the proper composition of the benefits provided by WV that are not settled by Rawls's theory. For example, what counts as the worst off group might vary depending upon different group-related weightings of primary goods. Although similar problems are raised by the diversity of individual preferences, pluralism adds a special dimension to the problem because it goes beyond questions of possibly arbitrary individual preferences and raises the issue of whether the basic structure is sufficiently neutral with respect to different religious, cultural, and ethnic traditions and commitments.

More generally, regardless of its other advantages, WV will not satisfy Fishkin's and O'Neill's proposal that the overall success rates of major social groups be equalized. For one thing, WV allows for inequalities, so long as the basic structure of society functions to maximize the position of the worst off. In a sufficiently pluralistic society, group differences in religion, cultural norms, and traditions, can operate to perpetuate inequality so long as WV is satisfied. Second, as we have seen, individuals may benefit differently from the compensating mechanism of the basic structure according to their membership in major social groups. Although it remains true that shares of primary goods are distributed according to WV, individual's chances of success, conceived more broadly in terms of the value persons ascribe to their shares, let alone their overall position in society, may vary along group lines.

Indeed, if group differences are sufficiently deep, there may be no common components of "success" to which all groups assign equal weight. There may be no single competition in which they are all engaged or one vision of the good life they share. If so, it will be difficult and in some cases perhaps impossible to find a common measure by which the relative standing of relevantly different groups even can be compared.

None of this is to say, however, that pluralistic diversity is a valuable, or even permissible, component of the democratic state. Perhaps it is to be reduced or even eliminated in the name of equal opportunity or equal life chances for all. Should assimilationism be encouraged in the name of liberal values and is pluralism something that at best is to be merely tolerated as a not easily eliminated vestige of primitive tribalism?

III. The Value of Pluralism

The value of diversity at the level of the individual can be defended on a variety of familiar grounds. For example, consequentialists can appeal to the arguments of J. S. Mill that different "experiments in living" help us detect harmful ways of life, create opportunities for improving existing arrangements, and enable us truly to appreciate what is satisfactory by forcing us to understand our choices in the face of alternatives available to us. From the perspective of fundamental rights and entitlements, we can argue that diversity is a natural outgrowth of human autonomy and liberty. Free persons are entitled to live as they decide, and have a right to live in ways that differ from the norm, so long as the rights of others are not violated.

Even if such arguments make a case for diversity at the individual level, however, they may not support an equally strong case for pluralism at the level of major social groups. What does diversity among cultures, traditions, religions, and ethnic groups add that we do not already obtain through individual diversity? In fact, isn't pluralism among groups actually harmful, in that it encourages intolerance, prejudice, stereotyping, and the oppression of minority groups by others? In view of these difficulties, let us consider arguments that might be given for some form of group assimilationism.

Orlando Patterson, for one, maintains not only that the case for individual diversity does not necessarily support pluralism of major social groups, it actually undermines it. According to Patterson, "an emphasis on group diversity . . . works against a respect for individuality." Indeed, Patterson maintains that "the greater the diversity and cohesiveness of groups in a society, the smaller the diversity and personal autonomy of individuals in that society."[15] As divisions among groups become sharper, groups compete more among themselves for power and influence, and hence become more internally cohesive. The greater the cohesiveness, the more their members share the group's norms and values and there is less room for individual dissent. Patterson concludes that "A relatively homogeneous society, with a high degree of individual variation and disdain for conformity, is a far more desirable social order than one with many competing ethnic groups made up of gray, group-stricken conformists."[16]

If the alternatives are indeed as restricted as Patterson suggests, his criticism is well taken. But are they? Perhaps to pose the alternatives in the way suggested may be no fairer than to equate individuality with mindless rejection of the values of others simply on the ground that others hold them, regardless of their justification.

If we equate individualism with degree of divergence from the behavior or beliefs of others, it follows tautologically that those who share a common culture, tradition, or other fairly cohesive set of values are not different in the areas that bind them together. But from the fact that they lack individuality in that sense, it does not follow that they lack individuality in the different sense of being mindless conformists. On the contrary, their allegiance to a tradition, a religion, or a set of norms comprising a cultural unit may reflect their deep beliefs about what is important in life. It seems no more fair to equate allegiance to a group with mindless conformity than it does to equate individuality with equally mindless non-conformity. Patterson's approach begs a crucial question by assuming the worst about pluralism or groups while assuming the best about assimilated individuals.[17]

Moreover, pluralists can argue that diversity among groups promotes values that cannot be secured through diversity at the individual level. For without the structure and framework constituted by groups, individuals would be unable to commit themselves to ways of life that involve more than minimal cooperation and allegiance, or which are held to express values worth upholding and passing on to later generations. Cultural, religious, and ethnic traditions, norms, and practices can be seen as crucial elements of Mill's experiments in living. Without them, we would lose not only the richness but also the experience to be gained from knowledge of contrasting ways of life. It is perhaps on such grounds that W. E. B. Du Bois recommended that black people—as well as other ethnic and cultural groups—should develop their particular culture so that each can give "to civilization the full spiritual message [it is] capable of giving."[18]

The kind of consequentialism suggested by Mill and Du Bois is not the only kind of defense available to the pluralist. Pluralists also can argue that it is through the existence of groups that embody norms, traditions, and values that individuals can commit themselves to ways of life and projects that extend beyond the life and particularistic concerns of one person. Without pluralism, the range of options open to individuals would be greatly impoverished. We could be individuals, but only so long as we did not commit ourselves to values or ways of life that involved extensive cooperation and that were designed to transmit values across generations. Adherence to a tradition, for example, can be seen as reflective allegiance to an inherited set of values that one regards as worth passing on to one's children, and that could not even exist were there not a major social group in which it is embodied. If so, assimilation, though it may allow a great range of individual choice in some directions, closes out significant options in others. Accordingly, while Patterson is right to warn us about nonreflective or even mindless loyalty to the group, pluralists can rejoin that Patterson's view of pluralism is oversimplified to the point of begging the question against the pluralist perspective.

This reply might seem unsatisfactory, however, for in fact we do not choose our group allegiances the way the perhaps mythical rational consumer selects a new car. Rather, we are born into groups, socialized to accept the values of those around us, and perhaps only rarely encouraged to question them. Thus, whatever its merits as a normative ideal, the reality of pluralism seems incompatible with individual autonomy to many philosophers. Wasserstrom criticizes pluralism with regard to sex on exactly these grounds; namely, that the socialization of women limits their autonomy.[19] His critique has more general application. It implies that whenever we adopt norms simply as a result of socialization, when they are in effect imposed upon us without our choice, we lack autonomy. Since groups socialize their members in precisely this way, pluralism is incompatible with autonomy of the person.

The first thing to notice is that, on one interpretation of autonomy, the kind of considerations advanced by Wasserstrom show that we would not be autonomous even in an assimilationist society. Even in such a society, children would need to be socialized, either by parents or some equivalent. If autonomy requires lack of socialization, it is not clear that it can be obtained in any kind of recognizably human society. On the other hand, if autonomy requires, not lack of socialization, but some means of reflecting upon it or evaluating it, it is far from clear that autonomy is any less available under pluralism than assimilationism. Moreover, reflection need not encompass critical scrutiny of all one's inherited values and allegiances as a whole from some neutral point of view. If that is what autonomy requires, it does become problematic whether the pluralist can attain it. The problem arises, however, not from pluralism but because autonomy has been conceived in such a way that it raises difficulties for pluralist and assimilationist alike. On the other hand, if autonomy is construed more modestly, perhaps along the lines of continued second order adherence to one's first order values in the face of specific challenges, then it is unclear why autonomy is necessarily any harder to achieve under pluralism than under other social arrangements favored by liberal democrats.

Although the idea of autonomy raises many more problems than can be considered here, perhaps the focus of discussion can at least be sharpened. What is at issue for our purposes is not whether anyone ever can be autonomous, an important question in its own right, but rather whether the socialization some receive precludes them from attaining the degree of autonomy allowed by the socialization of others. Wasserstrom's critique of sexual pluralism, therefore, is best construed not as an argument to the effect that socialization in itself precludes autonomy but rather that the kind of socialization women typically receive in our society precludes their achieving the same degree of autonomy as men.

An approach to autonomy that has the merit of explicating it through comparison of kinds of socialization has been advanced recently by Irving Thalberg. Thalberg asks us to consider why we refuse to characterize the behavior of victims of brainwashing as autonomous. Surely, he claims, it is because they would not have behaved in such a way were it not for the special and abnormal conditioning to which they had been subjected. His overall suggestion, then, is not that autonomy precludes lack of socialization, but rather that it presupposes absence of abnormal socialization or elimination of its effects when it already has occurred. For example, Thalberg maintains that the traditional socialization of females in our society precludes or significantly restricts the opportunity for autonomous choice by women. Autonomy would be restored, in his view, not by eliminating all socialization but rather by socializing men and women in the same way, perhaps in a way significantly similar to present male socialization.[20]

Thalberg's approach has at least two major problems. First, it lacks an independent criterion of which groups lack autonomy other than the fact that some other group finds their values unacceptable.[21] If fewer women would hold traditional values if they were socialized roughly like males, fewer males would hold traditional male values if their socialization were altered in causally relevant ways. Similarly, many of us would hold different religious beliefs if we had been socialized in relevantly different cultural settings. This hardly shows that these beliefs are not our own or that we are like brainwashed people. Since it provides no criterion for identifying "abnormal" conditioning, Thalberg's approach makes it far too easy to use the label of brainwashing arbitrarily to dismiss the views of others simply because we reject the values they happen to hold.

A second, but not unrelated point, is that Thalberg's account has questionable implications concerning pluralism. If autonomy requires socialization roughly equivalent to that of dominant groups, or simply similar socialization for all, little if any place is left for group diversity. Common socialization seems incompatible with the existence of significant group differences. Moreover, if the way the dominant group is socialized is taken as the norm for all, the values of the dominant majority illicitly are assumed to be the proper values for everyone. On the contrary, so long as we value diversity of groups, we may not dismiss some values as merely products of conditioning simply because they differ from what other groups regard as reasonable or normal.

In this context, consider the case of *Friedman v. New York.*[22] The case concerns a young unmarried Orthodox Jewish woman who went skiing with a male friend. When the ski lift on which they were riding malfunctioned, due to operator negligence, the couple was left stranded at some distance above the ground as the sun set over the Catskills. In the (false) belief that her Orthodox Jewish principles forbade her from spending the night with a male, even in the unusual circumstances in question, the young woman jumped and suffered extensive injuries. The question at issue in the case is whether the negligent operator should be held liable not only for the harm caused by the stalled lift but also for the injuries suffered by the young woman as the result of her jump. The operator's defense was that her injuries were her own fault; that it would be wrong to expect the operator to anticipate the consequences of any odd or unusual set of beliefs passengers might hold.

Guido Calabresi argues that a decision favoring the operator would have illustrated "the ugly side of the melting pot. It declares . . . that newcomers . . . may indeed have equality in this land, but only if they give up those tenets of their faith that do not fit (with what the majority regards as reasonable)."[23] In fact, the courts rejected the operator's defense, presumably on grounds related to those cited by Calabresi.

The point I want to make about this case is related to but different from Calabresi's. Is it not equally questionable to assume that adherents of the norms of a religious, ethnic, or cultural group lack autonomy and individuality as it is to assume that they alone must accept the consequence for their beliefs in certain circumstances just because their beliefs differ from the majority's? In particular, are we not begging important issues if we simply assume that the young woman's decision to jump was not truly her own, or not autonomous, let alone that she lacked opportunity equal to that of other passengers to avoid injury because of her upbringing, a mere accident of the socioeconomic lottery?

On the contrary, her decision might well have reflected her deepest personal commitments precisely because they have arisen from values imbued through earlier socialization; a process of development with which she continues to identify. On the other hand, it surely is possible that the young woman is a victim of a kind of mindless conformity and lacks true autonomy. My point has not been to make a priori assumptions about a particular case but to indicate the dangers of construing such notions in ways that beg the question against pluralism, or of defining them so rigidly as to make autonomy and individuality unattainable for us all.

IV. PLURALISM AND EQUALITY

We started out by considering the view that differences in religious, ethnic, or cultural inheritance are barriers to equality of opportunity since they promote different chances of success. Our consideration of pluralism suggests that such a view may stand things on its head. It takes as barriers to equality of opportunity the very features, such as character, motivation, and values that are most central to our nature as persons. Perhaps, then, the proper liberal conception of equality should dispense with the conception of moral arbitrariness underlying the lottery principle, and recognize that in a pluralistic society, the commitments that many of us autonomously affirm and through which we express our personhood, may arise from our moral development in the social groups into which we have been born.

To put the point another way, the lottery argument presupposes a radical separation between individuals and their characters, aspirations, values, and talents. Even if this separation is construed politically, as an assumption from which to reason about the principles that should govern the liberal state, rather than as a metaphysical account of the person, it raises problems.[24] It leads us to political analysis that construes these qualities as morally arbitrary from the point of view of respecting persons, except in so far as their use promotes the well being of us all, particularly the most disadvantaged. The suggestion made here, however, is that by viewing such characteristics as central to personhood, we need not abandon the liberal principles of equal opportunity or respect for the individual. Rather, these principles can be understood as incorporating a richer conception of the individual, one that takes the commitments of individuals in a pluralistic society seriously. The price for not adopting such a conception is conflict between liberal attachment to the less rich conception of the individual and traditional liberal regard for pluralism and cultural, ethnic, and religious diversity.

These considerations certainly can be misused as when inequalities due to discrimination or oppression are explained away by reference to alleged cultural differences among groups.

Focus on alleged group differences can form part of an invidious ideology that blames the victim for what really are the consequences of unjust social institutions. The possibility of misuse does not, however, imply that pluralism is an unimportant value but only that respect for pluralism needs to be carefully distinguished from rationalization for injustice, a complex task that raises many difficult philosophical issues of its own.[25]

If the admittedly rough suggestions made here raise questions worth pursuing, philosophers interested in the topic of minorities and majorities in democracy need to deal more fully with the evaluation of pluralism in the liberal democratic state. Does pluralism have an ethical foundation? How are we to distinguish those individuals who have an autonomous commitment to group life from the brainwashed adherents of a mere cult? How are the special loyalties that arise in a group to be reconciled with universal moral principles of equal respect for persons?

Clearly, pluralism raises major problems. Nevertheless, reduction of all initial differences among families, religions, ethnic groups, cultures, and perhaps between genders to morally arbitrary results of a lottery may be even more problematic. The view of ourselves as victims of a lottery implies that what may be most central to our personhood is purely arbitrary from the moral point of view. By so doing, it requires us to be untrue to our status as separate persons and as social beings alike.

NOTES

1. James S. Fishkin, *Justice, Equal Opportunity, and the Family* (New Haven: Yale University Press, 1983), 4.

2. Onora O'Neill, "How Do We Know When Opportunities Are Equal?" in *Sex Equality,* ed. Jane English (Englewood Cliffs, N.J.: Prentice-Hall, 1977), 148.

3. For example, Asian-Americans, who make up only 2 percent of the nation's college age population, constituted 11 percent of the Ivy League's freshman class in 1987. *Newsweek* (February 9, 1987), 60.

4. O'Neill, "How Do We Know," 151–52.

5. In particular, see Brian Barry, "Equal Opportunity and Moral

Arbitrariness" in *Equal Opportunity,* ed. Normal Bowie (Boulder, Colo.: Westview Press, 1988), 23–44.

6. Richard Wasserstrom, "Racism and Sexism" in *Today's Moral Problems,* ed. Richard Wasserstrom (New York: Macmillan, 1985), 20–21.

7. John Rawls, *A Theory of Justice* (Cambridge: Harvard University Press, 1971), 104.

8. I am indebted here to George Sher's similar formulation in his paper, "Effort, Ability, and Personal Desert," *Philosophy & Public Affairs* 8 (1979): 365.

9. As Fishkin has pointed out, a similar argument may be presented against the autonomy of the family. However, the parallel problem concerning groups may be even more intractable. This is in part because a significant part of the variance in socialization provided by the family can plausibly be attributed to the family's membership in broader social groups, but even more because differences in outcome correlated with differences in religion, culture, or ethnicity seem more of a practical problem in liberal democracy than differences based on family autonomy alone. That is, assimilation does seem to be an actual option for many groups in a way that significant restriction of the autonomy of the family is not a genuine option in our society.

10. Rawls, *A Theory of Justice,* 101.

11. I have argued that Rawls's use of the lottery argument does not cohere with his adherence to other liberal values in "An Indirect Defense of the Merit Principle," *The Philosophical Forum* 10 (1978–1979): 224–41.

12. For arguments of this kind, see Robert Nozick, *Anarchy, State, and Utopia* (New York: Basic Books, 1974), 213ff, Michael Sandel, *Liberalism and the Limits of Justice* (New York: Cambridge University Press, 1982), esp. chap. 2. See also the discussion by Anthony T. Kronman, "Talent Pooling," in *Human Rights,* ed. J. Roland Pennock and John W. Chapman, NOMOS 23 (New York: New York University Press, 1981), 58–79.

13. Kronman makes a similar point in "Talent Pooling," 64–71.

14. It might be objected that WV can be justified directly by argument from the original position, without any reference to LP. This may well be so, although I suspect that the idea of deriving principles of justice from an original position faces as least as serious difficulties as LP. In any case, if my argument has force, it is questionable whether lottery arguments, such as those based on LP, can be used to give independent intuitive support to conclusions derived from the original position, or to show that such conclusions are in harmony or in reflective equilibrium with our considered judgments in this area.

15. Orlando Patterson, "Ethnic Pluralism," *Change: The Magazine of Higher Learning* 7 (March, 1975): 10, 11.

16. Ibid., 10.

17. Of course, Patterson, may not be merely describing what he takes to be the effects of membership on members of major social groups but rather might be making a normative claim to the effect that rational autonomous choice by individuals is superior to nonreflective conformity to the dictates of a group. If that is his claim, few would dispute it. But once again, the question should not be begged by assuming that pluralism as a normative ideal is committed to endorsing mindless allegiance to the group.

18. W. E. B. Du Bois, "The Conservation of Races," in *Negro Social and Political Thought 1850–1920: Representative Texts,* ed. Howard Brotz (New York: Basic Books, 1966), 487. For discussion, see Bernard Boxill, *Blacks and Social Justice* (Totowa, N.J.: Rowman & Allanheld, 1984), chap. 8.

19. Wasserstrom, "Racism and Sexism," 28. See also Sharon Hill, "Self Determination and Autonomy," in *Today's Moral Problems,* ed. Richard Wasserstrom (New York: Macmillan, 1985), 69. For a critique of the view that women with traditional values lack autonomy, see George Sher, "Our Preferences, Ourselves," *Philosophy and Public Affairs* 12 (1983): 34–50.

20. Irving Thalberg, "Socialization and Autonomous Behavior," *Studies in Action Theory: Tulane Studies in Philosophy,* vol. 28, ed. Robert C. Whittemore (New Orleans: Tulane University Press, 1979), 32–36.

21. On this point, see also Sher, "Our Preferences, Ourselves," *Philosophy & Public Affairs* 12 (1983): 34–50.

22. *Friedman v. New York,* 282, N.Y.S. 2d 858, 54 Misc. 2d 448 (1967), discussed in Guido Calabresi, *Ideals, Beliefs, Attitudes, and the Law* (New York: Syracuse University Press, 1985), 51.

23. Ibid., 57.

24. See John Rawls, "Justice as Fairness: Political not Metaphysical," *Philosophy & Public Affairs* 14 (1985): 223–51, for an argument, in my view already implicit in *A Theory of Justice,* that the Rawlsian account of the person is justified on normative political grounds rather than metaphysical ones.

25. I owe this point to Joseph Carens, who developed it in his original commentary on my paper presented in Chicago and in his contribution to this volume (chap. 9).

9

DIFFERENCE AND DOMINATION: REFLECTIONS ON THE RELATION BETWEEN PLURALISM AND EQUALITY

JOSEPH H. CARENS

Can we respect differences among groups without blindly endorsing existing patterns of inequality? Can we distinguish between domination and diversity without forfeiting our claim to pluralism? These are the sorts of questions we should ask ourselves as we reflect on the relation between pluralism and equality.

Robert Simon offers an eloquent defense of pluralism in his contribution to this volume. But in his eagerness to avoid the Charybdis of egalitarian assimilationism he embraces the Scylla of inegalitarian pluralism. To choose between these two is to succumb to a myth. The right sort of egalitarianism does not require us to make everyone like everyone else or to make minorities conform to the dominant majority. The right sort of pluralism rarely entails inequality. Pluralism and equality are usually compatible and often mutually reinforcing. To see why,

I wish to thank Frank Cunningham and the editors of NOMOS for comments on an earlier draft of this chapter.

we have to examine Simon's abstract principles in concrete social and political contexts and we have to pay attention to a
variable he overlooks—power.

IN DEFENSE OF MORAL ARBITRARINESS

Let me begin by trying to rehabilitate what Simon calls the
concept of "moral arbitrariness" as a tool for criticizing inequality. Simon begins his chapter by saying that James Fishkin claims
that one should not be able to predict the eventual social position of children on the basis of "class, race, sex, or other arbitrary characteristics."[1] In rebuttal, Simon mentions the above-
average success of Asian-Americans in higher education, which
he implicitly attributes to their cultural heritage. He goes on to
argue that it is mistaken to see cultural heritage as an arbitrary
characteristic because it is often central to a person's identity
and sense of self. I agree with Simon that we should not treat a
person's culture as an arbitrary characteristic of the self. But
Simon's approach leaves no basis for challenging any aspect of
anyone's culture and he too easily discards the concept of moral
arbitrariness, ignoring its power in Western liberal democratic
culture.

When Fishkin says that we should not be able to predict social
position on the basis of class, race, or sex, he does not have
successful Asian-Americans in mind but members of the working class (as opposed to the upper class), blacks (as opposed to
whites), and women (as opposed to men). For each pair, we can
predict that members of the first group will do less well on
average than members of the second with respect to such things
as education and income. Why would anyone think that is a bad
thing? Should we regard these inequalities as the benign, or at
least morally neutral, outcome of group differences?

The answer depends in part on how one thinks the differences and inequalities are linked. Recall Malcolm X's story about
his experience in the eighth grade. He was at the top of his
class, a class with both white and black students. His teacher,
whom Malcolm describes as a well-meaning person full of advice on how to succeed in life, asked him if he had given any
thought to a career. Malcolm said that he wanted to be a lawyer.

His teacher replied, "Malcolm, one of life's first needs is for us to be realistic. Don't misunderstand me, now. We all like you here, you know that. But you've got to be realistic about being a nigger. A lawyer—that's no realistic goal for a nigger. You need to think about something you *can* be. You're good with your hands—making things. . . . Why don't you plan on carpentry?"[2] Similar stories can be told by and about women. A friend of mine whose first name did not reveal her gender was about to be offered a professional position only to have the offer withheld when it was discovered that she was a woman.

It is impossible to hear such stories without having the reaction that this sort of thing is so unfair, so arbitrary. It is arbitrary not in the sense that it is random or that we cannot offer social explanations of the phenomenon or that it does not contribute to the preservation of patriarchy and racial domination. Rather it is arbitrary from the moral point of view, arbitrary in the sense that there is no morally legitimate reason for treating people this way. To call race and sex arbitrary characteristics in this context then is not to deny that they may be central to a person's identity and sense of self. It is to say that they are illegitimate criteria of social selection and exclusion. To say "because you are a woman" or "because you are black" is not to offer an adequate reason for denying someone an opportunity to develop his or her talents or to pursue a career. If group differences and inequalities are connected in this way, they are morally wrong.

The view I have just described is a commonplace of contemporary liberal democratic societies. Simon clearly shares it, too, although his rejection of the language of moral arbitrariness eliminates one of the standard ways of articulating and defending this view and he offers no alternative formulation. But suppose group differences and inequalities are not linked in this way. What if it is not a question of restrictions and exclusions imposed on people against their will, but of the way in which being raised in a group shapes one's talents, character, motivation, and values? That is the sort of connection Simon wants to talk about.

We might draw on a useful distinction that Fishkin makes between two components of the idea of equal opportunity: the principle of merit ("There should be widespread procedural fairness in the evaluation of qualifications for positions") and the principle of equality of life chances ("The prospects of children for eventual positions in society should not vary . . . with their arbitrary native characteristics").[3] Simon might reasonably say that it is only the latter he wants to challenge. The very concept of equal life chances presupposes a consensus on what is important in life, a consensus that is incompatible with pluralism. Moreover, equal life chances would require "equal developmental conditions,"[4] which could be created only by eliminating all differences among groups, that is, by assimilation. Would this clarification make Simon's argument work?

ADVANTAGED GROUPS:
ASIAN-AMERICANS AND THE UPPER CLASS

Let us start with the group Simon mentions, Asian-Americans. One might object that this category is insufficiently sensitive to pluralism because it lumps together many different ethnic groups and cultural traditions. But leave that aside. Simon notes that Asian-Americans made up only 2 percent of the U.S. population in 1987, but 11 percent of the Ivy League's first year class. He does not elaborate upon the connection, but the implication seems to be that Asian-American culture, assuming that to be an appropriate category, places great emphasis on higher education and perhaps on related values like work, discipline, and achievement, and that this cultural pattern accounts for the higher than average success rate of Asian-Americans in applications to prestigious universities. Let's assume that to be true. We might conclude that it is an advantage to be born an Asian-American. It is an accident of birth, but it improves your chances of success in life. What is wrong with that? "Nothing," Simon implies, and I agree. The success of Asian-Americans is something we can rightly celebrate as a triumph of pluralism. But let us pause for a moment to consider why this example works so well for Simon's argument.

Notice first that the example supports one part of Simon's argument, the legitimacy of different starting points, by undercutting another, the diversity of group goals. What makes the idea of equal life chances attractive in the first place is the assumption that there are some things that almost all people in our society want. Simon questions that, and we can think of some cases that support him, as I will point out in the next section. But what makes the Asian-American example effective as an illustration of a legitimate inequality is the implicit assumption that most people, and not just Asian Americans, would find an Ivy League education and the opportunities it brings highly desirable. We care about the equality or inequality of starting points only with respect to things that are widely desired.

One important reason why it seems morally unobjectionable for an Asian-American cultural heritage to increase one's chances of conventional success is that, as a group, they have not enjoyed power and privilege in our society. On the contrary, they have been the targets of racial hostility and oppression, both overt and covert. No one can suppose that they have rigged the rules of the game in their own favor or that they have tailored the definition of merit to fit their own particular characteristics. Indeed, it sounds ironic to say, as I did above, that to be born an Asian American is advantageous. Their success has come in spite of the disadvantages the larger society has imposed upon them. That is why it does not seem problematic. But all this is a contextual judgment. If Asian-Americans had had a long history of disproportionate success and had not been subjected to racial oppression, we might view their advantaged position more skeptically.

Consider another example of disproportionate success that evokes more doubt about its legitimacy: the upper class. Recall that Asian Americans constitute only 2 percent of the population but 11 percent of the first year Ivy League class. I have no precise statistics on the financial background of Ivy League students, but I do have some experience with them, and I think it safe to say that at least 11 percent of the Ivy League student population, and probably a much higher proportion, comes from the richest 2 percent of the population. Should we celebrate this as a triumph of pluralism, too? Presumably not, but why not?

Part of the answer is that we may suspect the success of the rich applicants has more to do with the size of the parents' bankbooks than the quality of the children's brains. I write this at the moment when Senator Dan Quayle, the Republican nominee for vice-president in the 1988 election, stands accused of having used his family's wealth and influence to gain a position in the National Guard, permitting him to avoid being drafted to fight in Vietnam. Whether this particular charge is true or not, the allegation seems plausible because wealth and power often provide this kind of advantage.

Let us assume away any suspicion of abuse of power or special treatment. After all, lots of rich kids don't get into Ivy League schools. Those who do are usually talented and hardworking. Working class applicants are rarely denied admission just because they are poor. It is a matter of grades, test scores, writing ability; in short, of merit. Would the knowledge that only merit counts eliminate the sense that the disproportionate success of this group is not somehow unfair? Not entirely, for we also know that the qualifications are, in large part, a product of the environment that money buys. Lots of working class kids are bright and hardworking but never get the chance to develop their talents. They may not be as qualified now, at the time of application to college, but if they had had the same sort of schooling when they were younger, they would be. So, it seems, dare I say, arbitrary that rich children should enjoy disproportionate success.

Under the feudal system, one's life chances were determined by the social position of one's parents. Critics derided the system as arbitrary, arguing that individuals should be able to make whatever they could of themselves by their talents and effort. But if one's life chances are largely determined by the wealth of one's parents, is capitalism all that different from feudalism? Is it much less arbitrary in practice? This is a familiar challenge, accepted in principle even by most defenders of capitalism who then use empirical studies of social mobility to try to show that family financial position is not all that significant in determining life chances.[5] I do not want to address the merits of that debate here. I introduce it only to show that dispensing with the concept of moral arbitrariness is not as easy as Simon suggests. The distinction between merit and life chances is not enough, in the end, because the concept of moral arbitrariness turns out to be relevant not only to questions about merit but also to questions about life chances. We do think we know what life chances matter to most people and we care about the origins of people's life chances.

This line of argument creates a puzzle about my earlier discussion of Asian-Americans. Should we consider cultural heritage to be morally arbitrary after all? If poor children can complain because they have not had the opportunities provided by inherited money, can Italian- or Irish-American children complain because they have not had the opportunities provided by an inherited Asian-American culture? Is the inherited cultural tradition of Asian-Americans a form of unfair advantage? If one starts down this path, the next step is for the less talented to object that they could have done better if only they had been born with more talents. This leads quickly to Rawls' formulation that everything we start with is arbitrary from a moral point of view and then to the familiar criticisms of that formulation that Simon draws upon.

I confess that I do not have a good solution to this puzzle. I do not think that anything is to be gained by abandoning the language of moral arbitrariness. It has a long and powerful history in our moral tradition. In any event, the moral problems to which the language points would not disappear even if one abandoned the language. None of the critics offers a satisfactory approach to these problems, despite the destructive power of their critiques.

Perhaps I can suggest this much. Intuitively, inheriting a culture seems different from inheriting wealth. We do not think of the advantages enjoyed by Asian-Americans and the upper class in the same way, and that is not just because Asian-Americans have been subjected to racism. We would not think of success due to the Protestant Ethic in the same way as success due to schooling at a fancy private academy, even though the lessons of both have to be internalized if one is to be successful. Perhaps it is because a genuine culture seems more central to the self, less detachable and transferable than the things that money can buy, including education at a preparatory school. But I do not want to press this too far. In what follows, I leave aside the general challenge of moral arbitrariness, as it applies to all cultural inheritances. I want to assume that a cultural inheritance like that of the Asian Americans is morally legitimate even when it leads to social inequalities and to explore other cases where inequalities are linked to cultural differences among groups to see whether we can draw the general lesson, as Simon seems to do, that cultural differences among groups legitimate inequality.

GROUP CULTURE AND LEGITIMATE INEQUALITY: THE AMISH

Consider first a case that I think generally supports Simon's view: the Amish in the United States.[6] They are people whose religious and cultural traditions lead them to live simple lives, largely independent of the technologies that most people in the United States rely so heavily upon and free from the consumerism that is so central to the dominant ethos. For the most part, they engage in farming and handicraft production. They place great emphasis on work, family, and community. They are opposed to higher education; indeed they have resisted even the compulsory education required of all children. So, the Amish have less of many things that most Americans want. We could reasonably predict that Amish children are less likely than most American children to acquire advanced degrees or enter prestigious, high-paying occupations.

Is this sort of inequality morally objectionable? I think not. The inequality derives largely from the values and practices of the Amish themselves, not from their treatment by others. It is significant that the Amish themselves do not complain about this inequality. They see it as an outcome of their way of life, and, for the most part, they do not want the things they have less of. Of course, the absence of complaint is not proof of the absence of injustice, but it is a relevant indicator. Moreover, individual members of Amish society are free to leave the local community and to seek other goals, including the conventional American dream. Those who stay in the society choose to do so.

One might object that the children do not choose to be brought up this way. By the time they are adults their options outside the Amish community may be severely restricted by their limited training and education. Thus they are deprived of life chances equal with other Americans, even if their own parents and community are the ones depriving them.

This objection should not be dismissed lightly. Indeed the state requires that Amish children be educated in certain ways and up to a certain age, in part to enable them to participate as citizens in public life, if they choose to do so, and in part to ensure that they will have some basic capacities relevant to the social and economic life of the larger society, if they choose to join it. But this can hardly be said to create equal life chances for these children to succeed in the ways most Americans think of success. Why not go further?

Here we encounter some of the internal tensions of liberal democratic culture with which Simon is concerned. One cannot make sense of the concept of equal opportunity without addressing the question "opportunity for what?". The answer to that question depends upon the liberal idea of the good life.

Liberalism is not neutral among competing ways of life, despite familiar claims to the contrary.[7] It values individual development and especially forms of development that involve rationality, purposiveness, and choice. In contemporary liberal democratic societies these ideals are conventionally linked to certain kinds of achievement, especially in the economic sphere. Not all ways of life encourage this sort of development. But liberalism also values diversity among ways of life for the sorts of reasons Simon has advanced, for example, the desirability of different experiments in living some of which are possible only in the context of a group life with shared traditions. Now it is obviously impossible for people to have an equal opportunity to participate in every experiment in living. If you are raised in one tradition, for example, Catholicism, you cannot simultaneously be raised in another, for example, Judaism, or if you are, as in a "mixed" marriage, that is a different experience and experiment from being raised in either alone. And no one can choose the tradition into which he or she is born. But these facts alone do not create a problem for the liberal ideal of equal opportunity, for there may be many different paths to development. For example, both Catholicism and Judaism may develop, in different ways, the characters, talents, and motivations needed to achieve those things that are widely valued in contemporary liberal democratic society. In this situation no conflict between equal opportunity and pluralism exists.

The conflict emerges only when a tradition or way of life does not offer a comparable path to conventional success, as in the case of the Amish.[8] Then whatever course is taken requires the sacrifice of something valued in liberal democratic societies. The approach adopted in the Amish case is a compromise, partially infringing upon the Amish way of life and yet not really providing the Amish children with equal opportunity in the full sense. Still, it is a reasonable compromise. It does not alter the core of the Amish tradition and yet it ensures that the Amish children have some of the basic capacities that liberal democratic societies value so highly. This course is far preferable to emphasizing only one of the competing values. That is why the inequality between the Amish and other Americans is not morally objectionable.

GROUP CULTURE AND ILLEGITIMATE INEQUALITY: BLACKS

Consider now another minority group that has less of what most Americans want: American blacks. This is a case that reveals some of the limitations and inadequacies of Simon's approach. Are the inequalities between blacks and other Americans morally objectionable? Again part of the answer depends upon what one thinks are the sources of these inequalities. No one denies that black Americans were oppressed and kept down both during slavery and after, and almost no one now defends that history. But what about today?

In my view, racism remains a powerful and pervasive force in American life, often openly influential, but even more often covertly and in ways the people involved do not themselves understand. It is not just a question of discrimination that violates the merit principle, although that is common enough. One of the reasons I support affirmative action programs, even the use of quotas, is that I do not think it possible in most spheres to create procedures for evaluating merit that are free of racism, at least of the unconscious variety. But the problem goes much deeper than the word discrimination suggests. In a multitude of ways, American society creates a hostile environment for blacks, one in which it is harder for them than for whites to develop their potential and to flourish.

These considerations have important implications for our understanding of pluralism. It is not just a group's own culture that may affect its members' life chances, but also the cultures of groups with which it interacts. When considering the legitimacy of inequalities between groups, we cannot simply assume that interactions among groups are benign and that all group cultures are equally legitimate regardless of their effect on those in other groups. In the Amish case it seems reasonable to say that Amish children have lower expectations, in conventional terms, primarily because of Amish culture and the values and motivations it inculcates rather than because of the way they are regarded and treated by the non-Amish majority. But that is not a plausible account of why the life chances of blacks are less than those of whites. One of the problems with Simon's approach is that it does not draw our attention to this sort of issue. But this is precisely what we must consider in making a moral judgment about group inequality in the real world.

This general point about what is relevant to the evaluation of pluralist inequality is valid even if one rejects my claims about racism in American society. Simon says nothing one way or the other about the issue, but others clearly disagree with me. Some claim that racial domination is a thing of the past. They point out that laws mandating segregation have been replaced by laws prohibiting discrimination in education, housing, and employment. They do not claim that racial prejudice has disappeared but rather that it no longer has any significant impact on the distribution of education, income, and employment. They point to the success of other groups like Jews and Asian-Americans who have also been the victims of discrimination and exclusion and who now do better in many ways than others. They conclude that the lower than average success rate of black Americans must therefore be due to cultural characteristics of black life. For example, some authors suggest that black culture does not promote educational achievement, an important key to employment and income. In their view, not domination but difference is the source of inequality between blacks and whites today.[9]

I have made clear my disagreement with the position I have just described, but I do not want to pursue that debate here. On the contrary, I want to assume for the sake of argument that my opponents are correct and black culture is the major cause of the continuing inequality between blacks and whites. After all, even if I am right about the ongoing force of racism, black culture could still be a contributing factor and it is important to see how this would affect the moral argument. Moreover, by framing the question in this way, we can focus on Simon's implicit suggestion that inequalities that can be traced to cultural differences are morally legitimate.

If black culture were the cause of black's lower rate of success in areas like education and income, would the inequality be as morally unobjectionable as the inequality between the Amish and other Americans? No, it would not. The connection between inequality and culture is different in the two cases, different in ways that are morally relevant.

Let us suppose that black culture does not encourage educational achievement. Why might that be? One plausible answer is that black culture is in important respects a culture of subordination. Socialization is a source of power, and cultural differences between groups may reflect and embody relations of domination and subordination. Children from dominant and subordinate groups receive different sorts of socialization. Children from subordinate groups are taught by schools, but also by their families and peers, not to aspire to positions possessed by members of the dominant groups, not to expect equal treatment from authorities, not to challenge the status quo or to show initiative, and so on. In some respects this reflects a prudent recognition of the dangers of excessive ambition, but it also reflects, at least in part, internalization of subordination. A group that has consistently been denied access to things the dominant groups in society value may come to say it does not want these things anyway. Jon Elster calls this adaptive preference formation, like the fox saying that the grapes out of reach were probably sour.[10] A group culture that has been signifi-

cantly shaped by this sort of adaptation cannot be used to legitimate the inequality of which it is a product.

All this applies to blacks much more than to the Amish. Black
culture has been shaped profoundly by the long and recent
history of racial domination. Even if we assume that the domination has not finally ended, we cannot set aside its cultural
legacy. If black culture contributes to lower rate of black success
in education, we should not simply accept this as a morally
legitimate by-product of pluralism, as part of the black way of
life. By contrast, the Amish opposition to technology, consumption, and higher education is not the result of an adaptation to
a recent history of deprivation and discrimination. This is not
to say that the Amish have not been subject to discrimination in
the United States, but rather that this has not been central to
the formation of their culture and values.

Someone might object that the Amish suffered from perse-
cution in Europe and this shaped their culture. Should it matter
from a moral perspective that this happened long ago and far
away? Yes, it should. The fact that the Amish have affirmed the
distinctive features of their culture over time under circumstances in which they were not primarily reacting to domination
gives legitimacy to the elements that differentiate them from
the majority. It makes their culture more a product of their own
inner life, of their own collective choice.

Does this mean that there is nothing of distinctive value in
black culture, that assimilation is, after all, the ideal, at least for
blacks and groups like them whose culture is in important ways
a response to recent domination? No. We have to avoid two
different dangers. The first would reproduce domination in the
name of pluralism by uncritically accepting the social consequences of a culture of subordination. The second would reproduce domination in the name of equality by uncritically accepting the culture of the dominant group as a valid norm for all. It
is characteristic of oppressed groups struggling for liberation
that they want to affirm the value of their collective experience
without endorsing the history of their oppression and to celebrate their distinctiveness without legitimating ongoing domination.

Unlike the Amish, blacks want to improve their educational

achievements and to take advantage of the opportunities offered by educational success. We do not find the same deep conflict between the goal of equal opportunity and respect for black culture. If black culture is an obstacle to educational success, blacks themselves want to transform it, but they want to do so without abandoning it altogether. This was clearly part of W.E.B. Du Bois' enterprise as it was of the later black-power movement. It remains a challenge for blacks today.

Again, we have a valid general lesson about pluralism even if one does not accept my specific claims about black culture. To show that inequality results from a group's own distinctive culture is not sufficient to establish the moral legitimacy of the inequality. We have to consider both the wider social context in which the group lives and the context in which the group's culture has developed before we can use distinctiveness of culture to legitimate inequality.

Culture and Gender: Are Differences Legitimate?

Now consider the issue of gender differences. What are we to think of cultural differences between men and women? If one is for pluralism, should one endorse these differences? If one is for equality, must one oppose them? Simon seems to suggest that the answer to both questions is "yes." He refers several times to "sexual pluralism" hinting that it is desirable without specifying what it entails and he suggests that the idea that males and females should receive the same socialization is incompatible with the pluralist ideal of group diversity.

As usual what is needed to deal with these issues is more attention to context. If we are asked how to respond to cultural differences between the sexes, we should begin by distinguishing between two cultural contexts: the culture of a religious or ethnic group and the public culture of a liberal democratic society such as Canada or the United States. A commitment to pluralism will require us to respect cultural differences between the sexes that emerge from the internal culture of a group. It does not require us to endorse differences between the sexes in the public culture. Pluralism is not relativism, and respect for diversity does not entail indifference to the way the public culture treats gender.

Let us begin with the issue of gender construction within groups. Different traditions have different conceptions of the proper roles of men and women and the proper relations between the sexes. For example, some religious and moral traditions sharply differentiate the roles of men and women, assigning women to the domestic sphere, thus limiting their public activities, and emphasizing the authority of the husband in the family. Other traditions, particularly as they have evolved in recent years, seek to minimize the differences between the sexes, encouraging both females and males to develop their talents and capacities whatever they might be and teaching that men and women have similar responsibilities in the public and domestic spheres. Within broad limits a liberal democratic society ought to tolerate these sorts of cultural differences among groups and thus cultural differences between the sexes when these emerge from a group's inner life. This follows from a general commitment to pluralism.

These differences may affect the life chances of group members. For example, other things being equal, women raised in the former kind of tradition seem less likely to pursue professional careers than women raised in the latter. But again these sorts of consequences of group differences are legitimate for the sorts of reasons mentioned above in connection with the Amish.

There are limits to toleration, of course. Some traditions might oppose formal education for women on principle, but, as in the case of the Amish, a liberal democratic state will override that prescription and insist on certain kinds of education for all children, girls as well as boys, up to a certain age. A liberal democratic state may also try to limit the ability of people to act on the basis of their group culture in their relations with those who do not share their views, at least in certain contexts. For example, laws that prohibit discrimination on the basis of sex are supposed to prevent men whose culture teaches that women belong in the home from acting on those beliefs in the public sphere.

Even where it does not impose formal limits on group cultures, the public culture is not neutral. For example, a liberal democratic regime will tolerate a patriarchal religion as part of its commitment to pluralism. But if it grants equal legal rights to women, it communicates a message about the status of women that is subversive of patriarchal values and creates a resource that makes it easier for a woman to leave a life based on that religion.[11] A young girl raised as an Islamic fundamentalist in Canada or the United States receives one image of what it is to be a woman from her family and another, quite different, from the larger society. Her socialization and her objective situation are very different from those of a girl raised in Iran, where public institutions support the values of Islamic fundamentalism. A liberal democratic regime ought to respect diversity, but it cannot be equally congruent with all values and ways of life and should not try to be. It will quite properly support some and undermine others simply by being true to itself.

What should the public culture of a liberal democratic regime communicate about gender? I cannot answer that question fully, but I can make a few general points. As the preceding analysis makes clear, equality must be central to the message. Gender is not a relevant difference when it comes to legal rights and social opportunities. No one seriously questions that now. As in the case of race, liberal democratic societies have become committed to gender equality in many areas where they previously tolerated or even enforced inequality. This sort of equality is not in conflict with pluralism. Pluralism does not require one always to favor difference over sameness, regardless of context.

I assume that Simon would not disagree with any of this. What could he mean then in suggesting that "sexual pluralism" is desirable? He criticizes two authors who have objected to traditional patterns of female socialization, claiming that they illegitimately take male socialization as a norm. The objection may be valid for the male authors whom Simon discusses, but it does not apply to most contemporary feminists who routinely criticize customary male socialization at least as sharply as customary female socialization.[12] For example, if female socialization is criticized for having discouraged women from fully developing their mental and physical capacities, male socialization is criticized for having discouraged men from developing their emotional and affective capacities. Women are to pursue careers and to act in the public sphere while men are to assume equal responsibility for childcare and domestic activities.

In challenging the critics of gender socialization, Simon seems sometimes to suggest that there is nothing we can say about anyone else's values except that they are different; there is no ground for distinguishing better from worse. That sort of argument is a self-defeating form of relativism. It has nothing to do with pluralism, which presupposes that there are good reasons for valuing diversity. He also seeks to defend differential gender socialization by arguing that women can act autonomously when they affirm the traditional roles and values into which they have been socialized. Even if that is true, it is irrelevant. The fundamental question is not whether particular women, and men, can autonomously embrace their socialization, but what that socialization ought to be.

Does our commitment to equality require that upbringing be the same for both sexes? Is every social difference between the sexes a form of domination?

To answer these questions we must first ask what a particular difference means in a concrete social context. We cannot answer that on the basis of a priori principles: "All differences of X type mean Y." Nor is it something that can be determined by the subjective will of an individual: "I do [or do not] experience this difference as a form of domination." Instead it is a matter of interpreting a culture, of understanding a social reality.

Let me offer an illustration.[13] In *Plessy v. Ferguson*, the Supreme Court majority who upheld the "separate but equal" doctrine contended that, if blacks found their separate treatment stigmatizing or degrading, that was their problem. Separation alone carried no implication of inferiority, so long as the treatment was equal, for example, comparable facilities. Given the actual disparity between the treatment of blacks and whites at the time, it would be kind to call this argument disingenuous. But later, in an attempt to maintain segregation, some communities did upgrade the facilities available to blacks, for example, physical plants and money spent on educational resources, so that the claim that the treatment was separate but equal was not absurd on its face, as it had been in the past. Still, everyone knew what segregation was all about. Whites regarded blacks as inferior. That is why the whites wanted them kept separate. Given the history of American race relations, for whites to keep blacks apart was inevitably stigmatizing and degrading. That is why the later Supreme Court was right to rule in *Brown v. Board of Education* that separate treatment of blacks was inherently unequal.

What is, or is not, stigmatizing is not merely a matter of the subjective perceptions of individuals. It is a social construction and a cultural reality. Particular claims about what is stigmatizing may be contestable, but some claims are clear beyond a reasonable doubt. That the segregation of blacks was stigmatizing is clear in that way.

The claim that separate but equal is inherently unequal is not, however, an analytic truth. Take the famous recent debate about what equality would require with regard to public toilets for men and women. Opponents of the Equal Rights Amendment argued that equal treatment of the sexes would require the elimination of separate toilet facilities for men and women, on the "separate is inherently unequal" ground. But in our culture, having separate public toilet facilities for men and women is not stigmatizing. The practice reflects a cultural norm about gender and privacy. It is perhaps a funny norm, as anyone who has seen *The Discreet Charm of the Bourgeoisie* can recognize. (Bunuel has a scene in which people retreat quietly to locked rooms to eat and sit on toilets around a common table to talk.) It may also be an incoherent norm, as many people suggested in noting that men and women normally use the same bathrooms in private homes. But no one, as far as I know, supposes that the separation of public facilities is in itself stigmatizing, or degrading, or disadvantaging to one sex over another.

The fact that the separation of toilets is not stigmatizing does not necessarily settle the question of what counts as equal treatment. If we measured equal treatment not by footage of lavatory space but by time spent waiting in line to use the facilities, we would indeed conclude that women are usually disadvantaged by the "separate but equal" treatment. But they are not stigmatized. So, in this case, separate but equal, is not inherently unequal. The inequality is something that could be fixed with additional plumbing. That is simply not the case with racial segregation, which included, not incidentally, public toilets. No improvement of facilities could have made separate toilets for blacks equal in the United States. The social meaning of that difference was plain.

This long excursus on toilets reveals both that it is difficult, but possible, to think of cases in contemporary North American societies where differences in social treatment between the sexes do not entail domination or objectionable forms of inequality. In my view, most differences in the ways males and females are treated in these societies, including gender-related patterns of socialization, embody and maintain patriarchal domination. But I will not try to support that claim here. If the claim is correct, it has important implications for the question of what the public culture ought to be with regard to gender. In general, distinctions based on gender should be suspect. In this context, equality does usually require the elimination of difference.

Let me immediately add two important caveats to that general conclusion. First, in a context of piecemeal social change, the elimination of difference in one area, while others remain intact, may actually aggravate patterns of domination. For example, the move to have men assume more responsibilities for child-rearing has been accompanied, in some legal jurisdictions, by a change in assumptions about who would get custody of the children in case of divorce. The traditional assumption was that the mother would normally get primary custody. Now some jurisdictions have eliminated that assumption, making it easier than before for fathers to get joint or even primary custody. But the social reality continues to be that, in most cases, women care much more than men about rearing their children. Often the man uses his potential legal claims to custody as a bargaining chip in negotiations over finances, agreeing to give primary custody to the woman if she will settle for a lower level of child support. So, the effect of the change has been to transfer power from women to men, leaving women in a worse position than they would have been under legal rules that assumed a tradi-tional sexual division of labor. A number of "egalitarian" re-forms in the area of family law seem to have generated this sort of inegalitarian outcome. This shows that we have to pay attention not only to the symbolism of a social arrangement but also to how it actually works. It also indicates why one cannot use the moral judgments offered here, even though they are themselves contextual judgments, as a simple blueprint for social change.

The second caveat concerns the androgynous ideal that is implicit in the arguments I have presented in this section. Some feminists have suggested that the ideal of androgyny is not sufficiently sensitive to women's differences from men.[14] It is not just that we have to avoid constructing the ideal primarily from a male model. Any plausible androgynous ideal will require that men become more like women as well as women more like men. It will require men to integrate traditionally female roles, values, motivations, tasks, and dispositions into their lives. But I take that much as implicit in what I said above. The new feminist challenge goes deeper still, suggesting that women have a distinctive voice that men cannot easily hear and perhaps not at all, that women have a distinctive and valuable way of being that risks being lost if men and women become too much alike. Some trace the difference to biology, while others emphasize the long history of enforced difference under patriarchal domination.

To speak of men and women as fundamentally different will remind many people of the traditional defenses of gender distinctions. The feminist writers are well aware of this and see it as a danger. They want to find ways to identify and respect women's differences from men without providing a justification for past and present subordination. They want to pay tribute to women's historical experience without simply endorsing women's traditional roles. I do not think that any of those struggling with this approach have yet succeeded entirely, but I do think they are asking the right questions. If an effective challenge to the androgynous ideal is mounted, one that emphasizes difference rather than sameness, it will come from this sort of inquiry not a retreat to traditionalism or an abstract general commitment to group pluralism.

CONCLUSION

Throughout this chapter I have not sought to challenge the basic framework of contemporary liberal democratic capitalist institutions. The question has been whether inequalities among groups could be legitimate within that framework. I adopted this approach because I thought that what is most interesting about Simon's chapter is the questions it raises about groups and that these could be pursued most effectively without raising the larger issues. Without challenging the basic framework, I have tried to show that we have to investigate the contexts in which differences among groups emerge in order to make substantive judgments about the legitimacy of inequality. In particular, I have tried to show that we must consider the ways in which power has shaped cultural differences before we rely upon cultural differences to legitimate inequality. The cases of blacks and women show that pluralism and equality can be complementary and mutually reinforcing, even within the limits of liberal democratic capitalist regimes. But I want to conclude by calling those limits into question in order to suggest that pluralism and equality are compatible at a much deeper level.

Simon argues that cultural differences are a legitimate source of inequality among groups. If he accepted my critique, he would have to modify that to say that morally legitimate cultural differences are a legitimate source of inequality among groups. The Asian-American and Amish cases can be used to support this modified claim. But Simon seems to think that if cultural differences are legitimate, whatever inequalities they might give rise to in a capitalist market society are also legitimate. That is a much stronger claim. It has an obvious affinity to the classical liberal argument that natural differences of talent and motivation among individuals legitimate the inequalities of market societies. Simon does not actually say any of this, but it seems implicit in his construction of a hypothetical Rawlsian case for limiting the inegalitarian effects of cultural differences and his rejection of that case. His discussion treats culture as an asset, and the issue is who owns it or the benefits that flow from it. Following Anthony Kronman and others, Simon criticizes Rawls' use of the idea of common assets.

In my view the whole debate that Simon draws upon is a dead end. The criticisms of Rawls are effective, but the critics have nothing persuasive to offer as an alternative.[15] The focus on ownership is fundamentally misguided. It is not the only way or the best way to reflect upon the relation between the individual and the collective, the legitimate scope of social inequalities, the development of human capacities, or the nature of the human good and the relation of social institutions to that good. One need not ground the case for equality on a claim to collective ownership. To think of the question in this way already reflects a narrow market mentality, one that C. B. Macpherson aptly labeled "possessive individualism."[16]

Many moral traditions share the view that the more gifted have a duty to contribute in accord with their capacities and to share the benefits of their good fortune and that it is appropriate for social institutions to require this of them in some ways though not in others. To see these demands as incompatible with respect for the individual or as a disguised form of utilitarianism is to adopt too constricted a conception of the human person.[17]

Simon's extension of the argument to groups is particularly problematic.[18] If anything is to be regarded as a common asset, surely a cultural tradition is. A cultural tradition cannot be maintained by a single individual, as Simon himself notes elsewhere. We cannot think intelligently about the proper place of distinctive cultures in society if we think in terms of individual ownership. But again it is a mistake to use ownership language in the first place. It obscures more than it reveals.

We ought to accept cultural differences as a good thing, within the limits discussed above, and to recognize that some cultures will emphasize certain forms of aspiration and accomplishment more than others. Cultures affect people's motives and values and goals, and achievements will vary from one cultural group to another. But this does not settle the question of what sort of social institutions and policies we should have, that is, of the framework within which these differences are to operate. A neutral social structure does not exist. We have to decide whether and to what extent and in what ways certain forms of achievement will receive rewards, in addition to the intrinsic rewards that come from the achievement itself. This obviously includes deciding what role the market will play in society and how it is to be constrained, if at all.

In my view we are most likely to encourage genuine diversity, both among individuals and among groups, if we minimize the role of the market as an arbiter of human worth. We should try to reduce invidious distinctions and differential material rewards in relation to education and occupation. People should be encouraged to develop those talents and capacities that offer an opportunity for personal growth and self-realization and to respect achievements in diverse fields. In the end, a society that permits relatively few inequalities among individuals, and hence among groups, will be the one in which the kinds of differences we want to affirm among individuals and groups are most likely to flourish.

NOTES

1. James S. Fishkin, *Justice, Equal Opportunity, and the Family* (New Haven: Yale University Press, 1983), 4. Simon's citation leaves out a word from the original. Fishkin actually says "arbitrary *native* characteristics" (emphasis added). This difference makes Fishkin less useful as a foil for Simon because one might question whether a cultural heritage can be a "native" characteristic. For a deeper problem with Simon's use of this phrase from Fishkin, see note 3.

2. Malcolm X, *The Autobiography of Malcolm X* (New York: Grove Press, 1966), 36.

3. Fishkin, *Justice,* 22, 32. Fishkin uses the term "arbitrary" as a qualifier in order to distinguish native characteristics that are not relevant to future qualifications from those, like I.Q., that are. In Fishkin's usage, IQ is not an arbitrary native characteristic and presumably neither is a cultural heritage that makes one more likely to develop qualifications.

4. Ibid., 32.

5. See, for example, Seymour Martin Lipset, *Social Mobility in Industrial Society* (Berkeley: University of California Press, 1966).

6. For information on the Amish, I rely upon Cornelius J. Dyck, ed., *An Introduction to Mennonite History* (Scottdale, Pa.: Herald Press, 1967).

7. Here I follow William Galston, "Defending Liberalism," *American Political Science Review* 76 (September 1982): 621–29. Simon appears to assume that liberalism's commitment to pluralism requires neutrality, an impossible demand that he then uses to criticize Rawls' notion of primary goods. In fairness to Simon, however, Rawls' theory invites this.

8. One could object that the Amish way of life comes closer to the fundamental liberal ideal than the conventional way of life, that is, that the former has more purposiveness and rationality to it than the latter with its blind dedication to acquisition, consumption, and meaningless and frivolous choice. The objection has merit but it conflates two issues. The first requires a substantive judgment about the fit between the deepest ideals of liberalism with regard to the development of human talents and capacities and the sorts of development most valued and encouraged by the institutions and social practices of contemporary liberal democratic societies. Here I agree with the critics that the fit is not very good. The second concerns the question of whether a liberal democratic society ought to ensure that all its members have access to the kinds of developmental opportunities that the society considers valuable. The answer is yes, even if the society is wrong about what is valuable. To act differently would be hypocritical.

9. See, for example, Nathan Glazer, *Ethnic Dilemmas* (Cambridge: Harvard University Press, 1983).

10. Jon Elster, *Sour Grapes* (Cambridge: Cambridge University Press, 1983).

11. I do not mean to suggest that legal equality is enough to overcome patriarchy or that patriarchal domination is not a powerful force in contemporary liberal democratic societies. But I do think that legal equality is a necessary step in overcoming patriarchy and that it makes a difference.

12. See, for example, Dorothy Dinnerstein, *The Mermaid and the Minotaur* (New York: Harper & Row, 1976).

13. The next four paragraphs are taken, with minor alterations, from my essay "Nationalism and the Exclusion of Immigrants: Lessons from Australian Immigration Policy," in *Open Borders? Closed Societies?*, ed. Mark Gibney (Westport, Conn.: Greenwood Press, 1989.

14. See, for example, Carol Gilligan, *In a Different Voice* (Cambridge: Harvard University Press, 1982).

15. It is possible to read Rawls in ways that make him somewhat less vulnerable to the criticisms. In "Rights and Duties in an Egalitarian Society," *Political Theory* 14 (1986): 31–49, I defend Rawls against Anthony Kronman on this issue. See Anthony Kronman, "Talent Pool-

ing" in *Human Rights,* ed. J. Roland Pennock and John W. Chapman, NOMOS 23 (New York: New York University Press, 1981), 58–79.

16. C. B. Macpherson, *The Political Theory of Possessive Individualism* (Oxford: Clarendon Press, 1962). In his later works, Macpherson explicitly argues that Rawls and other contemporary liberal theorists are in the grip of possessive individualism. See, in particular, *Democratic Theory* (Oxford: Clarendon Press, 1973) and *The Rise and Fall of Economic Justice* (Oxford: Oxford University Press, 1985).

17. See my article, "Rights and Duties," for a development of this argument.

18. Simon's criticism of what he calls the weak version of the Rawlsian case rests primarily upon the argument that any redistribution that does not compensate perfectly for differences in initial assets and tastes is a form of theft and hence unjust. This reveals the extent to which he is a captive of the language of ownership. It is surely implausible to claim that a compensation mechanism that does not work perfectly is ipso facto, unjust. The relevant question, assuming compensation to be a desirable goal in principle, is whether the compensation mechanism works better than the alternatives, including no compensation mechanism. I have explored this issue in "Compensatory Justice and Social Institutions," *Economics and Philosophy* 1 (1985): 39–67.

10

ELECTORAL POWER, GROUP POWER, AND DEMOCRACY

ANDREW LEVINE

It has been suggested that the tendency of American courts in recent years to acknowledge discrimination only in cases where an intent to discriminate can be demonstrated has exacerbated social inequalities; and the application of this standard to voting rights has diminished the electoral strength of blacks.[1] I have no quarrel with this suggestion, though I would emphasize, as a realist would, that the decline of progressive social movements in the United States and the rise of the right to commanding positions in the state apparatus, including its courts, are largely to blame. It is beyond my competence to provide arguments, grounded in Constitutional doctrine, for redressing this situation. I am confident that with sufficient ingenuity, compelling legal arguments can be produced, and that in the right political conditions they can prevail. I shall therefore leave Constitutional questions for others to worry over, and address the issue of group rights directly to electoral power. I ask: How do measures for empowering racial minorities fare from the standpoint of democratic theory? The short answer is that they fare well. The longer, more nuanced answer, not surprisingly, is that it all depends.

The issue central to proposals for according blacks (and per-

haps other disempowered groups) special electoral rights is not
quite the same as in affirmative action or "reverse discrimination" debates. There the crucial consideration is justice. In evaluating claims for group rights to electoral power, the principal
concern is democracy. To address our question, then, it is well
to focus on democracy as an ideal; and on means, in particular
historical circumstances, for implementing democratic values.

From the time the ancient Greeks invented the word until
roughly two hundred years ago, "democracy" was universally
despised. Nowadays, it is endorsed by everyone, from celebrants
of the American system of government to defenders of popular
democracy in the Third World and Eastern bloc. The change
reflects a profound transformation in human history: the entry
of the *demos*, the (ordinary) people, into the political arena. But
beyond the recognition that the claim of "we the people" to rule
ourselves is legitimate and incontrovertible, what democracy is
remains contested.

Democracy is susceptible to many interpretations, of varying
degrees of cogency and historical legitimacy. But for the term
to retain some connection with its original meaning and its
historically important uses, it must in some way designate popular rule. The democracy that was despised was the rule of the
demos. The democracy that has come to be universally endorsed
has lost this class-based connotation. Today, a political community is democratic to the extent that its collective choices are
functions of the choices of its citizens, where citizens' votes
count equally and where rights of citizenship are enjoyed regardless of such irrelevancies as class, gender, ethnicity or race.
These definitions are connected, given the size and composition
of the *demos*. But it is plain that the modern understanding, to
its detriment, obscures social divisions in a picture of universal,
political equality. Still, if only to be faithful to how the word is
used nowadays, it will suffice to think of democracy not as rule
of the people in contrast to elites, but as rule of the people *tout
court*.

Democracy in this sense has been investigated by many political theorists, but never so perspicaciously as by Rousseau. Implicitly, Rousseau's views provide a sound purchase on the ques-

tion of group rights to electoral power. I will therefore refer to
Rousseauean positions throughout what follows.

1

Direct democracy is plainly impracticable except in small political communities. It is commonly supposed that this fact warrants recourse to representative institutions—to governance
through elected officials and mass-based electoral parties. Ostensibly, representative institutions approximate direct democracy without succumbing to its impracticability. They implement
democratic ideals in a world where political communities are
too large and heterogeneous for the entire citizenry to assemble
and deliberate together.

If this rationale for representative government is accepted,
we have a prima facie case against according special rights to
groups in elections. In direct democracies, all citizens count
equally in the determination of collective choices. Presumably,
this feature should carry over to its second-best approximation.
In principle, each person should be accorded one and only vote.

But, as Rousseau long ago pointed out,[2] representative governments do not in fact approximate direct democracy. At best,
they provide a mechanism through which "we the people" can
select those who make laws for us—quite a different prospect
from making laws ourselves.[3] This observation, stated directly,
should go without saying. It is, however, neither trivial in its
consequences nor is it generally accepted in our political culture. It would be a useful exercise in "ideological criticism" to
investigate the forces that sustain the widespread disregard of
what is virtually a truism. For now, it must suffice to insist on
the obvious, and to focus on some implications of the evident
differences between direct democracy and representative government for the question of group rights to electoral power.

Mainstream democratic theory characteristically joins mainstream politics in identifying "democracy" with the governmental forms in place in the "Western democracies."[4] Western democracies do have electoral mechanisms for selecting legislators
and (some) other government officials. To some degree, there-

fore, voters in Western democracies register consent to the measures their rulers undertake, and therefore hold public officials accountable for what they do. Needless to say, consent can also be conferred and accountability achieved through other institutional forms. But to the extent the people collectively control their own political affairs through representative institutions, the Western democracies are indeed democratic—in substance, and not just by definition.

Even ardent defenders of Western democracy would concede that, in the sense in question, the institutions they promote are barely democratic. We citizens of Western democracies can reasonably persuade ourselves that we enjoy a measure of control over those who rule us. But it requires enormous capacities for self-deception to see this control as a practical implementation (or approximation) of democratic self-rule. It is a signal achievement of the political order under which we live to have sustained this self-deception in the face of what is, after all, perfectly obvious.

The idea that representative institutions approximate direct democracy typically coexists, uneasily, with nondemocratic justifications for representative government. It is sometimes held, for example, that the *demos* are incapable of governing wisely and are therefore in need of rulers. With representative institutions, the requisite degree of skill in governance can be cultivated by those who assume politics as their vocation. At the same time, the citizenry, through the electoral and party systems, can help guide the rule to which they submit. Representative government would then be an institutionalized benevolent despotism. This view is commonly joined with the conviction that politics is best not made a permanent focus of human life, as it was, say, for Aristotle or Rousseau. Rather, it is best set to the side or relegated to professional politicians. Representative government, precisely because it depoliticizes human affairs, frees individuals from the burdens of political life, allowing them to pursue private ends outside the state, in "civil society."

However this may be, if representative government is not, in fact, a close approximation of direct democracy but only a distant simulacrum—and *a fortiori* if it is something else entirely—then even a prima facie case in favor of "one person-one vote" cannot be sustained. A commitment to our existing system of government has no immediate bearing on the question of group rights to electoral power.

2

I have thus far assumed that democracy is indeed a worthwhile value. This assumption could be false. It is, in fact, a widely known secret of mainstream political theory that sophisticated defenders of representative government implicitly deny, or severely mitigate, democracy's standing as an ideal. As already noted, representative government is often defended for anti-democratic reasons. But its democratic trappings nevertheless play an important political role.

Representative governments accommodate popular aspirations for self-rule by conferring the franchise on the citizenry at large, and holding elections at periodic intervals. But in Western democracies, collective decision making, though enshrined in popular self-representations, amounts to much less than is commonly supposed. Above all, voting helps legitimate the order in place. That is, voting encourages the belief that the existing order is legitimate. Needless to say, the question of the real (de jure) legitimacy of political institutions, the issue central to Rousseau's political philosophy, is logically independent of the prevalence of such beliefs, just as the question of the existence of God is independent of the prevalence of the belief that God exists. If there is a causal connection, it runs the other way: voting helps legitimate de facto arrangements because voters at some (not fully articulated) level subscribe to political theories according to which voting legitimates institutions de jure.

However voting and participation in general can be perilous if not kept strictly in bounds. To legitimate existing regimes, what matters is the appearance of popular rule, not the substance. Citizens will obey better if they think themselves in control. But beyond that degree of control sufficient for (de facto) legitimation, democracy is, at best, unnecessary and, very often, dangerous. Far from encouraging as much democracy as is practicable, given the size and heterogeneity of political communities, proponents of representative government effectively

advocate minimal democracy: as much democracy as is needed
for stability and order, but no more.

Representative government, in this view, is a "golden mean"
between a permanent legitimation crisis, given popular aspirations for self-rule, and real democracy, which threatens stability.
Defenders of Western democracy generally regard the undif-
ferentiated citizenry in much the way pre-nineteenth century
political theorists regarded the *demos:* as a mob lacking competence to govern—mercurial, prone to assault individuals' rights,
liable to despotic usurpation of customary and legal restraints
and, in a word, insufficiently wise. These claims undoubtedly
have merit, particularly if "the people" are identified with the
depoliticized citizenry of the Western democracies—or their
counterparts in the existing socialist countries. I here register
the conviction however, that pro-democratic arguments, stress-
ing the beneficial transformative effects of popular participation
in collective deliberation and choice, finally prevail over the
mainstream case for minimal democracy. In whatever way we
finally assess traditional justifications for political representation
in general or for Western democracy in particular, it is only fair
to acknowledge that democracy—popular self-rule—is hardly
the value that moves its more discerning defenders. Quite the
contrary. The democracy that representative government allows
is a necessary evil, a requirement of civil order, and not a
positive ideal.

3

It requires ingenuity and wisdom, and sensitivity to particular
social, political, and economic circumstances, to contrive genuinely democratic institutions or, in a more reformist vein, to
move existing institutions in democratic directions. To democratize is to undertake a struggle over institutional forms, over
the tendency of political arrangements to enhance or diminish
self-rule. For democrats, the point is to empower. Democratic
politics is always a struggle for "peoples' power."

If rights of citizenship were fully and equally enjoyed, and
citizens were generally equal in their respective conditions, the
principle "one person-one vote" would provide the greatest fea-

sible degree of popular control over public policy consistent with the requirement that citizens count equally in the determination of social choices. But, of course, nothing like equality of condition exists in the United States or in any political community. And the United States has hardly been exemplary in providing citizenship rights to persons of color. First slavery, then discrimination (formerly protected by law, now largely extralegal) and, of course, material inequality (which works to the detriment of people of all races and ethnicities, but particularly victimizes blacks and other racial minorities) have affected the political sphere through a variety of familiar mechanisms, including the party system. In these circumstances, countervailing political measures are indispensable for democratization. According special group rights in elections to blacks and other disempowered groups is not necessarily an effective remedy. But it may be a good remedy in some cases. All that can be claimed in general is that, for democrats, the question to ask of particular proposals of this kind is whether or not they help in the broader project of empowering the disempowered.

It is worth noting that existing electoral systems generally do accord special group rights in voting, though seldom, if ever, to enhance popular control. The bicameral legislature of the United States is an example. By prescribing that one of two legislative branches be comprised of two representatives from each state, regardless of the state's size or population, the U.S. Constitution confers disproportionate power to small or underpopulated states. Perhaps this system is only a product of political compromises, and therefore no mark against a theoretical commitment to "one person-one vote." Perhaps it can be defended by appeal to extra-democratic considerations that swamp the presumption against diminishing the electoral power of citizens of larger states. However this arrangement might be explained or justified, the practice is sufficiently pervasive—in addition to the U.S. Congress, all but one state legislature is bicameral—to suggest that, despite what is widely assumed, the "one person-one vote" principle is not even a regulative ideal of our political culture. Our representative institutions regularly and typically belie the principle. For democrats reconciled to representative government, whether in despair of implementing direct democ-

racy or in genuine enthusiasm for the non- or extra-democratic
virtues of political representation, the point is therefore not so
much to defend the propriety of deviating from "one person-
one vote"—that point is already effectively conceded—but to
insist that deviations advance democratic aspirations.

4

Thus far I have followed Rousseau in impugning representative
government from the standpoint of a democratic theory that
"takes men as they are and laws as they might be."[5] I have also
endorsed Rousseau's pessimistic assessment of the likelihood, in
view of our past and present condition, of implementing institutional arrangements consistent with the theory of a just state.
Rousseau sometimes did recommend representative institutions; he was not, in practice, a doctrinaire opponent of political
representation.[6] I would suggest that, in fact, Rousseau conceded too much; that, even now, it is feasible to approximate
direct democracy through a system of delegation that concen-
trates power at the actual interstices of social life and economic
organization. I have argued elsewhere that there is a defensible
strain of political theory, of Marxian provenance much indebted to Rousseau, that defends precisely such arrangements.[7]
Still, where no good approximation to direct democracy is on
the political agenda, representative government is at least a
straw for democrats to grasp and build upon. For democrats,
the principal political objective is to democratize. If, in particular circumstances, existing (undemocratic) arrangements cannot
be replaced with institutions that accord with democratic convictions, then, so far as possible, democrats should seek to democratize what is already at hand. This democratic imperative is in
line with Rousseauean theory and practice, even if it is at odds
with the pessimism that pervades many of Rousseau's reflections
on political life. Thus it is in a generally Rousseauean spirit that
I have suggested that claims for group rights in elections be
assessed—and, where possible, supported—according to how
well they advance the ideal of citizenship that is fundamental to
Rousseau's account of political right and obligation, and to democratic theory generally.

I have not yet broached the most important respect in which Rousseauean political theory bears on our topic.[8] At one level, Rousseau conceived of politics as an eternal human drama, a struggle where reason and passion contend for dominance over individuals' wills. At this level, politics is timeless, and pessimism over prospects for approximating ideal outcomes inexorable. But Rousseau also maintained, implicitly throughout his copious reflections on political life, that actual political struggles are essentially localized in time and place, and therefore that the assessment of political measures can only be historically specific. If he was right, as I believe he was, little can be said in general about what is or is not empowering. Politics is essentially conjunctural. Following Rousseau, the wise democrat will be loath to make a fetish of particular institutional forms. For politics is not a matter of technical manipulations of political arrangements. What is required of democrats is sensitivity to the exigencies of tradition and circumstance, flexibility, and what Pascal called *l'esprit de finesse*. Only in this way can a protracted struggle over institutional forms be waged successfully, and "peoples' power" finally made real.

What we can learn from Rousseau, then, is this: in assessing practical political measures, actual or proposed, the general rule is that it all depends. According group rights to blacks or other disempowered groups probably is empowering in a range of likely circumstances. But not necessarily. And not necessarily any attempt at according special rights to disempowered groups will further democratic objectives. Only careful analysis and practical experimentation can determine what policies democrats should support in particular conjunctures. Philosophical reflection cannot provide sure answers, if only because the level of abstraction appropriate for thinking philosophically about democracy and representation is inappropriate for thinking effectively about how, in particular times and places, the struggle for democracy can be pursued with some likelihood of success.

I shall nevertheless venture some inconclusive speculations, in full awareness, after Rousseau, that my remarks, whatever their merit, are only tenuously connected to what I have so far maintained. Philosophical arguments can rebut opposing philosophical arguments. But it is one thing to defend proposals for

according special voting rights to blacks from (purported) philosophical refutation, and something else again to endorse such
proposals. I shall proffer an endorsement, but with only a bare
indication of what would need to be shown in a full-scale defense. In doing so, I appeal again to Rousseau's example. For
Rousseau often found it illuminating, even in expressly philosophical contexts, to reflect on "what is to be done?" despite a
clear realization that a sure answer will inevitably remain elusive.

5

Consider proportional representation. If blacks or other disempowered groups were to vote *en bloc,* there are conceivable
proportional representation schemes that would indeed enhance their collective power in the political arena. But would
blacks vote *en bloc?* I do not know. I am fairly sure, however,
that in the American context proportional representation would
have an even more unsettling effect on the established order: it
would undermine the unofficial hegemony the two-party system
exercises over political life. New political parties could finally
escape marginalization, and political ventures that now seem
utopian might actually become feasible. In such a changed political landscape, the nature and extent of black participation in
public life could hardly fail to be transformed—in ways impossible now to imagine.

In my view, the prospects for democracy implicit in moves
beyond the two-party system, not just for blacks, but for all of
us, is reason enough to support such measures. But would
proportional representation empower blacks as such? The answer depends, among other things, on the extent to which racial
identifications would take precedence over class interests and
ideological commitments, including party identifications. And it
depends on the consequences, in circumstances that cannot now
be envisioned, of favoring some identifications over others. I
would argue that, in the world as we find it, black power politics
generally is constructive—not least from a strictly democratic
perspective. But even small changes in our political system could
prompt a quite different assessment.

In any case, proportional representation is not the only route to rectifying black disempowerment. Arguably, there are even circumstances in which traditional coalition politics, of the sort once commonplace in many city governments, could enhance the power of black voters beyond what would be possible through proportional representation. In short, there are no institutional panaceas, no substitutes for *l'esprit de finesse*. For proponents of black power, as for democrats generally, *what* is wanted is clear. But how it might be achieved is a question only practice can determine.

Even as practical politics takes its rightful place, however, a philosophical point is worth bearing in mind: namely, that what matters for democrats is not so much the nature of institutions per se—not, for example, whether offices are awarded in proportion to votes received or according to the principle "winner takes all"—but the tendency of institutions, their role in the permanent struggle for peoples' power. Democratization is a process. If in some circumstances machine politics would help to empower blacks, then so long as black empowerment remains a democratic objective, this is a mark in its favor. But machine politics has generally been cooptive: historically it has helped integrate potentially insurgent constituencies into an already established order. Proportional representation schemes are less likely to have this effect, particularly insofar as they permit new political formations freer entry into the political arena. Since the established order is barely democratic, this is a mark in favor of proportional representation, perhaps a decisive mark.

6

Democrats want democracy, power to the people, but the implementation of peoples' power depends on particularities of circumstance forever elusive to speculative thought. In a world of formal political equality and real political inequality the guiding principle is to empower the disempowered—but which disempowered? To this point, I have assumed that, in the United States of America, blacks are the proper beneficiaries of the measures in consideration. This assumption is hardly beyond dispute. It will not be possible to address this question at all adequately here. Instead, by way of conclusion, I will offer a perfunctory "philosophical" comment as a contribution to the discussion that must eventually be joined.

My comment is just that rectification of past injustice is not a good reason for conferring special voting rights on blacks, even supposing that a proper rectificatory project would favor blacks over other historical victims of injustice. The guiding principle for democrats is, again, empowerment, not rectification of injustice. The question is: what, if anything, in the social, political, and economic organization of the United States—as it is *now*—supports policies favoring blacks over other racial or ethnic minorities or over economic classes or other groupings of individuals? This is a large and complex question, calling for an analysis of American society and of the historical tendencies at work in it, and for a sober assessment of what is politically feasible in the United States at present and in the foreseeable future. For now, I can only register the view that a sustained analysis would support the conclusion that black empowerment must remain an important component of any democratic agenda in this country because blacks continue to occupy a place in the political economy of the United States that makes their oppression special and their empowerment crucial for democratization.

It should be noted, finally, that there is no a priori reason why race-specific strategies for empowering blacks must be more successful than race-neutral strategies. Indeed, my conclusions do not depend upon the efficacy of race-specific policies. I have only argued in support of the objective of black empowerment, and for the legitmacy of according special voting rights to blacks. If, in particular circumstances, these or other race-specific measures could not be expected to bring about the intended objective, what I have said in support of their legitimacy would nevertheless remain. Only the wisdom of resorting to these means would be impugned.

7

The aim of the democratic project is full and equal real, not just legal, citizenship. Is this objective legally possible, given the state our Constitution established and the very unequal society it superintends? To repeat a conviction already expressed: with lawyerly ingenuity and the right political situation, virtually anything is possible within the framework of our Constitution. Indeed, Constitutional law is itself a terrain for waging the battle for democracy. For the foreseeable future it is, of course, unlikely to be a hospitable terrain. But this sad legacy of the Age of Reagan is not an insurmountable obstacle. Even if the Supreme Court were still controlled by liberals, Constitutional initiatives for according special voting rights to blacks would likely not succeed. For the real battle is not in the courts, but in society. The courts, even the Supreme Court in the best of times, follows the battle in the streets and the struggle in and over institutions. That struggle is temporarily in eclipse, but still viable. It is still possible therefore to bring the law along. Legal remedies can again ratify new victories, and the law can once more become a means for advancing democratic ideals. Despite the misfortunes of the past decade—in the law and in society at large—the struggle for democracy can still be won.

NOTES

1. This view was defended in a talk by Professor Randall Kennedy, entitled "Group Rights to Minimal Electoral Power," delivered at the meetings of the American Society for Political and Legal Philosophy in Chicago, September 3, 1987. The present paper is descended from a comment on Kennedy's presentation.

2. See Jean-Jacques Rousseau, *The Social Contract*, book 3, chap. 15, in Rousseau, *Basic Political Writings*, trans. Donald A. Cress (Indianapolis: Hackett, 1987).

3. In Rousseau's view, when others make laws for us, our autonomy is forfeit; our wills are heteronomously determined and we are, in Rousseau's term, slaves. So far as what matters for the theory of the just state, it is therefore irrelevant that the lives of citizens under representative institutions are likely to be more comfortable than, say, the lives of black slaves in the antebellum South. Among other things, we who live under representative institutions are able, to some degree, to choose our own masters; slaves could not. We therefore have more protections against the oppressiveness of subordination than they did.

But we are alike in having lost our essential autonomy, the sine qua non of legitimate political institutions.

4. The *locus classicus* for this misleading definitional move is Joseph Schumpeter, *Capitalism, Socialism, and Democracy* (New York: Harper & Row, 1942).

5. Rousseau, *The Social Contract*, 141.

6. See Richard Fralin, *Rousseau and Representation: A Study of the Development of His Concept of Political Institutions* (New York: Columbia University Press, 1978).

7. See Andrew Levine, *The End of the State* (London: Verso, 1987).

8. What follows draws on Levine, *The End of the State*, 39–41.

PART IV

THE AMERICAN EXPERIENCE

11

AMERICAN DEMOCRACY AND MAJORITY RULE

JONATHAN RILEY

I

Robert Dahl points out that "the Framers [of the U.S. Constitution] intended . . . to impede the operation of majority rule. In few other democratic countries are there so many obstacles in the way of government by electoral and legislative majorities."[1] These antimajoritarian obstacles include indirect methods of election or appointment for some government officials; intragovernmental checks designed to maintain a degree of separation of powers among the legislative, executive, and judiciary branches and between the two houses of the legislative branch; a federal division of powers between national and state governments; and a complex supermajoritarian constitutional amendment procedure. More specifically, electoral majorities have no authority directly to name the President or Supreme Court justices: these popular "representatives" may actually be opposed by a majority of the people at large.[2] Indeed, prior to the 17th Amendment in 1913, electoral majorities did not even have the power to choose their representatives in the Senate:

I am grateful to John Chapman and Alan Wertheimer for helpful editorial suggestions and comments. Responsibility for the views expressed remains mine.

the two senators from each state were chosen by the legislatures.[3] Legislative majorities have no authority to enact ordinary legislation, let alone constitutional changes. Given bicameralism, a House or Senate majority cannot by itself legitimately present legislation for presidential signature: a one-house majority is checked by a contrary majority of the other house. A two-house majority can be checked by the executive branch which has authority partially to control the predominant legislative branch. The President is empowered to veto the acts of a Congressional majority, although the veto can be overridden by a special two-thirds majority of both houses. Presidential authority to stop a simple (but not special) two-house majority helps the executive branch to maintain a degree of separation of powers doctrine as enunciated by James Madison in *The Federalist,* numbers 47 through 51. The same doctrine grants the Supreme Court authority to declare unconstitutional (and therefore *ultra vires* any branch of government) not only statutes enacted by a two-house majority and signed by the President but also supermajoritarian legislation enacted to override the executive veto.[4] It is true that the Court may be more more able than the President to stop a determined legislative supermajority given the ultimate Congressional weapon of impeachment (requiring two-thirds majority in the Senate to convict). Yet the power of the Court to control Congress may also become very nearly complete if newly appointed Justices feel sufficiently bound by precedent to follow the reasoning of their impeached brethren.[5] Apart from these intragovernmental checks involved in separation of powers and bicameralism, the federal structure imposes additional checks on legislative majorities at the state if not national level of government.[6] And finally, apart from all else, even a Congressional supermajority cannot by itself amend the fundamental constitutional rules: any proposed amendment must be ratified by legislatures or special conventions of three-fourths of the states as per Article 5 with the caveat that "no state, without its consent, shall be deprived of its equal suffrage in the Senate."[7]

These antimajoritarian constitutional constraints are applauded by some as the bulwarks of individual liberty, justice, and productivity in America. According to writers usually classified as "conservative," Americans have good reason to demand not only these constraints but perhaps others including constitutional limitations on government's fiscal, monetary, and welfare relief or transfer powers.[8] Unconstrained democracy is associated with disastrous long-term consequences given that special interests can be expected more or less to control Congress: "The point of constitutional constraints on government is to prevent people from doing through government that which they would do in the absence of government. . . . As desirable as democracy is in comparison to the alternatives, allowing government to do anything agreed to by a majority of the voters, or by a majority of their elected representatives, does not provide an adequate constraint on government power."[9] But others condemn the antimajoritarian obstacles as antidemocratic devices that largely frustrate majority coalitions (including political parties) in order to protect minority privileges and transfer the real power of government to other institutions, particularly capitalistic enterprises. According to these "liberal" critics, major constitutional reforms are required (often as part of a broader package of social and political reforms) to bring about true democracy in the United States.[10] This reformist perspective is currently dominant in the literature, due largely to the influential work of Dahl. He gives the perspective its most sophisticated expression and nicely summarizes the distaste for the sheer number of antimajoritarian obstacles in the United States.

> The elaborate system of checks and balances, separation of powers, constitutional federalism, and other institutional arrangements . . . are both adverse to the majority principle, and in that sense to democracy, and yet arbitrary and unfair in the protection they give to rights. However laudable their ends, in their means the framers were guilty of overkill. . . . Because they succeeded in designing a system that makes it easier for privileged minorities to prevent changes they dislike than for majorities to bring about the changes they want, it is strongly tilted in favor of the status quo and against reform.[11]

In his view, Americans should seriously consider "possibilities . . . such as abolishing the presidential veto . . . [and] creating a

unicameral Congress" in order to inject more democracy into
the political system, as well as arrangements such as worker-
controlled socialistic firms in order to inject more democracy
into the government of economic enterprises.[12]

The antimajoritarian features of the Constitution raise the
question: what kind of democracy is American democracy? My
present purpose is to suggest an answer to the question. In
section II, I argue that the Constitution can be interpreted as a
logically coherent form of just majority rule, where justice connotes protection of equal basic rights. This interpretation of
American democracy is taken for granted in the writings of
eminent founders such as Madison and Jefferson. Yet it often
seems to disappear from view in recent literature on democratic
theory. Section III argues that American democracy is distinctive only in the means employed to constrain the legislative
branch from violating basic rights. Unlike a sovereign parliament, Congress has no legal authority to pass certain types of
legislation. Unless the great contrast between popular and parliamentary sovereignty is kept in mind, the distinctive nature of
American democracy cannot be appreciated. Section IV clarifies
my interpretation of American democracy in the course of rebutting Dahl's influential criticisms of the Constitution. His criticisms are misplaced. American democratic theory remains a
logically coherent doctrine that seeks to temper majority rule by
certain considerations of justice. Moreover, the institutional means
prescribed by the doctrine for achieving its goal cannot be shown
to be imprudent on the basis of the empirical evidence. Section
V briefly summarizes my argument and draws attention to three
topics for further research.

II

Evidently, American democracy is not simple majoritarian democracy. But this fact alone does not vitiate its claim to be called
democracy or justify James Bryce's charge that it is "the least
democratic of democracies."[13] As Dahl himself says, "the argument that democratic procedures uniquely specify the majority
principle . . . is doubtful."[14] In this connection, Arend Lijphart
points to two "dramatically opposite models of democracy: the

majoritarian model (or the Westminster model) and the consensus model."[15] The majoritarian model consists of nine elements that allegedly facilitate rule by electoral and legislative majorities: homogeneous society; two-party system; unitary government; plurality system of electing representatives from single-member districts; concentration of executive power in majority party; fusion of powers in a group of officials like the Cabinet; unicameralism or at least asymmetric bicameralism; unlimited legal authority of government; and no vestiges of direct democracy. In essence, popular sovereignty is delegated entirely to any party with a majority of seats in the national legislature, that is, popular sovereignty becomes Parliamentary sovereignty between elections. In contrast, the consensus model consists of eight elements that restrain electoral and legislative majorities to promote rule by "as many people as possible": pluralistic society; multi-party system; federal government; proportional system of representation; sharing of executive power among key parties or other groups (religious, ethnic, economic); division of government powers among distinct groups of officials; balanced bicameralism; and legal authority of government limited by a written constitution, the visible symbol of popular sovereignty. In essence, popular sovereignty is not delegated entirely to any party with a majority of seats in the national legislature. Instead, sovereignty is shared among various groups designated by a constitution, including perhaps political parties, linguistic and ethnic groups, or the officials of different branches of government at different levels. Each of these designated groups exercises some portion of constitutional authority and to that extent represents the people. A consensus (or near-consensus) among these groups is required for consensus democracy, even though failure to achieve the required agreement will frustrate electoral and legislative majorities.

Lijphart characterizes the majoritarian and consensus models as logically coherent polar opposites that may help to guide "democratic constitutional engineers" in different societies. He suggests, for example, that "majoritarian democracy is especially appropriate for, and works best in, homogeneous societies, whereas consensus democracy is more suitable for plural societies."[16] At the same time, his empirical study of twenty-two democratic regimes in twenty-one Western countries reveals that no actual regime conforms perfectly to either of the two models. Any Western democracy seems to be a mixture of elements from both, the nature of the particular mixture apparently depending on degree of social pluralism, population size, and cultural heritage.[17] Nine distinct kinds of democratic regimes are identified and the U.S. Constitution is labeled a "majoritarian-federal" democracy. This kind of democracy more or less mixes five elements of the majoritarian model (homogeneous society, two-party system, single-member-district plurality system of elections, concentration of executive power in one party, and fusion of government powers in a Cabinet) with three elements of the consensus model (federal government, balanced bicameralism, and written constitutional limitations on government authority). Moreover, American democracy is not so distinctive after all: Canada, Germany, Austria, and Australia are also "majoritarian-federal" democratic regimes.[18]

According to Lijphart, American democracy is a complex form that ultimately seems to be a logical muddle. As he puts it, "the majoritarian-federal category [of which the U.S. is a member] . . . is a mixture of two logically opposite models of democracy."[19] I think this interpretation of the U.S. constitutional system is open to at least three objections. First, one of the most salient aspects of the U.S. government—its remarkable degree of formal separation of powers—does not distinguish it from other members of the majoritarian-federal category whose systems exhibit a formal fusion of powers in a Cabinet, for example, Canada's parliamentary system. But if a presidential veto and judicial review are no more or less efficient than social mores and customs at checking a national legislature, then the fuss made by so many critics as well as defenders of these constitutional checks seems misplaced. Although this is certainly possible, it is also possible that Lijphart's empirical analysis is too crude to display the effects of this distinctive aspect of American government.[20]

Second, the basic Westminster and consensus models do not seem to differ in kind but only in degree. Even the Westminster model is not a simple majoritarian regime. Single-member districts are a feature of the model. But geographical districting is clearly a device for ensuring representation to various local groups, each of which is a national electoral minority even if a majority in its district. Lijphart seems to recognize this point when he suggests that the majoritarian model strictly implies at-large elections "in a single national district," that is, no districting.[21] But even if every representative is elected by a popular majority in a nation-wide race, legislative majorities may make decisions that are often at odds with popular majority opinion. For example, if a bloc of 51 percent of the voters elects the whole slate of representatives, then bare majority decisions by the representatives may accord with the opinions of only about a quarter of the people on any issue. This means that the idea of a simple majoritarian model of representative democracy is itself problematic. Majority rule applied twice over (once to elect representatives, then to make government decisions) is often popular minority rule and thus antimajoritarian, particularly if minimal winning Cabinets are favored. In short, popular majority rule generally requires that we sacrifice either legislative majority rule or election of representatives by majority and plurality rule. Of course, "democratic constitutional engineers" might stipulate nation-wide majoritarian elections together with unanimity rule in the legislature on the assumption that each elected representative should feel constrained to follow popular majority opinion on every issue. But in practice this simply gives a veto to any elected representative. Alternatively, the engineers might prescribe some system of proportional representation (PR) to enable legislative majority decisions to reflect popular majority opinion.[22] But PR is yet another device for constraining electoral majorities and is a feature of Lijphart's consensus model.

The Westminster and consensus models of democracy seem to differ merely in the degree to which they rely on antimajoritarian devices to encourage popular participation in the political system. Neither model is simply majoritarian. In each, electoral or legislative majorities are shackled by constraints that virtually everyone (including the popular majority) must agree to endorse. Both models presuppose a popular consensus endorsing some antimajoritarian constraints. This suggests a third criticism of Lijphart's analysis: American democracy is not a mixture of elements from two logically incompatible models. The American model is just as logically coherent as the basic Westminster or consensus models. But it is a distinctive model. On the one hand, it retains a non-PR system of election similar to that of a Westminster parliamentary regime. On the other hand, it also involves many intragovernmental constitutional checks implying a remarkable degree of formal separation of powers in addition to balanced bicameralism. Lijphart notes that only the U.S. Constitution embodies this degree of formal separation of powers together with balanced bicameralism. Other regimes of the majoritarian-federal type fail to exhibit one if not both of these elements.[23]

The rationale for this distinctive American model is not self-evident and requires clarification. In this regard, a logical point discussed earlier deserves re-emphasis. If democracy is defined as rule in accord with popular majority wishes, then representative democracy or republican rule is possible only if the popular majority accepts some constraints on electoral or legislative majorities. The key question for any "democratic constitutional engineer" in this representative context is: which antimajoritarian constraints are justified? In that sense, a theory of justice must underlie (at least implicitly) any representative democratic regime: "justice is the end of government [and] of civil society."[24] Since reliance on some theory of justice is unavoidable, further questions must be faced. What standards of justice are taken for granted by citizens of the society under consideration?; What standards are implicit in their customs and mores?; and Is their theory of justice in some sense universal or specific to that society? Given answers to these questions, democracy may be defined as popular majority rule with the caveat that the popular majority wishes only to live in accordance with certain standards of justice. It follows that engineers of representative democratic constitutions must devise political institutions that are likely to be the most expedient for keeping the popular majority just.

Questions about justice seem to have been answered in more or less similar ways by Anglo-American countries having a British common law heritage. More specifically, justice in these countries is generally conceived in terms of fundamental equal rights.[25] Hence, democracy is majority rule limited by these individual rights. Alexis de Tocqueville, for example, evidently saw the U.S. Constitution in this light:

> What is understood by a republican government in the United States is the tranquil rule of the majority. . . . It is a conciliatory government, under which resolutions are allowed time to ripen, and in which they are deliberately discussed, and are executed only when mature. . . . But the majority's power itself is not unlimited. Above it in the moral world are humanity, justice, and reason; and in the political world, vested rights. The majority recognizes these two barriers; and if it now and then oversteps them, it is because, like individuals, it has passions and, like them, it is prone to do what is wrong, while it discerns what is right.[26]

Tocqueville dismissed what he called "a discovery of modern days" that the majority has a right to do whatever it chooses, that is, a right to absolute power or tyranny. "Until our time it had been supposed that despotism was odious, under whatever form [including the popular form] it appeared."[27] He defended the antimajoritarian constraints in the Constitution as "a sort of appeal" to the common sense and moral virtue of the people. Intragovernmental checks help popular majorities control legislative majorities, for example, because presidential veto and judicial review "signal" the people when to evaluate carefully the conduct of their elected legislators. Evidently, these checks presuppose that citizens generally are interested in holding their representatives accountable to standards of prudence and justice. But "there is no country in which *everything* can be provided for by the laws, or in which political institutions can prove a substitute for common sense and public morality."[28]

Tocqueville's assessment of American democracy has been echoed by eminent American political thinkers. Madison, who is still usually held to be the father of the Constitution, defended the original indirectly elected Senate as a check against unjust measures demanded by factious popular majorities:

As the cool and deliberate sense of the community ought in all governments, and actually will in all free governments ultimately prevail over the views of its rulers; so there are particular moments in public affairs, when the people stimulated by some irregular passion, or some illicit advantage, or misled by the artful misrepresentations of interested men, may call for measures which they themselves will afterwards be the most ready to lament and condemn. In these critical moments, [a well constructed Senate may be] salutary . . . to suspend the blow meditated by the people against themselves, until reason, justice and truth, can regain their authority over the public mind.[29]

Thomas Jefferson also spoke of "this sacred principle, that though the will of the majority is in all cases to prevail, that will to be rightful must be reasonable; that the minority possess their equal rights, which equal law must protect, and to violate would be oppression."[30] And Abraham Lincoln held that "a majority held in restraint by constitutional checks and limitations, and always changing easily with deliberate changes of popular opinions and sentiments, is the only true sovereign of a free people."[31]

Nevertheless, despite this common goal of majority rule limited by fundamental individual rights, American democracy differs essentially from the Westminster parliamentary model in the means employed to constrain legislative majorities from violating these rights. Parliamentary regimes rely solely on customary moral constraints: because government itself is sovereign, legislative majorities are legally unlimited. In effect, the popular majority is assumed to delegate legal supremacy to the legislative branch with the caveat that legislative majorities should not violate norms of justice despite possessing legal authority to do so. Unlike the parliamentary regimes, American democracy gives at least some moral constraints the force of constitutional law: the written constitution is sovereign and so legally constrains legislative majorities. In effect, the sovereign constitution is the legal embodiment of a just majority will. In the American perspective, the popular majority divides its sovereignty as follows: (1) rights are reserved permanently to all the people (i.e., individual rights as indicated if not fully enumerated by the Bill of Rights), and (2) political authority is delegated temporarily to various representatives including officers of the different branches and levels of government as well as delegates to special constitutional conventions. The legislative branch at the national level is assigned a share of sovereignty for enumerated purposes and has no legal authority to touch sovereign rights. If the legislature violates enumerated individual rights, for example, then it not only invades an inalienable domain of popular sovereignty but also negates constitutional norms of justice.

III

This American conception of popular sovereignty, in which legal supremacy is vested in a just popular majority assumed to divide and delegate authority to various representatives for limited purposes as enumerated in a written constitution, renders American democracy distinctive.[32] Still, contemporary thinking tends to be sharply critical of American democracy. Even Garry Wills rejects any suggestion that sovereignty can be so divided and assigned. After debunking the conventional portraits of Alexander Hamilton and Madison, he recasts their arguments in *The Federalist* as follows: (1) the Madisonian separation of powers doctrine is merely a criterion of legitimate government ("the right to rule") and is logically distinct from (indeed, at odds with) any intragovernmental system of checks and balances used to maintain separate branches; (2) the national legislature cannot be checked by the other branches and should be supreme in a federal republican government; (3) bicameralism in the legislature is the only check that can possibly maintain a degree of separated powers; (4) even bicameralism will not work if House and Senate members are moved by a joint ambition to push through legislation; (5) the danger of legislative oppression can be removed only by a suitable "refining process" of elections that serves to "distill" impartial and virtuous representatives from the population; so that (6) popular sovereignty is limited in accord with the customary moral virtues of the popular majority.[33] In short: "The distinguishing note of a republic is public virtue, which encourages all to participate in decisions for the common good. . . . The classical zeal for republican virtue [is] . . . at the very heart of *The Federalist*."[34]

By playing down mechanical constitutional constraints on legislative majorities and playing up public virtue in citizens and legislators, Wills offers a constitutional vision that at once sidesteps Dahl's influential critique and forces us to reconsider the relevance of the Framers' plan. If Wills is right, then Dahl is wrong to attribute to the Framers the key psychological hypothesis that leaders are at least sometimes motivated largely by self-interested ambitions to dominate others.[35] The American system really presupposes generally virtuous leaders. Moreover, despite all the rhetoric about constitutional checks and balances, the Framers did not really try to impose legal constraints on leaders. Legal constraint is not necessary to get this virtuous elite to follow the dictates of reason and justice. But if Wills is correct, then Dahl should have saved himself the trouble of his critique in the first place: the notion of a virtuous elected elite might have been appealing in 1787 but it is not relevant today.[36]

I think that Dahl is right to emphasize the weakness of honor and virtue as motives.[37] Both Hamilton and Madison are explicit on this point.[38] Moreover, Wills raises at least three major problems of interpretation by his insistence on the salience of virtue. First contrary to his assertions, balanced bicameralism plus virtue cannot alone maintain any degree of formal separation of powers among the different branches. Presumably, virtuous representatives in a bicameral legislature will display wide agreement in their virtuous intentions, in which case the bicameral check will not even maintain a separation between the House and Senate. Given that this virtuous Congress will surely override executive vetoes and impeach wayward justices, Wills must conclude that all power really inheres in the same group of leaders, the very definition of illegitimate government (that is, tyranny or despotism) for Madison.[39] But if virtuous legislators with absolute power are still despots (albeit benevolent despots), then this suggests that the Framers do not rely on virtue as a predominant motive. Otherwise, why be so concerned about separation of powers as a criterion of legitimate government? By implication, even virtuous despots are not likely to remain virtuous very long: like anyone else in their position, they are likely to be corrupted by their omnipotence.

Second, it is misleading to disparage the executive veto and judicial review because they may not stop the legislative branch altogether. These checks do stop Congressional majorities and can only be overridden by supermajorities. Moreover, Madison does not expect the Senate to contain completely the popular House of Representatives: he takes for granted "the irresistable [sic] force possessed by that branch of a free government, which has the people on its side."[40] The bicameral check itself, in other words, is at best a partial check on the House. The significance of intragovernmental constitutional checks is not that they must paralyze the legislature but that they are fundamental legal as opposed to merely religious or moral constraints on legislative procedures. In effect, these checks are the girders of legal opposition to legislative majorities. In particular, the president and Supreme Court have *legal* weapons to block Congressional majorities, weapons that are not shared by the Loyal Opposition in any parliamentary regime. To the extent that the binding force of religious and moral constraints is enhanced when they are transformed into fundamental law, American legislators will be more disposed to look askance at the conduct of their elected representatives when so opposed. If the average person is not predominantly virtuous but is at least inclined to obey the law, then legal constraints are likely to be more effective than extra-legal constraints. Self-interested persons may well be law-abiding. Suitable legal penalties (including fines and loss of liberty if not life) enforced by means of state coercion will render law-breaking contrary to self-interest. Moreover, any infamy associated with these penalties may further deter ambitious public officials and office-seekers in a democracy.

Finally, it is misleading to claim that popular sovereignty is equivalent to legislative supremacy. Wills, after pointing out that Hamilton's concern in *The Federalist* No. 78 is not to defend judicial review (since nobody really challenged its legitimacy) but rather to deny that judicial review implies judicial supremacy, claims that "Hamilton argues . . . that judicial review demands a theory of legislative supremacy—in the constitution-

making act."[41] "Hamilton does not argue for a *judicial* check on
the legislature."[42] Instead, he argues that "the people's legislative act" (i.e., making a constitution) checks the legislative acts
of their elected representatives. The Court merely gives priority
to the legislative will of the people when voiding statutes at odds
with "the manifest tenor of the constitution." But with all due
respect, this *is* a judicial check on the legislative branch. The
power of judicial review is delegated to the judiciary by the
people for the purpose of keeping the legislative branch within
the limits established by the constitution. The people themselves
do not exercise this check on the legislature; their agents, the
federal judges, do. The judiciary is nevertheless not superior to
the legislature (or vice versa) because the legislature has no
constitutional authority to enact unconstitutional laws in the
first place. Congress is not a sovereign parliament. Instead, the
members of Congress are also merely agents whose delegated
authority extends no further than the making of laws in accord
with ("in pursuance" of) the "manifest tenor" of the Constitution. Moreover, it begs the question to classify the people's
"constitution-making" power as merely legislative, suggesting
that it might somehow devolve entirely upon the national legislature. No single branch of government at any level has final
legal say over the federal constitution. Instead, the constitutional authority to amend the Constitution is sui generis, being
divided among various national and state representatives as per
Article 5. These representatives are jointly authorized to enact
higher laws plainly binding on both Congress and the Supreme
Court. Even then, a new round of constitutional changes is
permitted in the unlikely event that widespread popular unrest
continues to exist over any amendment approved by these national and state representatives. Apart from any extra-constitu-
tional moral right to rebellion, the people themselves permanently retain a share of sovereignty—including their inalienable
First Amendment rights to propose and discuss changes in their
form of government as they see fit—even though the authority
actually to amend the Constitution is delegated at any one time
to the various representatives designated under Article 5.[43]

Wills appears to be under the impression that unless impartial
motives are held to dominate partial ambitions, Dahl's critique

of the U.S. Constitution inexorably follows.[44] But this impression is not warranted. I present my interpretation of American democracy in the next section with particular reference to Dahl's work. His views have changed somewhat since he first published his admirably precise model of "Madisonian democracy" in 1956, and I have tried to allow for these changes where relevant to my analysis. For convenience, my interpretation is summarized in an appendix by means of a set of formal definitions and hypotheses directly comparable to the set comprising Dahl's Madisonian model.[45]

IV

Dahl suggests that democracy in general "poses some fundamental dilemmas" and that American democracy in particular poses additional dilemmas of its own. In his view, any democracy faces hard choices on at least six general fronts: rights-based versus utilitarian theories of justice; criteria for citizenship or membership in the *demos;* equal voting rights for individuals or for organizations; uniformity versus diversity; centralization versus decentralization; and concentration versus dispersion of power and political resources.[46] Given conflict among the members of society with respect to these six issues, democratic constitutional engineers cannot expect to resolve them in some painless ideal manner: "For we live in a world where ideal solutions frequently cannot be found, even at the theoretical level."[47] More specifically, it does not seem possible to prescribe a satisfactory general solution to many jurisdictional issues that commonly arise in a democracy. To hold that the popular majority should invariably prevail in these matters "is easily rebutted by counterexamples." Yet if minorities should invariably prevail whenever they believe their fundamental rights are threatened, then by extension we seem to be driven to anarchism, a dubious principle given the harm that minorities (including minorities of one) might inflict on others (including popular majorities) in the name of rights.[48] No satisfactory general solution seems to be forthcoming. Instead, any democratic regime apparently must develop its own particular solutions to these jurisdictional issues. Moreover, any solution probably has a nonrational component: "a nonrational loyalty to the integrity of a particular historical collectivity . . . [is] probably . . . required if democracy is to exist in the government."[49] Lincoln's ultimate justification for the jurisdictional framework embodied in the U.S. Constitution, for example, "was not a rational principle at all, but rather a primordial attachment." It is not that these primordial loyalties are necessarily incompatible with rational deliberation. But "beyond some point, loyalties are no longer open to rational discussion."[50]

Granted that democracy probably requires a degree of nonrational patriotism, reasonable citizens may nevertheless come to see that their patriotism is attached to a wholly unreasonable object. In particular, Dahl argues that the loyalty felt by Lincoln and other Americans to the Constitution is misplaced and not likely to endure. The reason is that the Constitution embodies an "unreasonable" Madisonian "ideology" rather than rational solutions to America's jurisdictional dilemmas: "Madisonianism, historically and presently, is a [logically and empirically flawed] compromise between . . . two conflicting goals," that is, majority rule and antimajoritarian constraints supposedly designed to protect privileged minorities.[51] Dahl later emphasizes that he "accepts the liberal argument . . . that certain rights are so fundamental to the attainment of human goals, needs, interests, and fulfillment that governments must never be allowed to derogate from them." But he rejects "the American constitutional argument that the . . . unique set of political arrangements embodied in our constitutional and political practices is necessary to preserve these rights."[52] Most recently, he argues that the right of self-government is "one of the most fundamental of all the rights to which human beings are entitled"; that "a set of basic political rights . . . *necessary to* the democratic process . . . can be derived" from this most fundamental right; that property rights are not so fundamental; and that the right of self-government (and derived political rights) should be extended to members of economic enterprises.[53]

The nature of Dahl's preferred solution to jurisdictional dilemmas of democracy is fairly clear. The idea seems to be be that a majority of adult residents should have final control over the public agenda including the degree of autonomy granted to various organizations in the society; and that in many if not all independent political and economic organizations, majority rule should obtain.[54] Jurisdictional disputes among these organizations would ultimately be referred to the popular majority.[55] Like any other representative democratic regime, this involves popular majority rule tempered by some more or less implicit theory of justice. For Dahl, justice entails a fundamental right of self-government (and associated political rights) for all nontransient adults in society; and similar rights of self-government for qualified members of some reasonable plurality of independent organizations. "Self-government" here means majority rule. In effect, a just popular majority will limit its own jurisdiction and delegate some authority to majorities in independent organizations. The latter majorities are, of course, popular minorities. Hence, the regime involves constraints on electoral and legislative majorities to safeguard the basic political rights of these minorities.[56]

This solution to democratic jurisdictional conflicts has powerful appeal as far as it goes. Indeed, defenders of the American constitutional rationale need not object to it.[57] But the solution is incomplete as it stands. The relevant antimajoritarian fetters remain to be specified. But Dahl is not precise. He claims that the Framers of the Constitution "were guilty of overkill" in the sheer volume of constitutional checks placed on legislative majorities. Moreover, he suggests that perhaps the executive veto and bicameralism ought to be abolished and some form of PR introduced. But he never speaks of abolishing judicial review and does not insist on a parliamentary regime. Instead, he merely asserts that "we ought to be able to design a way of preserving fundamental rights that is not so biased in favor of existing privilege and against reform."[58] Yet he also doubts whether Americans can ever be expected to "have the knowledge and skills to excel the performance of the framers."[59]

In my view, Dahl's rejection of American constitutional design is not compelling. A proper model of American democracy (summarized in the appendix) shows why the constitutional scheme has appeal even for those who accept his otherwise incomplete democratic solution to jurisdictional issues. My purpose in what follows is to clarify the appeal of the constitutional arrangements rather than provide a detailed model. Here, it is important to recognize that Madison (like Dahl) warns that "no government of human device and human administration can be perfect." Madison defended the Constitution even though he admitted that its "departure from the rule of equality . . . may be abused in various degrees oppressive to the majority of the people . . . and in modes and degrees so oppressive as to *justify* ultra- or anticonstitutional resorts to adequate relief."[60]

To begin, it is fair to assume that the Constitution seeks to achieve a just representative democracy, that is, majority rule that respects justice. Dahl essentially agrees, although he confuses things by equating justice with nontyranny. For Dahl, "tyranny is every severe deprivation of a natural right."[61] But for Madison, tyranny is "despotic government." He supports Jefferson's remark that "the concentrating [of] . . . all the powers of government, legislative, executive and judiciary, . . . in the same hands is precisely the definition of despotic government."[62] Nontyranny is free government such that "usurpations [of government power by the same group of leaders] are guarded against by a division of the government into distinct and separate departments."[63]

Two aspects of this Madisonian definition of tyranny cannot be overemphasized. First, tyranny is logically unrelated to any particular conception of injustice and, indeed, carries no necessary ethical connotation whatsoever.[64] It might seem odd that despotic government does not necessarily mean unjust government for Madison. But "benevolent" despotism in which a group of leaders holding all government power uses that power to protect the basic rights of their subjects is as logically conceivable as an "oppressive" despotism in which the leaders "severely deprive" the people of their basic rights. Whether tyranny is just or unjust depends on the empirical consequences of a complete fusion of government power in the same hands, and can only be answered on the basis of experience. Similarly, "nontyranny" or "free government" does not necessary mean just government.

Second, the Madisonian definition of tyranny is independent of any particular form of government. For example, a representative democracy without any separation of powers is an "elective despotism." As Madison, again quoting Jefferson, asserts: "It will be no alleviation that these [concentrated] powers will be exercised by a plurality of hands, and not by a single one. . . . As little will it avail us that they are chosen by ourselves."[65] On the other hand, the contemporary British constitutional monarchy (a nonrepublican form of government on Madison's definition of a "republic") is nontyrannical and might even be styled (to use Montesquieu's expression) "the mirrour of political liberty" because it incorporates some separation of powers.[66]

Given that tyranny and injustice are not logically related in the American model, it makes sense to introduce a separate definition of injustice. One possibility is "highly congenial to the whole cast" of Dahl's thought: Injustice consists of violations of basic political rights. Once injustice and tyranny are distinguished in this way, the logical coherence of the American constitutional system is not in doubt: (1) Justice is the end of government (axiom); (2) security of basic political rights is justice (definition); (3) a nontyrannical republican government, that is, a representative democracy exhibiting a degree of separation of powers, is most likely to protect the basic political rights of Americans (empirical generalization); hence, (4) a nontyrannical republican constitution is most desirable for the United States.[67] What might be doubted is whether (3) is supported by historical evidence. In this regard, Madison evidently concludes that tyranny—absolute power in the same group of rulers—is likely to result in injustice: tyrants will probably violate the basic political rights of their subjects. His conclusion holds for representative democracies as well as for non-republican forms of government. Indeed, there is a danger that elected despots might be instructed by popular majority factions to violate the rights of minorities. Elected officials might not desire to act unjustly but do so anyway merely to satisfy their constituents. Thus: "It is of great importance *in a republic,* not only to guard the society against the oppression of its rulers; but to guard one part of the society against the injustice of the other part. . . . If a majority be united by a common interest, the rights of the minority will be insecure."[68]

Madison acutely fears the possibility that an unjust popular majority will easily control any republican government whose

powers are fused in the same group of elected legislators. Surprisingly, Dahl complains that this "acute fear" of majority tyranny suggests a contradiction in American constitutional justification. Surely, he suggests, minority tyranny is "equally
undesirable." But Madison's focus on the danger of majority
tyranny is hardly unreasonable. Popular minorities simply cannot gain control of a unified (i.e., tyrannical) republican government and abuse its power. The majority can always prevent this
by virtue of the "republican principle" of majority voting in
elections. The only fear is that a popular majority will instruct
the omnipotent representatives to act unjustly towards the minority. Thus, Dahl is on very thin ice when he accuses Madison
of inconsistently holding "a highly partisan viewpoint" in favor
of a wealthy minority elite.[69]

Evidence that elected despots will at times violate minority
rights, whether or not instructed to do so by popular majorities,
is derived from two related sources. One is the historical record.
Madison claims, for example, that during the post-revolutionary
decade "a tyrannical concentration of all the powers of government" in state legislatures facilitated unjust legislation including
bills of attainder, ex post facto laws, and laws impairing the
obligation of contract.[70] State constitutions were merely "parchment barriers" against the elected tyrants because few if any
intragovernmental checks maintained separation of powers. Defenders of the Westminster model might retort that modern
parliamentary regimes present counter-examples: unlimited legal authority concentrated in a Cabinet (tyranny in Madison's
sense) need not lead to deprivations of basic rights if the Cabinet respects customary norms.[71] But the parliamentary experience is difficult to interpret one way or the other because absolute concentration of legal power is actually rare. As Lijphart
notes, perfect examples of the Westminster model are not to be
found: some degree of separation of powers inevitably exists
because traditions to that effect are recognized by the Cabinet.[72]
Perhaps Madisonian tyranny is observed nowhere but in the
post-revolutionary experience of the American states. At that
time, extraordinary circumstances combined to produce a situation where "the legislative department is everywhere extending

the sphere of its activity, and drawing all power into its impetuous vortex."[73]

History does suggest, however, that it may be unnecessary to introduce *all* of the intragovernmental checks of the American model to prevent unjust legislation in countries other than the United States. This seems to be Dahl's real point. But it does not affect the logical coherence of the American constitutional argument or cast doubt on its validity for the United States. Perhaps America is or was different in relevant ways from these other countries, particularly with respect to socioeconomic structure and political attitudes such as deference to traditional authority. Perhaps if customary political values begin to lose their hold in parliamentary regimes, then the American constitutional regime will become more applicable to them. Until these difficult questions are settled, the historical record is at best inconclusive.

The other source of evidence for the likelihood of injustice by way of elective despotism is psychological. The Framers did take for granted the salience of self-interested ambition as a motive. But if any individual is driven largely by considerations of self-interest, then he will act unjustly towards others unless restrained by external checks, that is, sanctions applied or threatened by sources other than himself. These sanctions might be derived from at least three sources—the law, religion and public opinion.[74] If society consists of a "variety of interests, parties and sects" over an extended area, then religious beliefs and public opinion might be sufficiently pluralistic at least partially to restrain formation of majority factions. Diversity of beliefs and opinions "makes it less probable that a majority of the whole will have a common motive to invade the rights of other citizens; or if such a common motive exists, it will be more difficult for all who feel it to discover their own strength, and to act in unison with each other."[75] But if majority factions form nevertheless, then their restraint will require legal sanctions. The election system per se can hardly be expected to protect minorities from unjust majorities. The elected representatives of majorities have every incentive to violate the rights of these minorities if this is what the majority wants. Legal restraint of popular majorities is only feasible by way of intragovernmental checks on their representatives. The executive veto, for example, checks a legislative majority instructed by a majority faction: the proposed legislation is nullified so that any individual or group acting on that inclination may be legally penalized. Moreover, even if Dahl and others are correct that pluralistic social checks are sufficient to prevent altogether the formation of cohesive popular majorities, the intragovernmental checks remain necessary at least partially to restrain corrupt government officials, in particular, legislative factions acting without instructions from their constituents.[76] Again, elections are hardly likely to check violations of minority rights by these unjust legislators because there is little reason to expect popular majorities to vote on behalf of the interests of minorities. Elections are at best an imperfect device for controlling corrupt government officials in any event, given the indivisibility of the vote and potential for strategic manipulation of outcomes.[77]

The entire American array of pluralist checks and constitutional constraints can be justified as external checks on self-interested motives. But we must also recognize that the operation of external checks will be halting and imperfect unless individuals are motivated by something in addition to opportunistic self-interest. Law, religion and public opinion will never perfectly control anyone who does not desire to obey the law, please a divine ruler, or sympathize with the goals of other members of his society. In general, external checks must be complemented by "internal checks" on self-interest, that is, sanctions applied by the individual's conscience and feelings of affection for others.[78] And the Framers do admit a role for these moral concerns despite the force of self-interest in human nature.[79] Hamilton refers to "a portion of virtue and honor among mankind, which may be a reasonable foundation of confidence."[80] And Madison says that "republican government presupposes the existence of these qualities in a higher degree than any other form."[81]

American democracy presumes that virtue and honor can be decisive for legislation despite the prevalence of self-interest. The trick is to design a prudent system of external checks that is self-enforcing in the sense that predominantly self-interested persons desire to exert the checks as required. In effect, one person's interest is made to counteract another's so that the basic rights of everyone (including the minority) are secure. Intragovernmental checks show "this policy of supplying by opposite and rival interests, the defect of better motives." The ambition of any official is connected to the constitutional authority of his branch. He evidently desires to defend this authority against usurpations. He will exercise his constitutional powers to prevent whatever he sees as unconstitutional actions of other branches.[82] Similarly, pluralistic social checks promote the same policy. The interest of any individual derives from the various social groups to which he belongs. He will defend his interests. So he will refuse to join any coalition that he thinks intends to act unjustly towards one or another of his associations. Moreover, he will refuse to vote for any candidate purporting to represent this faction. "The rights of individuals or of the minority, will be in little danger from interested combinations of the majority . . . [because] a coalition of the majority of the whole society could seldom take place on any other principles than those of justice and the general good."[83]

Underlying the American scheme is the optimistic assumption that the "dictates of reason and justice" are compatible: by deliberately pitting ambition against ambition (whether through interplay of divided government powers or through competition among social groups), justice can generally be led to triumph over faction. Rational pursuit of self-interest underlies the exercise of social and constitutional checks whose outcome is to keep majority rule from violating basic rights. Nevertheless, it must be reiterated that the scheme is not perfect. For example, it is clear that supermajoritarian factions (popular or legislative) are only partially restrained by the constitutional barriers. If a legislative supermajority overrides a presidential veto to trample on minority rights, the victims may face lengthy judicial proceedings and perhaps ultimately a "packed" Supreme Court. Indeed, as Wills notes, one of Madison's chief objections to the constitutional arrangements is that insufficient power to veto legislation is granted to the executive and judiciary.[84]

It is also clear that intragovernmental checks are liable to abuse.[85] A popular minority faction might successfully lobby the

President to veto just legislation passed by Congress. As a result, this minority prevents the rectification of some existing injustice (in the laws or elsewhere) suffered by the majority. Even in the absence of popular minority factions, a corrupt President or Supreme Court might abuse their veto powers unjustly to prevent reform. These potential sources of injustice are certainly present in the American regime. But as Madison and Dahl both point out, no perfectly just system of government can be humanly designed. Moreover, at least two considerations suggest that the legislature is the most dangerous fount of injustice. First, unjust laws can be enacted only by the legislature. Unfortunately, vetoes might nullify subsequent attempts by the legislature to rectify its mistakes. But these unjust laws are hardly likely to sanction minority privileges, given the power of majorities to elect legislators. Initial passage of unjust laws presupposes unjust legislative majorities if not unjust popular majorities. The very fact that oppressive legislation is on the books testifies to the great need for intragovernmental checks to protect the rights of minorities. Second, and perhaps even more important, legislative majorities can produce injustice by continually changing the laws without necessarily intending to deprive minorities of basic rights. These incessant changes impair property rights and destroy the security of expectations required for commerce. Moreover, as Madison emphasizes, unstable laws also impair the basic political rights of the popular majority: "It will be of little avail to the people that the laws are made by men of their own choice if the laws . . . undergo such incessant changes that no man, who knows what the law is today, can guess what it will be tomorrow."[86] Indeed, this instability gives an unjust advantage to the wealthy minority: "Every new regulation concerning commerce or revenue, or in any manner affecting the value of the different species of property, presents a new harvest to those who watch the change, and can trace the consequences; a harvest reared not by themselves but by the toils and cares of the great body of their fellow citizens. This is a state of things in which it may be said with some truth that laws are made for the *few* not for the *many*."[87] Whether we most fear injustice to the minority or to the majority, prudence recommends constitutional checks like the executive veto and judicial review for their stabilizing influence: "The injury which may possibly be done by defeating a few good laws will be amply compensated by the advantage of preventing a number of bad ones."[88]

V

In brief, my argument is that American democracy is a logically coherent and distinctive conception of just majority rule. Like parliamentary democracies, the American regime takes for granted that reasonable majorities wish to respect certain basic rights held equally by all citizens: "There is a portion of virtue and honor among mankind, which may be a reasonable foundation of confidence."[89] Its distinctiveness lies only in the means employed for attaining this end. Unlike the parliamentary alternatives, it deploys a system of intragovernmental constitutional constraints to supplement traditional political values and pluralistic social checks. In consequence, popular majorities and their elected legislators are prevented by law (not merely by religious values or public opinion) from unjustly depriving people of their basic rights. The antimajoritarian legal constraints are enforced by rational self-interested officials of the other government branches. These officials are not required to display an unusual degree of moral virtue or impartial concern for the general good. Instead, their ambitions are connected to their constitutional powers whose reasonable exercise implies that legislators will be bound by some reasonable interpretation of the basic equal rights of citizens. Therefore, the American rule of law is not left solely to the virtuous characters and honorable opinions of majorities and their legislative representatives. It also is buttressed by prudence and rational self-interest.

American democracy is aptly characterized as a form of deliberative majority rule, with the understanding that deliberative connotes the "mild voice of reason pleading for [justice and] an enlarged and permanent aggregate interest."[90] Madison and Hamilton as well as Tocqueville and Lincoln refer to "the deliberate sense of the community" as something emerging from the antimajoritarian checks embedded in the Constitution. As Joseph Bessette suggests, constitutional "checks on popular inclinations do not violate majority rule properly understood, that is, the rule of the deliberative majority. . . . Such checks are absolutely essential to the formation, expression, and effective political rule of informed and reasoned majority judgements."[91] The constitutional checks enable rational self-interested government officials legally to block the irrational passions of unjust popular and legislative majorities so that "reason, justice and truth" can retain whatever legal standing they already have.[92] Pluralistic social checks might not completely block the formation of popular majority factions and cannot reach legislative factions in any event. "Auxiliary precautions" are required. Thus, even if perfect justice is not to be expected, Madison and his colleagues do not seem to have been arbitrary or confused in their choice of means to promote good government. This is not to say that no better means could have been found. But it is to say that the Constitution is worthy of great respect from popular majorities with the same desire for justice.

In closing, I wish to draw attention to three general issues worthy of further study. If my general conception of American democracy is correct, then we might go on to ask: Does the imperfect U.S. regime have pragmatic appeal in the sense that rational self-interested agents have incentives actually to exercise the constitutional checks as conceived? Does the regime have normative appeal in the sense that its equilibrium outcomes can be shown to satisfy some criteria of justice or aggregate utility-maximization? And should the regime be reformed in major ways? In my view, we still know so remarkably little about the first two issues that strong opinions about the third are premature.

The issue of pragmatic appeal is a complex exercise in game theory. Unfortunately, existence of constitutional equilibria cannot simply be taken for granted. It is not implausible to conjecture that situations can arise where predominantly self-interested leaders will waive rather than exercise their constitutional rights in order to yield an equilibrium outcome. For example, government officials of all three branches might choose simultaneously to waive their constitutional powers so as to generate unjust cooperative outcomes. If self-interested agents do not have incentives to follow the constitutional rules, then this sort of collusion can be expected and the constitutional system will simply not work as planned.[93]

The normative appeal of the Constitution is contestable even if rational self-interest is generally compatible with the constitutional machinery. As Dahl points out, conflicting theories of justice plague the engineers of any democratic regime and the U.S. Constitution can be no exception. In particular, modern commentators are fond of emphasizing an irreconcilable gulf between utilitarian and rights-based theories of justice: "justification based only on utilitarian considerations . . . will . . . clash with claims . . . justified by appeals to fundamental rights."[94] There is little doubt that the Framers conceived of justice in terms of fundamental moral rights even if explicit reference to "natural rights" seems to have been studiously avoided by the authors of *The Federalist*.[95] But plenty of evidence also exists that some sort of proto-utilitarian theory of justice was afoot. As Martin Diamond suggests, Madison used "the happiness of the people" interchangeably with "justice" to describe the goal of republican government: "A good government implies two things: first, fidelity to the object of government, which is the happiness of the people; secondly, a knowledge of the means by which that object can be best obtained."[96] Madison apparently saw no necessary schism between utility and rights because for him " 'Ultimate happiness' . . . is qualified with every necessary moral ingredient."[97] Unfortunately, it is not entirely clear what is meant by ultimate happiness so that this ethical basis for the Constitution remains problematic.[98]

Finally, the issue of fundamental constitutional reform cannot properly be addressed until more precise answers to the pragmatic and normative puzzles are forthcoming. But it is worth repeating that the Framers have no illusions that the Constitution is a perfectly just republican regime. Some injustice is inevitable given human nature. Madison clearly believed that the American regime is not even a second-best representative democracy, being in part the product of a pragmatic compromise.[99] In his view, judicial review as exercised under the current arrangements is an imprudent constitutional check. On the one hand, Congress has no opportunity prior to enactment to override the Court's interpretation of legislation and instead must wait until the Court decides some relevant case at an indefinite date after enactment. This permits the Court arbitrarily to revise the express constitutional intentions of the legislature on a case by case basis, thereby impairing the stability of reasonable laws. Congress ultimately has no recourse except impeachment, a crude and unwieldy weapon of uncertain consequence. On the other hand, victims of unjust legislation contrary to the "manifest tenor" of the Constitution are also forced to wait for a relevant Court decision, perhaps rendered long after the legislation. As Wills calls to our attention, Madison consistently argued for a stronger veto on proposed legislation thought to be unconstitutional by the judiciary and/or the executive.[100]

This Madisonian idea that some expert body should be empowered to review and if necessary thwart the will of elected legislators, is anathema to many modern democrats. But the idea is not so easily dismissed by defenders of limited government, and comes in many guises. Indeed, John Stúart Mill's proposal to establish a permanent Commission with sole legal authority actually to *draft* legislation, has the same practical effect of injecting competence, authority, and stability into a liberal democratic regime.[101] Each member of the Commission is appointed for a fixed renewable term and is excluded from political office. In this way, the legislature is prudently confined (as was the Roman assembly) to its proper functions of deliberation and enactment. Legislators retain authority to deliberate over a representative sample of conflicting opinions on any public issue; and to enact or reject (without power to amend) bills drafted by a professional civil service. Mill's Commission (suitably revised) could be a valuable addition to the American regime.[102] For example, the Constitution could be amended to create what amounts to a professional Cabinet, appointed for a renewable term (say, seven years) in more or less the current manner involving executive nomination and Senate confirmation. Cabinet members would have sole authority (perhaps with the advice of the Supreme Court) to draft bills concerning any public matter (including the budget) as requested by a Congressional majority or (if the president vetoes the request) by a Congressional supermajority. But neither Congress nor the president would have any power to alter proposed legislation. Congress would retain the power to enact or reject whole proposals yet (like the president) would essentially be forced to accept the permanent Cabinet's budgetary proposals. Once a constitutional amendment of this sort is in place, some additional changes, including a unicameral legislature and some form of proportional representation (as suggested by Dahl, among others), might make a lot of sense.[103]

APPENDIX: THE AMERICAN MODEL OF DEMOCRACY
(for comparison with Dahl's "Madisonian" model in *A Preface to Democratic Theory*, 32–33)

I. The basic definitions:

Definition 1. A republic or representative democracy is a government that (a) derives all of its powers directly or indirectly from the great body of the people, and (b) is administered by persons holding their office during pleasure, for a limited period, or during good behavior.

Definition 2A. An "external check" for any individual consists of sanctions (legal, religious or social) or the expectation of same, applied by some agent other than the given individual.

Definition 2B. An "internal check" for any individual consists of sanctions applied by his own conscience and feelings of affection for other persons.

Definition 3. A faction is "a number of citizens, whether amounting to a majority or a minority of the whole, who are united and actuated by some common impulse of passion, or of interest, adverse to the rights of other citizens, or to the permanent and aggregate interests of the community."

Definition 4. Tyranny is despotic government or, what is the same thing, the complete concentration of all powers, legislative, executive, and judiciary, in the same group of leaders.

Definition 5. Injustice consists of violations of basic moral rights, for example, basic political rights.

II. The basic axiom: The goal that ought to be attained, at least in the United States, is a just representative democracy.

III. The argument:

Hypothesis 1. If unrestrained by external checks, any given individual or group of individuals will act unjustly towards others.

Hypothesis 1A. If unrestrained by external checks, a minority of individuals will act unjustly towards a majority of individuals.

Hypothesis 1B. If unrestrained by external checks, a majority of individuals will act unjustly towards a minority of individuals.

Hypothesis 2. At least two conditions are necessary for any republican government to act within limits of justice:

First Condition. The accumulation of all powers, legislative, executive, and judiciary, in the same hands, whether of one, a few, or many, and whether hereditary, self-appointed, or elective, must be avoided.

Second Condition. Factions must be so controlled that they do not succeed in acting adversely to the rights of other citizens or to the permanent and aggregate interests of the community.

Hypothesis 3. Frequent popular elections will not provide an external check sufficient to prevent injustice by popular factions and their legislative representatives.

Hypothesis 4. If factions are to be controlled and injustice is to be avoided, this must be attained by controlling the effects of faction.

Hypothesis 5. If a popular faction consists of a minority of private citizens, then it can be controlled by "the republican principle" of majority rule in the legislature even if all government powers are completely fused in a unicameral legislature (in which case a tyrannical republic exists).

Hypothesis 6. If a popular faction consists of a majority of private citizens, then it cannot be controlled if a tyrannical republic exists. The popular majority faction will act unopposed through its elected representatives to commit injustice against the popular minority.

Hypothesis 7. The development of popular majority factions can be limited if the electorate is numerous, extended, and diverse in interests.

Hypothesis 8. To the extent that the electorate is numerous, extended, and diverse in interests, a majority faction is less likely to exist, and if it does exist, it is less likely to act as a unity.

Hypothesis 9. If a popular majority faction exists, then its legislative representatives can be controlled by suitable intragovernmental checks giving rise to separation of powers and bicameralism. More specifically,

   a. a legislative faction consisting of a minority of elected representatives in either house can be controlled by the "republican principle" of majority voting in that house;

   b. a legislative faction consisting of a majority of elected representatives in one house can be controlled by a contrary majority in the other house;

   c. a legislative faction consisting of at least a majority but less than two-thirds of elected representatives in both houses of the legislature can be controlled by the Presidential veto;

   d. a two-house legislative majority faction in combination with the President can be controlled by judicial review; and

   e. a legislative faction consisting of a two-thirds majority of elected representatives in both houses ultimately cannot be controlled unless the Supreme Court continues to follow precedent despite repeated impeachments of justices.

Hypothesis 10. A factious President or Supreme Court majority can be controlled by a two-thirds majority of both houses of Congress, that is, this supermajority of both House and Senate can override the executive veto or impeach corrupt officials including the President and justices.

NOTES

1. Robert Dahl, *Dilemmas of Pluralist Democracy: Autonomy vs. Control* (New Haven: Yale University Press, 1982), 190.

2. The fact that the electoral college might select a president opposed by an electoral majority underlies proposals to further democratize the presidential selection procedure. Theodore Lowi argues that the Framers of the Constitution probably intended to establish a quasi-parliamentary procedure: a House majority (each state delegation having a single vote) would usually select the president because the electoral college was not expected to determine winning candidates very often. For discussion of the Framers' intent, evolution of the selection procedure, and proposals for reform, see James Ceaser, *Presidential Selection: Theory and Development* (Princeton: Princeton University Press, 1979); James Ceaser, *Reforming the Reforms: A Critical Analysis of the Presidential Selection Process* (Cambridge: Ballinger, 1982); and Theodore Lowi, "Constitution, Government and Politics," in *Before Nomination*, ed. George Grassmuck, (Washington, D.C.: American Enterprise Institute, 1985), 9–23.

3. Under the current method of direct election, further problems arise given that state representation in the Senate is not apportioned to state population size. Thus, Senators from different states represent electoral majorities of very different sizes, with the implication that the weight of a person's vote depends on his geographical location. For a particularly useful analysis of apportionment problems in the context of the House of Representatives, see Michael Balinski and H. Peyton Young, *Fair Representation: Meeting the Ideal of One Man One Vote* (New Haven: Yale University Press, 1982).

4. In my view, it is absurd to pretend that the power of judicial review is not built into the U.S. constitutional system. This power is necessary for the judicial branch to remain immune to any degree from the authority of Congress or the president. As Hamilton remarks in *The Federalist* No. 81, 543: "The constitution ought to be the standard of construction for the laws, and . . . wherever there is an evident opposition, the laws ought to give place to the constitution. . . . This doctrine [of judicial review] is . . . deducible . . . from the general theory of a limited constitution." This reference and all subsequent references to *The Federalist* are taken from Jacob E. Cooke, ed., *The Federalist* (Middletown, Conn.: Wesleyan University Press, 1961).

5. The weight of precedent is emphasized by all but the most "liberal" or "radical" theorists of judicial review. For an introduction to the

debate over what comprises an appropriate theory of judicial review in the American context, see, for example, Ronald Dworkin, *Law's Empire* (Cambridge: The Belknap Press of Harvard University, 1986); John Hart Ely, *Democracy and Distrust: A Theory of Judicial Review* (Cambridge: Harvard University Press, 1980); and Walter F. Murphy, James E. Fleming and William F. Harris III, *American Constitutional Interpretation* (Mineola, N.Y.: Foundation Press, 1986).

6. In principle, Congress is delegated authority to enact legislation only with respect to objects enumerated in the Constitution. For objects not so enumerated, legislative authority (if not prohibited altogether) is reserved to the states under the 10th Amendment. In practice, however, this intergovernmental check on Congress has become less and less visible (it may now have almost vanished) as the Court has generally adopted a very broad reading of the authority granted to Congress (including the power delegated under the "necessary and proper clause" of art. 1, sec. 8). For discussion, see Murphy, et al., *American Constitutional Interpretation*, 255–84, 397–470. Some commentators suggest that this more or less complete supremacy of the central government vis-à-vis the state governments, was intended by the Framers, including Madison. But contrast *The Federalist* No. 39; and Madison, "Notes on Nullification 1835–1836," reprinted in *The Mind of the Founder: Sources of the Political Thought of James Madison,* ed. Marvin Meyers, rev. ed. (Hanover: University Press of New England, 1981), 417–42.

7. The extraordinary amendment procedure makes clear that popular sovereignty is not delegated entirely to Congress or indeed any single branch of government at either the national or state level. I return to this point later.

8. These "conservative" writers include traditional conservatives as well as more radical libertarians devoted to a free market capitalistic economy. For the traditional argument that existing constitutional constraints promote deliberation in democratic decision making, see Martin Diamond, "Democracy and The Federalist: A Reconsideration of the Framers' Intent," *American Political Science Review* 53 (1959): 52–68; Martin Diamond, "Conservatives, Liberals and the Constitution," in *Left, Right and Center: Essays on Liberalism and Conservatism in the United States,* ed. Robert A. Goldwin (Chicago: Rand-McNally, 1968), 60–86; George Carey, "Separation of Powers and the Madisonian Model: A Reply to the Critics," *American Political Science Review* 72 (1978): 151–64; and Joseph M. Bessette, "Deliberative Democracy: The Majority Principle in Republican Government," in *How Democratic is the Constitution?,* ed. Robert A. Goldwin and William A. Schambra (Washington,

D.C.: American Enterprise Institute, 1980), 102–116. For the libertarian or contractarian argument that unconstrained legislators are inevitably corrupted by their power, see James Buchanan, *The Limits of Liberty: Between Anarchy and Leviathan* (Chicago: University of Chicago Press, 1975); Geoffrey Brennan and James Buchanan, *The Reason of Rules: Constitutional Political Economy* (Cambridge: Cambridge University Press, 1985); Dwight R. Lee and Richard B. McKenzie, *Regulating Government: A Preface to Constitutional Economics* (Lexington, Mass.: Lexington Books, 1987); and Vincent Ostrom, *The Political Theory of a Compound Republic: Designing the American Experiment,* 2d ed. (Lincoln: University of Nebraska Press, 1987).

9. Lee and McKenzie, *Regulating Government,* 8, 31.

10. These "liberal" writers are a diverse assortment of political and social reformers including Anglophiles, populists, socialists, and advocates of a strong party system. Even the original anti-Federalist opponents of the Constitution might be termed "liberals" in this loose sense. For an indication of the assortment of views, see Herbert J. Storing and Murray Dry, eds., *The Anti-Federalist: Writings by Opponents of the Constitution* (Chicago: University of Chicago Press, 1985); Gordon S. Wood, *The Creation of the American Republic 1776–1787* (New York: Norton, 1969); Woodrow Wilson, *Congressional Government* (Baltimore: Johns Hopkins University Press, 1885); James Bryce, *The American Commonwealth,* 3 vols. (London: Macmillan, 1888); James Allen Smith, *The Spirit of American Government* (New York: Macmillan, 1907); Charles Beard, *An Economic Interpretation of the Constitution of the United States* (London: Macmillan, 1913); E. E. Schattschneider, *Party Government* (New York: Farrar and Rinehart, 1942); James MacGregor Burns, *The Deadlock of Democracy* (Englewood Cliffs, N.J.: Prentice-Hall, 1963); Burns, *The Power to Lead* (New York: Harper & Row, 1984); Charles M. Hardin, *Presidential Power and Accountability: Toward a New Constitution* (Chicago: University of Chicago Press, 1974); Donald L. Robinson, ed., *Reforming American Government* (Boulder: Westview Press, 1985); and James L. Sundquist, *Constitutional Reform and Effective Government* (Washington, D.C.: Brookings Institution, 1986).

11. Robert Dahl, "On Removing Certain Impediments to Democracy in the United States," in *Democracy, Liberty and Equality,* ed. Robert Dahl (Oslo: Norwegian University Press, 1986), p. 133.

12. Dahl, "On Removing Certain Impediments," 149. See also Robert Dahl, *Dilemmas,* 166–205; and Robert Dahl, *A Preface to Economic Democracy* (Berkeley: University of California Press, 1985). For recent discussions of democratic approaches to governance structures in American economic enterprises, see Lester C. Thurow, *The Zero-Sum*

Solution: Building a World Class American Economy (New York: Simon & Schuster, 1985), esp. 135–82; and Warren J. Samuels and Arthur S. Miller, eds., *Corporations and Society: Power and Responsibility* (Westport, Conn.: Greenwood Press, 1987). For a contrasting view, see Oliver E. Williamson, *The Economic Institutions of Capitalism* (New York: Free Press, 1985).

13. Bryce, *The American Commonwealth*, vol. 1, 407.

14. Dahl, *Dilemmas*, 89.

15. Arend Lijphart, *Democracies: Patterns of Majoritarian and Consensus Government in Twenty-One Countries* (New Haven: Yale University Press, 1984), 3.

16. Ibid., 3–4; see also 209.

17. Ibid., esp. 211–22. With some exceptions, majoritarian elements tend to be found in more homogeneous societies with British cultural heritage and relatively small population size, whereas consensual elements tend to be found in more pluralistic societies with relatively large population size and no British cultural heritage.

18. Ibid., 32–36, 216, 219.

19. Ibid., 219.

20. For Lijphart's treatment of the relevant variables (labelled "executive dominance" and "constitutional flexibility"), see Ibid., 212–15. In essence, presidential veto gets buried in the two-party system variable whereas active judicial review is captured by the federalism variable; see Ibid., 67–89, 187–96.

21. Ibid., 209.

22. Dahl, for example, recommends PR. On various systems of PR, see Vernon Bogdanor, *What Is Proportional Representation?* (Oxford: Martin Robertson, 1984).

23. Lijphart, 219–20. The Canadian parliamentary system, for example, exhibits a formal fusion of powers in the national Cabinet, together with a highly asymmetric bicameralism in favor of the House of Commons.

24. Cooke, ed., *The Federalist* No. 51, 352.

25. In my view, the most illuminating discussion of this point is still J. S. Mill, *Utilitarianism* [1861], in *Collected Works of J. S. Mill*, vol. 10, J. M. Robson, gen. ed. (Toronto: University of Toronto Press, 1969), 240–48. See also Bernard Schwartz, *The Great Rights of Mankind: A History of the American Bill of Rights* (Oxford: Oxford University Press, 1977). Bryce goes so far as to claim that Americans are able to transcend their flawed constitutions only because American customs and mores are imbued with a British respect for common law. See Abraham S. Eisenstadt, "Bryce's America and Tocqueville's," in *Reconsidering*

302   JONATHAN RILEY

Tocqueville's Democracy in America, ed. Abraham S. Eisenstadt (New Brunswick: Rutgers University Press, 1988), 229–73, 303–9.

26. Alexis de Tocqueville, *Democracy in America,* vol. 1, ed. Phillips Bradley (New York: Vintage, 1945), 433–34.

27. Ibid., 434.

28. Ibid., 127 (emphasis added). For a more general discussion, see 116–79, 264–342.

29. Cooke, ed., *The Federalist* No. 63, 425. See also Madison's letter of October 5, 1786, to James Monroe, reprinted in *The Papers of James Madison,* vol. 9, ed. Robert A. Rutland and William M. E. Rachal (Chicago: University of Chicago Press, 1975), 141; and his draft letter of 1833 on "Majority Governments," in *The Mind of the Founder,* ed. Meyers, 408–417.

30. Jefferson, "First Inaugural Address," in *Thomas Jefferson: Writings,* ed. Merrill D. Peterson (New York: Library of America, 1984), 492–93.

31. Abraham Lincoln, "First Inaugural Address," in *Complete Works of Abraham Lincoln,* vol. 6, ed. John G. Nicolay and John Hay, Bibliographical ed. (New York: Tandy, 1905), 179.

32. For a provocative discussion of this point, see Edmund S. Morgan, *Inventing the People: The Rise of Popular Sovereignty in England and America* (New York: Norton, 1988).

33. Garry Wills, *Explaining America: The Federalist* (London: Athlone, 1981), esp. 108–247. Wills acknowledges his debt to Douglass Adair's work. The latter is largely collected in *Fame and the Founding Fathers,* ed. Trevor Colbourn (New York: Norton, 1974).

34. Wills, *Explaining America,* 20, 193; see also 179–92.

35. Almost all commentators agree with Dahl on this point. Wills traces the controversy between Dahl and himself to an apparent conflict between Hume and Hobbes or Locke: "Hume rejected the theories of 'Hobbes and Locke, who maintained the selfish system of morals' " (Wills, *Explaining America,* 191). Morton White interprets *The Federalist* as an uneasy compromise between Locke's rationalism in ethics and Hume's empiricism in political science. According to his interpretation, the Framers infer from observation that self-interest predominates over moral virtue as a motive for any "ordinary" individual. But the reverse holds for "speculative" individuals like themselves because they habitually act in accord with certain self-evident moral beliefs deduced from "the God-created essence of ideal man." This suggests rule by a Lockean virtuous elite. But the details of Locke's philosophical psychology and how it differs from Hume's are (perhaps necessarily) left murky by both Wills and White. Thomas Pangle argues that the differ-

ences between Locke and Hume have been exaggerated in the literature. See Morton White, *Philosophy, The Federalist and the Constitution* (New York: Oxford University Press, 1987); and Thomas Pangle, *The Spirit of Modern Republicanism* (Chicago: University of Chicago Press, 1988).

36. Wills recognizes this point; see *Explaining America*, 265–70.

37. Dahl is willing to admit a significant role for virtue here provided it does not completely negate the need for constitutional checks. Dahl, *A Preface to Democratic Theory* (Chicago: University of Chicago Press, 1956), 5–8, 17–22.

38. Madison says in *The Federalist* No. 10, 61: "If [passion or interest] and opportunity be suffered to coincide, we well know that neither moral nor religious motives can be relied on as an adequate control." See also Cooke, ed. *The Federalist* No. 15, 96; and No. 51, 349.

39. Ibid. No. 47, 324.

40. Ibid. No. 58, 394–96; and No. 63, 430–31.

41. Wills, *Explaining America*, 135.

42. Ibid. 133.

43. If a constitutional amendment to, say, repeal the First Amendment is ever proposed and ratified, then the various representatives designated under Article 5 will have legally but unjustly deprived the people of some of their inalienable rights. The only recourse in this unlikely situation is revolution.

44. Wills, *Explaining America*, xiv–xxii, 121–25, 187–92, 208–215, 224.

45. Dahl, *A Preface to Democratic Theory*, 4–33. I do not adopt Dahl's phrase "Madisonian democracy" because Madison clearly regards the Constitution as a second-best or even third-best compromise rather than a first-best political system. I return to this point later.

46. Dahl, *Dilemmas*, 96–107.

47. Ibid., 168.

48. Ibid., 85–96, 166–70.

49. Ibid., 96.

50. Ibid., 95–96.

51. Dahl, *A Preface to Democratic Theory*, 31.

52. Dahl, "On Removing Certain Impediments," 132.

53. Dahl, *A Preface to Economic Democracy*, esp. 20–26, 82–83, 161–63.

54. See Dahl, "On Removing Certain Impediments," 139–52; Robert Dahl, "Procedural Democracy," in *Democracy, Liberty and Equality* (Oslo: Norwegian University Press, 1986), 191–225; Dahl, *Dilemmas of*

Pluralist Democracy, 166–205; Dahl, *A Preface to Economic Democracy,* 52–163.

55. Dahl suggests that jurisdictional disputes between these organizations will tend to be mitigated by the introduction of internal majoritarian procedures. See, for example, Dahl, *A Preface to Economic Democracy,* 107–110, 136–60.

56. Dahl's approach is compatible with basic nonpolitical rights such as a right to freedom of religious belief and a right to freedom of personal way of life, although he ignores them. These latter rights can be derived from a fundamental right of self-government for any individual in his purely private concerns. "Self-government" here means individual liberty as opposed to majority rule. By ignoring violations of these rights, Dahl may miss much of the point of Tocqueville's fear of majority oppression in mass democracies such as the United States. See Mill, "On Liberty" [1859], in *Collected Works of J. S. Mill,* ed. J. M. Robson, vol. 18 (Toronto: University of Toronto Press, 1977), 213–310.

57. Dahl's approach is not compatible with capitalism, in my view, because members of his self-governing economic enterprises have equal votes independent of their individual capital contributions and cannot alienate their voting rights. But the American constitutional argument per se does not logically commit its defenders to capitalism anyway.

58. Dahl, "On Removing Certain Impediments," 134; see also Dahl, *Dilemmas of Pluralist Democracy,* 190–93.

59. "On Removing Certain Impediments," 149–50.

60. Madison, "Majority Governments," 416.

61. Dahl, *A Preface to Democratic Theory,* 52; see also Dahl, *A Preface to Economic Democracy,* 14–22.

62. Cooke, ed., *The Federalist* No. 48, 335.

63. Ibid. No. 51, 351.

64. James Fishkin proposes to modify Dahl's definition such that tyranny is the destruction of anyone's "essential interests" when this destruction could have been avoided by some alternative government policy. This tyranny is not necessarily involved in tragic situations where someone's essential interests (or basic rights) must be violated no matter what policy is chosen. But Fishkin's definition (like Dahl's) is a definition of injustice, not tyranny in Madison's sense. The development of a fully adequate theory of justice is notoriously difficult. But it is not Madison's concern in the present context. See James Fishkin, *Tyranny and Legitimacy: A Critique of Political Theories* (Baltimore: Johns Hopkins University Press, 1979).

65. Cooke, ed., *The Federalist* No. 48, 335.

66. Ibid. No. 47, 324–27. Wills argues that both Madison and Hamilton display general reverence (derived from Hume) for the British constitution. See Wills, *Explaining America*, 34–45, 79–93.

67. Compare Dahl, *Preface to Democratic Theory*, 10–11.

68. Cooke, ed., *The Federalist* No. 51, 351.

69. Dahl, *Preface to Democratic Theory*, 8–10, 27–32.

70. Cooke, ed., *The Federalist* No. 44, 300–2; 48, 332–38. He specifically cites Virginia and Pennsylvania.

71. See, for example, Dahl, *A Preface to Democratic Theory*, 13; and Dahl, *A Preface to Economic Democracy*, 7–51. Contrast William Riker, *LIberalism Against Populism* (San Francisco: W. H. Freeman, 1982), 247–53.

72. See Lijphart, *Democracies*, 1–20, 46–105; and William Gwyn, "Separation of Powers and Modern Forms of Democratic Government," in *Separation of Powers: Does it Still Work?*, ed. Robert A. Goldwin and Art Kaufman (Washington, D.C.: American Enterprise Institute, 1986), 65–89. Madison argues that the British parliamentary regime of his day exhibits separation of powers (Cooke, ed., *The Federalist* No. 47, 324–27).

73. Cooke, ed., *The Federalist* No. 48, 333.

74. See, for example, Jeremy Bentham, *Principles of Morals and Legislation*, in *The Works of Jeremy Bentham*, vol. 1, ed. John Bowring (Edinburgh: Tait, 1843), 14–15.

75. Cooke, ed., *The Federalist* No. 10, 64; see also No. 51, 351–53.

76. For development of this argument, see especially Carey, "Separation of Powers and the Madisonian Model." Unfortunately, Carey follows Dahl in conflating tyranny with injustice.

77. See Riker, *Liberalism Against Populism*.

78. Dahl himself suggests that the distinction between external and internal may be problematic; see *Preface to Democratic Theory*, 19–22; "Impediments," 150–52; and *Dilemmas*, 138–65.

79. Dahl is correct, however, to emphasize the relative weakness of these impartial motives. His own relative weighting of motives seems roughly similar; see "On Removing Certain Impediments," 150–52; and *Dilemmas*, 138–65.

80. Cooke, ed., *The Federalist* No. 76, 513–14.

81. Ibid. No. 55, 378.

82. Ibid. No. 51, 349.

83. Ibid. No. 51, 351–53.

84. Wills, *Explaining America*, 151–55.

85. Dahl emphasizes this point in *Preface to Democratic Theory*, 27–29.

86. Cooke, ed., *The Federalist* No. 62, 421.

87. Ibid.

88. Ibid. No. 73, 496.

89. Ibid. No. 76, 514.

90. Ibid. No. 42, 283.

91. Bessette, "Deliberative Democracy," 106. John Chapman argues that a "theory of the deliberative state" is central to Rousseau's political doctrine and, more generally, modern liberalism, See John Chapman, *Rousseau—Totalitarian or Liberal?* (New York: Columbia University Press, 1956), esp. 124–44.

92. Wills attacks conservative and liberal versions of this argument, the former holding that delay per se is good, the latter that delay is good as a means for promoting some sort of compromise among competing interests. As he suggests, the real goal is justice, that is, impartial legislation that does not violate basic moral rights due equally to everyone. Nevertheless, the attainment of justice does presuppose legislative delay and deliberation given the existence of legislative majority factions. See Wills, *Explaining America*, 193–216.

93. Despite this possibility, some preliminary work indicates that the constitutional structure may have pragmatic appeal. See Thomas H. Hammond and Gary J. Miller, "The Core of the Constitution," *American Political Science Review* 81 (1987): 1155–1174. As these authors note (p. 1156), there is a serious need for further study in this area.

94. Dahl, *Dilemmas,* 168; see also 96–97. As Dahl notes, there is a vast inconclusive literature on this theme of rights versus utility.

95. On the general point, see, for example, White, *Philosophy, The Federalist, and the Constitution;* on the absence of natural rights language in *The Federalist,* see Constant N. Stockton, "Are There Natural Rights in The Federalist?," *Ethics* 82 (1971–1972): 72–82.

96. Cooke, ed., *The Federalist* No. 62, 419, quoted by Diamond, "Democracy and The Federalist," 63. See also Cooke, ed., *The Federalist* No. 37, 232; No. 40, 260, 267; No. 41, 269; No. 43, 297–98; No. 45, 309; and No. 63, 424.

97. Letter to Monroe in *Papers of James Madison,* vol. 9, ed. Rutland and Rachel, 141.

98. David Epstein emphasizes that the republican end of public happiness is distinct from the liberal goal of justice in the sense of secure "private rights"; and that justice is the more fundamental end if the two come into conflict. See David Epstein, *The Political Theory of the Federalist* (Chicago: University of Chicago Press, 1984), esp. 60–66, 162–66. I have shown elsewhere in the context of J. S. Mill's thought that there is no necessary contradiction between these two ends given a

suitable conception of "ultimate happiness." See Jonathan Riley, *Liberal Utilitarianism* (Cambridge: Cambridge University Press, 1988). The extent to which Hume or Madison may be interpreted to anticipate J.S. Mill's ethics is, of course, a separate matter.

99. On the latter point, see Calvin C. Jillson, *Constitutionmaking: Conflict and Consensus in the Federal Convention of 1787* (New York: Agathon Press, 1988).

100. Wills, *Explaining America*, 151–55.

101. J. S. Mill, *Considerations on Representative Government* [1861], in *Collected Works,* vol. 19, Robson, gen. ed., 422–34.

102. Woodrow Wilson, in *Congressional Government,* argued that some form of Commission of Legislation in Mill's sense is essential to modern democratic government; and defended the British cabinet structure as being superior to the Congressional committee structure in that respect.

103. Mill agrees with Dahl here. See J. S. Mill, *Considerations,* esp. 435–66, 513–19. In my view, the *Considerations* is a particularly useful companion to *The Federalist.*

12

"YES, BUT . . .":
PRINCIPLES AND CAVEATS
IN AMERICAN RACIAL ATTITUDES

JENNIFER L. HOCHSCHILD
and MONICA HERK

Analysts of Americans' racial attitudes agree on four points. Whereas a majority of whites expressed overt racism in the 1950s, only a small minority do in the 1980s. Whereas a minority of whites supported the principles of racial equality and racial integration in the 1950s, a large majority do in the 1980s. White endorsement of specific means for implementing those principles still varies tremendously. Finally, blacks have become increasingly pessimistic during the past three decades about ending racial prejudice and discrimination, and blacks see much more persistent white racism than whites do.

Beyond these points of agreement, controversy rages. Some analysts, mostly black, argue that prejudice has declined little and discrimination hardly at all.[1] Others see old-fashioned biological racism declining, but new forms of prejudice rising in its place. Attempts to describe these new forms of prejudice evoke academic war among exponents of symbolic racism, group conflict, self-interest, or stratification beliefs.[2] Debates over whether education reduces racism or merely increases ideological sophistication and sophistry occupy a slightly different battleground. Still others change the subject, claiming that the issue is not race at all, but the federal government's or courts' illegitimate intervention in local or private choices. Scholars disagree on whether (especially well-off) blacks' increased sensitivity to discrimination is an accurate perception or merely an emotional response to uncertainty, guilt over those left behind, or a result of ever-rising expectations.

In this chapter we choose "not to have a dog in that fight," as a wise dissertation advisor once urged. We believe that, except for the claim that overt racism has not declined, all of these views are partly right. Certainly none lacks eloquent defenders flanked with powerful evidence.

We are persuaded that endless disputes over the nature and correlates of changing racial attitudes are miscast. The important question is not "Does symbolic racism explain whites' racial attitudes better than group conflict?" or "Which people are most prone to symbolic racism (or group conflict)?," but "What is implied by the fact that white Americans increasingly accept racial equality and integration in principle, but disagree with each other, with black Americans, and sometimes with themselves, on how to implement those principles?" If the question is unwieldy, it simply reflects the unwieldy, even byzantine, nature of American racial attitudes.

In short, it is the very variety of white Americans' racial attitudes, the very absence of an overarching explanation for the extent and content of hesitation about racial policies that is the issue to be examined. More precisely: most whites now say "yes" to racial equality and integration, then add some sort of "but . . ." to their affirmation. It is that phalanx of "but . . . s" that blacks see when they decry white racial hypocrisy, and it is the combination of "yes" and "but" that makes American racial politics so difficult to negotiate.

If we are right, the implications of this view for social scientists and philosophers reach past American race relations. Our argument suggests the need to move beyond aggregating data about individuals to considering the collective impact of different, even contradictory, views. More particularly, it suggests to social scientists a way to use survey research to raise, if not resolve, issues of social structure and policy choice. It also suggests to philosophers ways to think about shifting the unit of analysis from individuals to collectivities without running into the classic problems of methodological reductionism and functionalism.

Our analysis has three parts. We first examine whites' waning racism and flourishing array of caveats to their affirmation of racial equality. We next examine blacks' views, including their responses to waning racism and flourishing caveats. Finally, we comment on the theoretical, normative and political implications of this new view of American racial attitudes.

White Racial Attitudes

We begin with a caveat of our own. For many reasons,[3] surveys are not the precise instruments for capturing variations and changes in public opinion that we sometimes pretend they are. We are working, not with a high resolution motion picture, but with a pile of fuzzy snapshots of different depths and ranges.

Even given the caveat, the first three conclusions cited at the beginning of this chapter are reasonably noncontroversial. First, dramatically fewer whites now express anti-black attitudes than did the previous generation. In 1942, 47 percent of those with an opinion agreed that blacks are just as intelligent as whites; by 1968, 77 percent did. In 1963, two-thirds saw blacks as less ambitious than "most other people"; by 1985, only one-quarter did (along with one-fifth of blacks). The proportion favoring segregation (over "desegregation" or "something in between") declined from 25 percent in 1964 to 5 percent in 1978.[4]

Second, along with decreasing overt racism has come rising white support for the principles of racial equality and integration. In 1964, 53 percent agreed that "blacks have a right to live wherever they can afford to"; that figure rose to 84 percent in 1978. Thirty-two percent expressing an opinion in 1942 and 90 percent in 1982 agreed that whites and blacks should attend the same schools. In 1944, 45 percent of whites with an opinion thought blacks should have "as good a chance as white people to get any kind of job"; by 1972, fully 97 percent agreed.[5]

Third, although racism has declined and support for integration has increased, neither trend is free of complexity. For one thing, the drop in overt white racism is not total. As late as 1978, 15 percent agreed that "blacks are inferior to white people" and 6 percent objected to sitting next to a black on a bus. In 1985, 11 percent objected strongly to a family member bringing home a black dinner guest.[6] The United States retains a small but not trivial group of hard-core racists—somewhere between 5 and 15 percent of the white population, if survey data can be believed.

Perhaps more important is the fact that even supporters of racial equality and integration retain a wide variety of caveats about how to get from here to there. In fact, views on implementing these principles vary so widely that measuring the level of remaining racism is a fool's errand, since the results will depend entirely on the definition of racism. It makes more sense to look directly at the varied views, while keeping in mind the decline in overt anti-black attitudes and rise in general support for racial equality.

Caveats about implementing racial equality take many, possibly independent, forms. Some whites are concerned about *time* —change should not occur too fast. Some pay attention to *space* —blacks can move into white neighborhoods, but not next door to me. Some are concerned about *social distance*—blacks can work with me but not marry my daughter. Some focus on *numbers*—a few blacks in my child's school are fine, but not too many. Some worry about *status*—middle class, but not poor, blacks may live near me. Some address the *agent of change*— individuals or private actors may foster reform, but not the federal government or the courts. Some are concerned about the *mechanism of change*—they support school desegregation but decry busing, or they support affirmative action but resist quotas. Some notice the *scope of change*—individual behaviors should change, but not the structures or institutions within which those behaviors occur. Some worry about the *cost of change*—the nation is spending too much money to improve the position of blacks. Whites differ in their concern about *the kind of racial threat*—some worry about their own job security, others about the dignity of their ethnic group, others about violations of cherished moral precepts.

Cognitions about race vary along with emotions. Whites' *perceptions of racial progress* have changed—most now see steady progress from the past and into the future, and most see discrimination as a thing of the past. They vary in their *explanation of racial differences*—some attribute persistent black disadvantage to God, luck, or genes; others think lazy individuals cause their own fate; others see persistent discrimination or elite conspiracies.

Finally, *education, income, occupation, age,* and *region of residence* affect some but not all views, affect different views differently, and have different effects over time. And so on; even this exhausting list is not exhaustive. Let us briefly illustrate each dimension before considering their collective implications.

Time. In 1964, 74 percent of whites with opinions felt that "civil rights leaders are trying to push too fast"; by 1980, 40 percent still concurred. In the early 1960s, the better-educated were most concerned about timing, but they were replaced in the 1970s by the less-well-educated and older respondents.[7]

Space. In 1963, 45 percent would definitely or possibly move (a very strong reaction, indeed) "if colored people came to live next door." Yet in the same year, only 33 percent would be "upset a lot" if "blacks moved into this neighborhood."[8] This finding may illustrate the "liberal distance function," in which "the degree of favorable support for a social reform will increase as the distance between the subject and the locus of reform increases."[9]

Social distance. By the late 1970s, fewer than 10 percent objected to casual interracial contact (sitting beside a black on a bus or at a lunch counter) or to some closer contacts (having one's child taught by a black, having black coworkers or supervisors). Roughly a quarter objected strongly or mildly to "a member of your family bring[ing] a black friend home to dinner" and roughly a third endorsed laws prohibiting racial intermarriage. Fully 80 percent would be "concerned" if their "teenage child dated a black" (a decrease of only 11 percentage points from 1963).[10]

Numbers. By 1988, only 4 percent objected to sending their children to a school with "a few" black students. An additional 15 percent objected to a half-black school, however, and a further 29 percent balked at a majority-black school, making a total of 48 percent who would object to a majority black school.[11]

Status. In 1974, 20 percent claimed that they would be unhappy if blacks of similar status moved into their neighborhood. (Presumably none would be unhappy about new white neighbors with similar status; the question was not asked.) Forty-five percent were unhappy with the thought of lower-status black neighbors (compared with 36 percent unhappy about lower-status white neighbors).[12]

Agents of change. In 1985, 58 percent favored a "community-wide" law to prohibit racial discrimination in housing sales, whereas a statistically significantly smaller proportion, 51 percent, favored identical federal legislation. Bostonians who claimed to endorse the principle and even some practices of school desegregation vehemently opposed "forced busing" imposed by a federal court, in part because they saw such intervention as denying their right to participate in public policy decisions.[13]

Mechanism of change. Most whites endorse school desegregation, but up to 95 percent oppose mandatory busing to achieve it.[14] Similarly, although most now support affirmative action in higher education and the workplace, opposition to specific means of implementing it run as high as 90 percent when the question suggests "quotas," "preferences," or "reverse discrimination."[15]

Scope of change. Despite hearing strong arguments to the contrary, from 37 to 50 percent claimed in 1978 that seniority systems, tracking in schools, and meritocratic college admissions do not represent constraints on racial equality. Not surprisingly, about the same proportions opposed changing those practices.[16] If this survey is valid (that is unclear, given its provocative question wording and small sample size), whites are more willing to change individual hearts, minds, and even behaviors than structures and institutional practices.

Cost of change. In 1973, 27 percent of whites with an opinion claimed that the United States was "spending too much money on improving the condition of blacks." In 1987, 9 percent fewer concurred, but still almost one-fifth of the white population balked at the financial costs of racial equalization.[17]

Kind of racial threat. Any newspaper reader knows that people resist direct racial threats to their school, home, or job. Nevertheless, survey research finds curiously little evidence of self-interest in racial attitudes. For example, parents of white children likely to be bused for school desegregation do not oppose mandatory busing more than people without children or parents of children not likely to be bused. Nor do the length of the bus ride and assignment to a heavily black school affect whites' views of busing.[18] Self-interest can be teased out of survey responses if the question wording highlights potential personal threats or if public debate currently emphasizes concerns about self-interest.[19] But if polls can be believed, the perception of direct racial threat plays little role in motivating caveats about implementing racial equality.

So surveyors have turned to broader notions of interest, and find that whites who see "widespread conflict between blacks and whites in American society, who believe that American institutions nudge blacks ahead and shunt whites aside, are as a consequence likely to oppose policies promoting racial equality."[20] For example, whites who believe that busing increases school costs and harms the education of white children are significantly more opposed to a mandatory busing plan than others. Especially if they are well educated, whites seem able simultaneously to cling to an assumption of white dominance and to recognize the moral and historical imperatives of racial equality. They reconcile these conflicting views by endorsing abstract racial equality but opposing concrete government policies that would change the racial balance of power in jobs, housing, and education.[21]

A third and even less direct form of racial threat is symbolic racism, a combination of "deep-seated feelings of social morality and propriety and . . . early-learned racial fears and stereotypes." Symbolic racism evokes a distinctive "moralistic tone: the sense that blacks are too demanding, that they have been handed advantages, that hard work, self-discipline, and sacrifice no longer count for much." Some researchers argue that survey questions that tap symbolic racism predict whites' opposition to affirmative action and to federal policies to promote racial equality better than questions that tap self-interest, group interest, or principles of individualism and the proper role of government.[22]

Whites' cognitions about American race relations generally reinforce their emotionally-based hesitations about implementing racial equality and integration. For example, consider *perceptions of racial progress:* Whites assess racial progress more and more optimistically over time. In the mid-1960s, 30 to 45 percent (depending on the year and question wording) felt that the country was making progress in solving its racial problems; by the 1970s, 50 to 70 percent concurred; and by 1988, fully 87 percent agreed that "in the past 25 years, the country has moved closer to equal opportunity among the races."

Anticipation of the future roughly resembles evaluation of the past. In the late 1950s and 1960s, 40 to 55 percent expected racial integration in the near future. Since the late 1970s, two-thirds or more expect further racial progress or complete racial equality soon.[23]

Whites are not only optimistic about ending discrimination, but they are also largely convinced that the effects of past discrimination no longer shape blacks' lives. In 1988, 60 percent saw blacks and whites as equally vulnerable to economic upheavals, and an additional 8 percent saw blacks as *less* vulnerable. Seventy percent believe blacks to have the same opportunities to live a middle class life as whites. On questions about discrimination in the courts and local communities, in wages, promotions, housing, and education, and by police, from 50 to 80 percent (depending on the year and the survey question) see neither continued bias nor harmful consequences of past biases. In both 1978 and 1988, about one-third felt that blacks received jobs or places in higher education even before whites.[24] In short, racial equality now exists, and opportunities are becoming even more equal all the time—so what is the problem?

That question leads us to *explanations for racial differences* in dissatisfaction and poverty. As one would expect from a population that perceives high levels of equal opportunity in general,[25] and much progress toward racial equality in particular, most white Americans see persistent black poverty as largely the fault of the poor. Since the late 1970s, roughly three-fifths have agreed that "most blacks don't have the motivation or will power to pull themselves up out of poverty." Two-fifths see past or present discrimination as the cause of black poverty, and (where offered the choice), half fault a lack of educational opportunities. Roughly one-fifth cite less inborn ability or the will of God.[26] The first group implies the need to direct policies at individual black psychologies; the second group implies the need to change social institutions and possibly individual white psychologies; and the last implies the futility of any policy intervention. And, for once, researchers have found what intuition suggests: individualists and especially biological determinists are most likely to oppose programs to compensate for past or current discrimination.[27]

By now the point should be more than clear: even though whites express much less biological racism and much more support for the principles of racial equality and integration than they used to, they can still find plenty of reasons to object to one or another form of actual change in the racial status quo. Some may rely on only one or a few caveats, others may have recourse to many; a few may express none. Education, age, or region of residence may incline people toward different caveats and amounts of them.[28] Our point is that the aggregate picture differs radically from a succession of portraits of separate individuals. Even if each person added only a very small number of "but . . .s" to their global "yes" to racial equality, the total number and array of "but . . .s" is formidable indeed. The fact that they may be independent of each other—some are cognitive, others affective; some rely on space, others on time, social distance, or numbers; some address particular and ephemeral mechanisms of change, whereas others make explicit basic beliefs about causation and human nature—makes the formidable array virtually impenetrable. At least that is how it must appear to blacks.

BLACK RACIAL ATTITUDES

Blacks perceive progress and discrimination exactly opposite from whites. Whereas the proportion of whites who see increasing racial equality has risen from three-tenths to nine-tenths over twenty-five years, the analogous proportion of blacks has *declined* from between 50 and 90 percent in the mid-1960s to between 20 and 45 percent in the late 1970s and 1980s. In the

1980s, from one-tenth to over one third report that the situation of blacks has worsened since some point in the past.[29]

Predictions about racial progress follow the same pattern: As more whites see an ever-better racial future, more blacks become discouraged. In the mid-1960s, 55 to 75 percent of blacks anticipated integration and full racial equality sometime in the future. Since the late 1970s, that proportion has dropped to 30 to 45 percent.[30]

Blacks also flatly disagree with whites about the speed of civil rights progress. Among those expressing an opinion, 27 percent thought that "civil rights leaders are going too slowly" in 1964, and 45 percent thought so in 1980. In contrast, only 3 percent of whites with an opinion felt that racial change was too slow in 1964, and the proportion had barely risen—to 9 percent—in 1986.[31] The full array of data show that as whites were shifting from concerns about moving too fast to satisfaction with the pace, blacks were shifting from satisfaction to concerns about sluggishness.

Finally, blacks mistrust whites' racial attitudes much more than do whites. Since 1963, about one-third have claimed that "whites want to keep blacks down"; slightly smaller proportions think "most whites want to see blacks get a better break" or "don't care." Central city residents see an even less benign white world, and their suspicions are rising. In contrast, to choose but one example, 52 percent of whites in 1988 (compared with 30 percent of blacks) thought whites wanted blacks to get some breaks; only 6 percent (but 25 percent of blacks) thought whites wanted to keep blacks down.[32]

What shapes these opposite trajectories in views of racism and racial progress? One answer is differing perceptions of discrimination. In 1943, 85 percent of blacks (compared with 50 percent of whites) saw discrimination in the "chance to make a good living in this country"; in 1988, 69 percent of blacks (and 37 percent of whites) continued to believe that blacks lacked "the same opportunities as whites." Questions about bias in employment, promotion and wages, treatment by courts and police, housing, and education show the same pattern; 50 to 80 percent of blacks perceive discrimination in each arena, compared with roughly one-third of whites.[33]

Blacks experience racial bias not only as an amorphous threat, but also as a concrete obstacle in their own lives. In 1970, over two-thirds reported being the recipient of discrimination, and one-quarter felt it "almost every day of my life." A 1980 survey of more-than-half-time workers provides illustrative detail. For 42 percent, being black was very or fairly important in "keeping [them] from getting the really good jobs"; 19 percent felt that they had not been hired for a particular job because they were black; 13 percent reported being denied a promotion; 21 percent reported "unfair" or "bad" treatment at work; 19 percent reported that blacks get worse jobs than whites in their current workplace and 22 percent reported the same for their previous workplace.[34]

Just as whites do, blacks develop explanations that fit perceptions and reinforce emotions. Thus it is not surprising that more blacks see structural causes for racial inequality than do whites. Whereas roughly 40 percent of whites see past or present discrimination and 60 percent cite lack of motivation, the figures are exactly reversed in black explanations for failure to "do well in life" or "get a good education or job."[35] About half of black respondents, like whites, cite lack of education to explain blacks' disadvantages, but blacks are more likely than whites to see poor schooling as itself a structural bias rather than an individual flaw.[36]

Blacks' growing assertiveness and frustration with dilatory whites translates infrequently into militant separatism but frequently into a preference for associating with other blacks. In 1966, only 5 percent supported Black Nationalism (although 32 percent were not sure). In the 1980s, being black is more important to 12 to 20 percent than being American (8 to 14 percent claim the reverse). Across the years, fewer than 20 percent have agreed that blacks should give up on working with whites.[37]

Nevertheless, blacks often and perhaps increasingly, differentiate themselves from whites when they can do so on their own terms. Support for "something in between" desegregation and strict segregation increased from 17 percent in 1964 to 38 percent in 1978, while support for desegregation was falling by the same number of percentage points (from 78 to 55 percent). Since the 1960s, between 10 and 55 percent prefer to work with, live near, shop from, date and marry, and educate their children among other blacks. Only 10 percent in the 1960s, but 50 percent in 1983 supported a separate black political party.[38] We know of no analyses indicating what combination of prideful black separatism, defeatist acceptance of white segregationism, or something else shapes these views.

The only data we know that give both races' perceptions of black and white attributes are similarly ambiguous (a serious flaw of survey questions isolated from open-ended probes). The Gallup Poll asked in 1986 whether certain virtues (such as "intelligent," "compassionate," "strong leader," "hard working") are more likely to describe an unnamed black or a white candidate.[39] The question is difficult and is easily misunderstood or answered by rote, so its validity is uncertain. Nevertheless, it suggests three things. First, whites make fewer global racial attributions than blacks; whether from an absence of racial consciousness, concerns about appearing racist, lack of comprehension, or something else we do not know. In any case, averaging the responses to thirteen traits, 57 percent of whites and 49 percent of blacks claimed that "it depends" or that, in the abstract, white and black candidates do not differ in virtue. Second, blacks are slightly more likely than whites to attribute more virtue to the other race; the averages on the same thirteen traits were 13 and 8 percent respectively. These results are also ambiguous, since the psychology of attributing more virtue to the other race probably differs by race. Third, blacks are also slightly more likely than whites to attribute more virtue to their *own* race, by a difference of 31 to 28 percent. These results seem the clearest: in the late 1980s, blacks are as ready as whites to express racial pride.

To the degree that survey data accurately depict people's views, blacks live in a different world from whites.[40] To blacks, racial discrimination is extensive and (at most) grudgingly yielding; the situation of blacks may be worsening; and black suffering results from structural biases and white indifference or hostility. To whites, racial discrimination has declined almost to the vanishing point; the future of racial equality is promising; and black suffering results as much from individual failings as from external impediments. Must one of these views be dismissed as wrong, or can they be reconciled? We turn now to that question.

THE WHOLE IS GREATER THAN THE SUM OF THE PARTS

Our evaluation of the sharp discrepancies in racial views distinguishes between emotions and cognitions. With regard to emotions, we conclude that neither race has a handle on virtue that the other has evaded or lost. These data, at least, give us no grounds for saying that blacks, or whites, are more internally consistent, honest, or compliant with social pressure. Rather than assigning virtue and blame, we find it more fruitful to examine the multiple truths that these conflicting emotions reveal. From one perspective, whites can justifiably claim that racism and discrimination have plummeted during the past thirty years. Most whites perceive correctly that they and their friends now endorse racial equality and feel little racial animus; they merely have particular concerns about how racial policies ought to be implemented, as they (and blacks) have about virtually all public policies. From another perspective, blacks can justifiably claim that racism and discrimination have changed more than declined. Most blacks perceive correctly that the aggregation of whites' particular concerns for implementing racial policies creates a massive, many-sided barricade. Whites see individual attitudes, which have changed; blacks see the aggregation of individual attitudes, which seems immovable.

The cliche heading this section captures our main point about race-related emotions: the total effect of white resistance to racial change is much greater than is indicated by simply summing individual whites' expressed resistance. The critical feature is the widespread prevalence of specific caveats combined with their broad array; that pattern of resistance in a pluralist political system with many veto points stymies every policy move beyond tokenism, even though many (most?) individual whites might not object to a given policy initiative.[41]

Efforts to improve American race relations and the status of blacks are faced, in short, with the tyranny of the status quo. Any change will attract some opposition, and any change complex enough to have significant effects will attract enough opposition to its various facets that it will be extremely difficult to enact. Charles Lindblom has noted this phenomenon in a different context:

> To succeed, . . . corporate molding of citizen volitions on grand issues does not need to accomplish tyranny over the mind, nor even a uniformity of opinion on the grand issues. . . . It need only persuade citizens not to . . . make demands in politics on . . . certain . . . issues. Hence on such an issue as the autonomy of the corporation, it succeeds if it persuades the citizen that the issue is not worth his energies, *or* that it is discouragingly complex, *or* that agitation on the issue is not likely to be successful, *or* that corporate autonomy is a good thing. Any one will do.[42]

In race relations also, "any one will do" to help whites escape the logic of Gunnar Myrdal's American dilemma, in which whites are torn between their belief in the "American creed" of freedom and equality for all, and the personal convenience and safety of having blacks remain subordinate.[43] Whites have, by our count, at least twelve reasons to choose among to enable them to slide out of the dilemma.

As the language of the previous few paragraphs suggests, we hold a different view on cognitions about race. Here, the dominant black view seems more correct than the dominant white view. Blacks' disproportionate poverty and dissatisfaction have clear structural as well as individual and cultural causes; the effects of past discrimination persist; racism and discrimination have not disappeared.[44] In our view, governments must act to help blacks overcome the obstacles that depress their quality of life and life chances. The point is not that whites want blacks to have a depressed quality of life—quite the contrary. The point is that some combination of structural obstacles, history, and the aggregation of white views combine to inhibit that achievement despite what whites want.

From that perspective, then, we turn to the question of what policymakers should learn from American racial attitudes. Government policies follow public opinion no more certainly than an individual's actions follow his or her expressed views. Furthermore, policies can produce new behaviors, which in turn change views. If the history of American race relations has taught us anything, it has taught us those two facts. After all, schools were desegregated in the face of tremendous white opposition, and whites' views changed only after their children attended desegregated schools.[45] Nevertheless, government policies do generally follow trends in public opinion,[46] and they are easier to enact and implement if they seem to follow it. Certainly few elected officials are prepared to ignore public opinion polls. Thus we do not have to assert any direct causal relation between attitudes and actions at either the individual or the societal levels in order to argue that policymakers ought to take seriously the pattern and content of American racial attitudes.

The most crucial task at this point for policymakers concerned with public opinion is to determine whether our implicit model of the distribution of caveats is correct. We have been arguing as though, setting aside unreconstructed racists and a handful of white radicals, most whites hold only a few reservations about racial change—they worry about *either* how many blacks are in their child's school, *or* what kind of blacks are moving in next door, *or* the speed or mechanism of racial change, *or* the preservation of traditional values. We have also been assuming that all caveats have roughly equal psychological and political force. This implicit "unpatterned model" may, however, be wrong. Some whites may hold many reservations and the rest almost none. A few reservations may have much more impact than the others. Certain reservations may have causal force, with others resulting from them.

The most powerful alternative is the "individualist model." In this view, a particular variant of the fundamental American ideology of individualism encompasses many of the other caveats. Americans are taught that people have the right and responsibility to control their own destiny, and that the government's purpose is to foster liberty and opportunity.[47] Such an individualist may resist government intervention in schools and jobs or reject expensive social welfare programs for fear that collectivism is undermining individualism. He or she may similarly oppose too many blacks or the wrong class of blacks moving into the neighborhood on the assumption that this many or that kind have not yet earned a place there. If many whites believe that individualism thus defined both describes American society and prescribes how Americans should behave, the individualist model may better explain the pattern and distribution of caveats than the unpatterned model.

This issue is not merely of academic interest, although it obviously is that.[48] If our implicit unpatterned model is correct, the hurdle facing an elected official is daunting. Given a white population expressing a wide and randomly distributed array of caveats, no educational or persuasive campaign could convince a majority to support a policy with any teeth. In that case, authoritatively imposing reforms even against the will of the majority may be the only way to have a real impact on persistent racial inequality.[49] It is barely possible that in such a circumstance, the disarray of whites' caveats may even facilitate the imposed change. If opponents cannot agree on whether they object to the speed, or the numbers, or the kinds of people, or the mechanism of change, then they may have as hard a time coalescing to resist change as proponents had to promote it. Once again, the status quo trumps—we are simply dealing with a new status quo.

Consider a variant on the unpatterned model: an identifiable minority of whites holds most of the reservations, but members of that group are unsystematic in the particular caveats they express. In that case—let us call it the "unpatterned racist model"— the politicians' task might be easier. They should target different campaigns at different white audiences. Those likely to support racial change should be given every encouragement to do so, ranging from reminders of the sanctity of Myrdal's American creed to participation in planning and implementing the change. Those with many reasons to oppose racial change probably cannot be persuaded to support it by any features of the policy proposal; they should instead be convinced that the rest of the polity is firmly behind the change, that it will occur despite their opposition, that their worst fears almost certainly will not be realized, and that it is in their interests to cooperate with a fait accompli.

If the individualist model is more accurate, the politicians' task is easier than that suggested by the unpatterned model but harder than that suggested by the unpatterned racist variant. Public officials must start by recognizing that actions based on the classic version of individualistic equal opportunity simply cannot overcome the historical gap between the average positions of whites and blacks.[50] Their job is then to try to redefine individualism to permit effective policies to slip under its umbrella. Doing so is not easy, and faces the constant danger that the conventional understanding of individualism will undermine the new policy rather than vice versa, as the history of affirmative action also shows.[51] In this case, the public official must seek to persuade a majority of whites to broaden and change their beliefs about what America stands for, even to the point of contradicting what they have always believed. Such a campaign has a chance to work only if political leaders forcefully present it and probably only if they make it clear that change is inevitable regardless of popular support.[52]

Readers may object that our proposed campaigns to change views during or after the imposition of policy changes are almost as heavy-handed as the authoritative imposition of change without any effort to change opinions. They are right. We are persuaded that further significant improvement in the status of black Americans will not occur without some sort of uncomfortably heavy-handed action. The question for us is which form will produce the greatest benefits to both races at the least cost; knowing the pattern and distribution of caveats would be a big help in answering that question.[53]

Our final observation is more philosophical, and the most speculative. These data argue, albeit obliquely, against the value of ideal theory abstracted from real world messiness. The reason is simple: detail is all. Knowing how white Americans feel generally about blacks, racial equality, equal opportunity, and integration just does not tell us very much. It is only at the level of specific implementation—*how* will the schools be desegregated? *where* will the blacks moving into your neighborhood live? who will *your* son or daughter date?—that a more complete picture of racial attitudes emerges. The general views are not immaterial, but they provide only an outline; it is the caveats that give the color and perspective to the American racial portrait. By analogy, ideal theory in political philosophy remains at such a high level of abstraction that it has little bite either philosophically or as a guide to politics. We do not claim that all philosophy must be argued with an eye toward immediate policy use; we do, however, urge philosophers to descend far enough from the heights of ideal theory to help us think about real world dilemmas full of awkward and unpalatable detail.

We end, therefore, with four pleas. We urge philosophers not to abstract so far from messy reality that their arguments become bloodless and irrelevant. We urge survey researchers, conversely, not to concentrate so much on debates among pet theories that they lose sight of the larger, aggregated picture. We urge public officials to lead and shape racial attitudes rather than merely responding to them. Finally, let us avoid unnecessary scholarly and political conflicts. We have enough real and intractable ones as it is.

NOTES

1. Alphonso Pinkney, *The Myth of Black Progress* (Cambridge: Cambridge University Press, 1984), esp. 58–80; Robert B. Hill, "The Illusion of Black Progress," *Social Policy* 9 (3) (November/December 1978): 14–25.

2. These four concepts mean, respectively, that whites see blacks as violating cherished (nonracially based) moral precepts, whites equate improving the status of blacks with lowering the status of whites, whites see raising the status of blacks as a direct threat to their own well-being, and whites believe that, since individual prejudice has declined, blacks now have the same chances as whites to succeed on their own.

3. Among these reasons are: (1) survey questions are often changed, so trend data do not exist; (2) samples are selected differently, so their deviations from the population as a whole deviate; (3) details such as the question's context and wording, interviewer's race, amount of probing for substantive answers, and interview method (face-to-face or by telephone), affect responses; (4) some respondents may be subject to response set (they always agree or disagree with any question), social desirability effects (they give the answer they think the interviewer wants to hear), or lapses of memory (in presidential elections, more people [especially blacks] report having voted, and having voted for the winning candidate, than was actually the case); (5) black samples

are almost always smaller than white samples, and black respondents are usually chosen through very dubious sampling procedures; (6) black non-response rates are often much higher than white non-response rates; (7) respondents typically hold, not a single, unmodulated view on political issues, but rather a variety of views from which they themselves "sample" when responding to survey questions. See John Zaller and Stanley Feldman, "Answering Questions vs. Revealing Preferences: A Simple Theory of the Survey Response." Paper presented at the annual meeting of the Political Methodology Society, Los Angeles, August 1988; Howard Schuman, Charlotte Steeh, and Lawrence Bobo, *Racial Attitudes in America* (Cambridge: Harvard University Press, 1988), 49–70, 95–96; Howard Schuman and Shirley Hatchett, *Black Racial Attitudes: Trends and Complexities* (Ann Arbor: University of Michigan, Institute for Social Research, 1974), 39–44.

4. Schuman et al., *Racial Attitudes*, 118, 119; Louis Harris, "Poll Results Contradict Claims that Prejudice Is Increasing," *The Harris Survey*, February 18, 1985, 3; Philip Converse, Jean Dotson, Wendy Hoag, and William McGee, *American Social Attitudes Data Sourcebook, 1947–1978* (Cambridge: Harvard University Press, 1980), 61.

5. Converse et al, *American Social Attitudes*, 66; Schuman et al., *Racial Attitudes*, 74–75.

6. In 1963, 31 percent of whites saw blacks as inferior, and 20 percent objected to sharing a bus seat. Louis Harris and Associates, "A Study of Attitudes Toward Racial and Religious Minorities and Toward Women," (unpublished report, New York: Louis Harris and Associates, Inc., 1978), 15, 16. In 1963, 31 percent strongly objected to a black dinner guest. "Opinion Roundup: The State of Intolerance in America," *Public Opinion* 10 (2) (July/August 1987), 24. For an analysis that parallels ours in its discussion of the complexities of racial attitudes, and that adds different dimensions, see Thomas Pettigrew, "New Patterns of Racism: The Different Worlds of 1984 and 1964," *Rutgers Law Review* 37 (4) (Summer 1985): 673–706.

7. Lawrence Bobo, "Attitudes Toward the Black Political Movements: Trends, Meaning, and Effects on Racial Policy Preferences," *Social Psychology Quarterly* 51 (December 1988), table 2; Converse et al., *American Social Attitudes*, 84, 85. Here and elsewhere, we present illustrative rather than comprehensive data.

8. Hazel Erskine, "The Polls: Negro Housing," *Public Opinion Quarterly* 31 (3) (Fall, 1967), 495; Harris, *A Study of Attitudes*, 34.

9. Myron Rothbart, "Perceiving Social Injustice: Observations on the Relationship Between Liberal Attitudes and Proximity to Social Problems," *Journal of Applied Social Psychology* 3 (4) (1973): 291–302. His

data show that the farther away a proposed public housing project or halfway house for prisoners are likely to be, the more respondents approve of them.

10. Harris, *A Study of Attitudes*, 15; James Davis and Tom Smith, *General Social Surveys, 1972–1982: Cumulative Codebook* (Chicago: University of Chicago, National Opinion Research Corporation, 1982), 101.

11. James Davis and Tom Smith, *General Social Surveys, 1972–1988: Cumulative Codebook* (Chicago: University of Chicago, National Opinion Research Corporation, 1988), 172. Resistance to a "few" or "half" black schoolmates fell steadily from 1958 (when the question was first asked) to 1970, mainly because Southerners' views changed dramatically. Resistance to "more than half" has declined much less, and shows less regional disparity.

12. William Watts and Lloyd Free, *The State of the Nation—1974* (Washington, D.C.: Potomac Associates, 1974), 280–82. For similar results in 1985, see Howard Schuman and Lawrence Bobo, "Survey-based Experiments on White Attitudes Toward Residential Integration," *American Journal of Sociology* 94 (2) (September 1988), 290. Well-educated whites were especially sensitive to the class of their putative new black neighbors.

13. Schuman and Bobo, "Survey-based Experiments," 279; D. Garth Taylor, *Public Opinion and Collective Action* (Chicago: University of Chicago Press, 1986), esp. 76–81. See also Douglas Gatlin, Michael Giles, and Everett Cataldo, "Policy Support within a Target Group: The Case of School Desegregation," *American Political Science Review* 72 (3) (September 1978): 985–95.

14. Responses vary with question wording, but pollsters can never persuade more than one-quarter to endorse "forced busing." Louis Harris, "Majority of Parents Report School Busing Has Been Satisfactory," *Harris Survey*, March 26, 1981; Gary Orfield, *Must We Bus?* (Washington, D.C.: Brookings Institution, 1978), 112–18. In this case, however, age and education dramatically affect racial attitudes. Agreement among college freshmen that "busing is OK if it helps to achieve racial balance in the schools" has risen every year from a 1976 low of 37 percent (when the question was first asked) to a 1987 high of 56 percent. (Roughly 90 percent of the respondents in any year are white; 5 percent are black, and 5 percent are other, mostly Asian.) Alexander Astin, Kenneth Green, and William Korn, *The American Freshman: Twenty Year Trends* (Los Angeles: Higher Education Research Institute, University of California at Los Angeles, 1987), 99, and Alexander Astin, Kenneth Green, William Korn, and Marilynn Schalit, *The American*

Freshman: National Norms for Fall 1987 (Los Angeles: Higher Education Research Institute, University of California at Los Angeles, 1987), 61.

15. Harris, *A Study of Attitudes*, 45–55; Stuart Jackson and Harris Collingwood, eds. "A Nation Divided on Black Progress," *Business Week/ Harris Poll*, March 14, 1988, p. 65; Louis Harris, "Big Shift in Single-Issue Voting Expected This Fall," *The Harris Survey*, March 11, 1982; "Black and White: A *Newsweek* Poll," *Newsweek*, March 7, 1988, 23; Media General/Associated Press, survey of June 22–July 2, 1988, tables 4 and 5; Donald Kinder and Lynn Sanders, "Pluralistic Foundations of American Opinion on Race," paper presented at the annual meeting of the American Political Science Association, Chicago, September 1987, table 1.

16. Over 90 percent agreed that the private sale of lawyers' services constrained blacks and the poor, but only 60 percent supported changing that feature of the legal system. About one-third also opposed changes in suburban zoning laws and redlining practices in bank mortgages. However, only one-tenth opposed changes in school funding formulas and bail systems. (Unfortunately, respondents were not asked if the four latter structures imposed constraints on blacks.) Steven Tuch and Marylee Taylor, "Whites' Opinions about institutional Constraints on Racial Equality," *Sociology and Social Research* 70 (4) (July 1986): 268–71.

17. Schuman, Steeh, and Bobo, *Racial Attitudes*, xii, 88.

18. Gatlin, et al., "Policy Support," 985–95; David Sears, Carl Hensler, and Leslie Speer, "Whites' Opposition to Busing: Self-Interest or Symbolic Politics?" *American Political Science Review* 73 (2) (June 1979): 369–84; Donald Kinder, "The Continuing American Dilemma," *Journal of Social Issues* 42 (Summer 1986): 151–72; John McConahay, "Modern Racism, Ambivalence, and the Modern Racism Scale," in *Prejudice, Discrimination, and Racism* ed. John Dovidio and Samuel Gaertner (Orlando: Academic Press, 1986): 91–125.

19. Kinder and Sanders, "Pluralistic Foundations," 23–24; Cardell Jacobson, "Resistance to Affirmative Action—Self-Interest or Racism?" *Journal of Conflict Resolution* 29 (2) (June 1985): 306–29. Better measures of self-interest, which tap whether a respondent has actually experienced harm from a given policy, might help to resolve this discrepancy between common sense and survey findings.

20. Kinder and Sanders, "Pluralistic Foundations," 14 (original text in past tense). See Lawrence Bobo, "Whites' Opposition to Busing: Symbolic Racism or Realistic Group Conflict?" *Journal of Personality and Social Psychology* 45 (6) (1983): 1196–1210; and "Group Conflict, Prejudice, and the Paradox of Contemporary Racial Attitudes," in *Eliminat-*

ing Racism, ed. Phylliz Katz and Dalmas Taylor (New York: Plenum Press, 1988): 85–114.

21. McKee McClendon and Fred Pestello, "White Opposition: To Busing or to Desegregation?" *Social Science Quarterly* 63 (March 1982), 77; Mary Jackman and Michael Muha, "Education and Intergroup Attitudes: Moral Enlightenment, Superficial Democratic Commitment, or Ideological Refinement?" *American Sociological Review* 49 (December 1984): 751–69. See also James Sidanius, "Symbolic and Group Conflict Theories of Racism: An Attempt at a Synthesis" (unpublished paper, Los Angeles: University of California at Los Angeles, Department of Psychology, 1988), 16–19.

22. The first quotation comes from Donald Kinder and David Sears, "Prejudice and Politics: Symbolic Racism versus Racial Threats to the Good Life," *Journal of Personality and Social Psychology* 40 (3) (1981), 416. The second quotation and survey results are from Kinder and Sanders, "Pluralistic Foundations," 11, 14–16. Other researchers reject these findings, claiming that the operationalization of the concept of symbolic racism is so broad that it encompasses rival concepts, and thereby causes them to appear less important in survey analyses than they actually are. See, for example, Paul Sniderman and Philip Tetlock, "Symbolic Racism: Problems of Motive Attribution in Political Analysis," and "Reflections on American Racism," both in *Journal of Social Issues* 42 (2) (Summer 1986): 129–50, 173–87.

23. Converse, et al., *American Social Attitudes,* 79; Media General/ Associated Press Poll, tables 2, 3, 3a; Hazel Erskine, "The Polls: Race Relations," *Public Opinion Quarterly* 26 (1) (Spring 1962), 138; Hazel Erskine, "The Polls: Negro Philosophies of Life," *Public Opinion Quarterly* 33 (1) (Spring 1969), 156; Harris, *A Study of Attitudes,* 56; *Los Angeles Times, "Los Angeles Times* Poll Number 71," 1983, table 86.

24. Jackson and Collingwood, "A Nation Divided;" Harris, *A Survey of Attitudes,* 4–13, 26–34; James Kluegel and Eliot Smith, *Beliefs about Inequality* (New York: Aldine de Gruyter, 1986), 186; "Black and White: A *Newsweek* Poll," 23; George Gallup, ed. *Gallup Poll: Public Opinion, 1987* (Wilmington, Del.: Scholarly Resources Inc., 1987), 36; Herbert Denton and Barry Sussman, "Blacks, Whites Agree Blacks Have Gained, Differ on What's Ahead," *Washington Post,* March 24, 1981, A2; Denton and Sussman, " 'Crossover Generation' of Blacks Express Most Distrust of Whites," *Washington Post,* March 25, 1981, A2; Jacobson, "Resistance to Affirmative Action," 315.

25. Joseph Feagin, "Poverty: We Still Believe That God Helps Those Who Help Themselves," *Psychology Today* vol. 5, November 1972, 101– 129; Kluegel and Smith, *Beliefs about Inequality,* 43–102; Jennifer L.

Hochschild, *What's Fair?: American Beliefs about Distributive Justice* (Cambridge: Harvard University Press, 1981); Sidney Verba and Gary Orren, *Equality in America: The View from the Top* (Cambridge: Harvard University Press, 1985).

26. The total sums to more than 100 percent because respondents give more than one explanation. Kluegel and Smith, *Beliefs about Inequality*, 185–96; Barry Sussman and Herbert Denton, "Lingering Racial Stereotypes Damage Blacks," *Washington Post*, March 26, 1981, A2; "*Los Angeles Times* Poll No. 71," Tables 88–91; Paul Sniderman and Michael Hagen, *Race and Inequality* (Chatham, N.J.: Chatham House Publishers, 1985), 29–39; Richard Apostle, Charles Glock, Thomas Piazza, and Marijean Suelzle, *The Anatomy of Racial Attitudes* (Berkeley: University of California Press, 1983), 38–44, 69–86.

27. Apostle et al., *The Anatomy*, 87–114; Sniderman and Hagen, *Race and Inequality*, 49–54.

28. This sentence, of course, uncovers only the tiny tip of a large iceberg. Generally, more highly educated, well-off, younger whites living outside the South express more liberal opinions than their opposites. These differences are diminishing over time, as individual attitudes are becoming more liberal, and as younger and more liberal cohorts are replacing older, more conservative, ones. Schuman et al., *Racial Attitudes*, esp. 199–200; for exceptions to this generalization, see Kluegel and Smith, *Beliefs about Inequality*, 207, 210; Mary Jackman, "General and Applied Tolerance: Does Education Increase Commitment to Racial Integration?" *American Journal of Political Science* 22 (2) (May 1978): 302–24; Jackman and Muha, "Education and Intergroup Attitudes."

29. William Brink and Louis Harris, *Black and White: A Study of U.S. Racial Attitudes Today* (New York: Simon & Schuster, 1966), 222–31; Gary Marx, *Protest and Prejudice: A Study of Belief in the Black Community* (New York: Harper Torchbooks, 1967), 5–11, 220; Schuman et al., *Racial Attitudes*, xiv, 141–43; CBS News/*New York Times* Poll, "The Kerner Commission—Ten Years Later," 1978, App., 8; James Jackson and Gerald Gurin, *National Survey of Black Americans Codebook* (Ann Arbor: University of Michigan, Institute of Social Research, 1980), 679; Thomas Cavanagh, *Inside Black America* (Washington, D.C.: Joint Center for Political Studies, 1985), 3; "Black and White: A *Newsweek* Poll," 23; Joint Center for Political Studies/Gallup Organization Survey, 1987 (Washington, D.C.: Joint Center for Political Studies, 1987), table 11. Not surprisingly, blacks are more sanguine about the longer run—the past several decades—but even here, fewer than two-thirds see significant progress: Katherine Tate, Ronald Brown, Shirley Hatchett, and

James Jackson, *The 1984 National Black Election Study Sourcebook* (Ann Arbor: University of Michigan, Institute for Social Research, 1988), table 15.5; Media General/Associated Press Poll, table 2.

It is important to keep in mind throughout this section that survey data for blacks are considerably less trustworthy than survey data for whites for a variety of (mainly methodological) reasons.

30. In 1984, 36 percent of blacks anticipated that blacks would never achieve equality; in 1988, one quarter of both races were equally pessimistic. Brink and Harris, *Black and White*, 258–59; Marx, *Protest and Prejudice*, 13–15, 220; CBS News/*New York Times* Poll, "The Kerner Commission—Ten Years Later," App. 19; Tate et al., *The 1984 National Black Election*, table 7.5; Media General/Associated Press Poll, table 3a.

31. Schuman, Steeh, and Bobo, *American Racial Attitudes*, xiii, 118–19, 146–47.

32. Some changes in the central cities samples may be due to the changing class structure of cities rather than to the changing attitudes of city residents, but we know of no analysis of this question. William Brink and Louis Harris, *The Negro Revolution in America* (New York: Simon & Schuster, 1964), 126; Jackson and Gurin, *National Survey*, 683; *Los Angeles Times* Poll No. 71, table 94; Tate et al., *The 1984 National Black Election*, tables 7.6 and 15.14; Diane Colasanto, "Black Attitudes," *Public Opinion* 10 (5) (January/February 1988), 47; "Black and White: A *Newsweek* Poll," 23; Castellano Turner and William J. Wilson, "Dimensions of Racial Ideology: A Study of Urban Black Attitudes," *Journal of Social Issues* 32 (2) (Spring 1976): 139–52. For central city samples, see Colasanto, "Black Attitudes," 47.

33. Hazel Erskine, "The Polls: Negro Employment," *Public Opinion Quarterly* 32 (1) (Spring 1968), 133; Media General/Associated Press Poll, table 1; Tate et al., *The 1984 National Black Election*, table 15.2; Harris, *A Study of Attitudes*, 2–34 passim.; Denton and Sussman, "Blacks, Whites Agree," A2; Denton and Sussman, " 'Crossover Generation'," A2; Jackson and Collingwood, "A Nation Divided,"; "Black and White: A *Newsweek* Poll," 23; The *New York Times* Poll, "New York City Race Relations Survey," March 8–11, 1987, tables 13–15, 23, 24; Gallup, ed. *Gallup Poll, 1987*, 36.

34. "The Black Mood: More Militant, More Hopeful, More Determined," *Time Magazine* (April 6, 1970), 28–29; *Los Angeles Times* Poll No. 71, table 29; 1980: Jackson and Gurin, *National Survey*, 161–66, 236–37, 268–73, 345–47; CBS News/*New York Times* Poll, "The Kerner Commission—Ten Years Later," App. 2–7, 17; *New York Times*/WCBS News, "New York City Race Relations Survey," April 27–May 3, 1985,

Tables 26, 27, 32a, 33; *New York Times* Poll, "New York City," tables 26, 32, 36, 40–43.

35. The proportion of blacks blaming blacks' lack of will power for racial inequality is rising, from roughly 20 percent in the late 1960s and 1970s to over 30 percent in the 1980s. In the early 1980s, a quarter of blacks—a higher proportion than is common among whites—even agreed that racial inequality is due to blacks' lesser "inborn ability to learn." Marx, *Protest and Prejudice*, 220–21; CBS News/*New York Times*, "The Kerner Commission—Ten Years Later," Appendix, 9; Sussman and Denton, "Lingering Racial Stereotypes," A2; *Los Angeles Times* Poll Number 71, Table 88; Tate et al., *The 1984 National Black Election*, table 15.8; Colasanto, "Black Attitudes," 49; "Black and White: A *Newsweek* Poll," 23.

36. Colasanto, "Black Attitudes," 49; Jackson and Gurin, *National Survey*, 239, 348.

37. Brink and Harris, *Black and White*, 260, 262; Jackson and Gurin, *National Survey*, 655; Tate et al., *The 1984 National Black Election*, table 15.7; Edwin Slaughter, "Gallup/*Newsweek* Poll: Race Relations," unpublished results from The Gallup Organization, Inc., Princeton N.J. 1988, table 8; Jeffrey Paige, "Changing Patterns of Anti-white Attitudes Among Blacks," *Journal of Social Issues* 26 (4) (Autumn 1970): 69–86. Residents of central cities were, however, much more willing than the general black population to endorse black nationalist leaders in the 1960s; see Marx, *Protest and Prejudice*, 217, 226–29; Schuman and Hatchett, *Black Racial Attitudes*, 9.

38. CBS News/*New York Times* Poll, "The Kerner Commission—Ten Years Later," 11, 15, 16, 17, 18; Jackson and Gurin, *National Survey*, 672–75; Converse et al., *American Social Attitudes*, 61; "Black and White: A *Newsweek* Poll," 23; Schuman, Steeh, and Bobo, *Racial Attitudes*, 144–45; Brink and Harris, *Black and White*, 91; *Los Angeles Times* Poll No. 71, table 83; Tate et al., *The 1984 National Black Election*, tables 3.12, 15.12.

39. We report data on thirteen of the fourteen cues offered in the survey since one of them, liberal, is a more ambiguous cue than the others, which are uniformly seen as virtues. Joint Center/Gallup Survey, 1987, table 9.

40. Demographic differences affect blacks' views, but in more complex patterns than among whites. In the 1950s and 1960s, low-income, non-Southern blacks were marginally more disaffected, sensitive to discrimination, and supportive of black nationalism than high-income blacks; the latter were marginally more optimistic about civil rights progress and changes in white attitudes. By the 1980s, the opposite

pattern held; working-class blacks were more optimistic, and well-off blacks more sensitive about racial bias. Virtually all blacks endorse civil-rights legislation, but low-income blacks are more enthusiastic about government intervention in the interests of blacks and the poor. W. S. M. Banks, "The Rank Order of Sensitivity to Discriminations of Negroes in Columbus, Ohio," *American Sociological Review* 15 (4) (August 1950), 533; Brink and Harris, *Black and White,* 224–35, 258, 260–63; I. A. Lewis and William Schneider, "Black Voting, Bloc Voting, and the Democrats," *Public Opinion* 6 (5) (October/November 1983), table 1; Denton and Sussman, " 'Crossover Generation'," A2; Diane Colasanto and Linda Williams, "The Changing Dynamics of Race and Class/*Public Opinion,*" 9(5) (January/February 1987): 50–53; Wayne Parent and Paul Stekler, "The Political Implications of Economic Stratification in the Black Community," *Western Political Quarterly* 38 (4) (December 1985): 521–38; Susan Welch and Lorn Foster, "Class and Conservatism in the Black Community," paper presented at the annual meeting of the American Political Science Association, Washington, D.C., 1986; Phillip Bowman, Alida Quick, and Shirley Hatchett, "Social Psychological Status of the Black Population" (unpublished report, Ann Arbor: University of Michigan, n.d.), table 4.

41. These data, when combined with more behavioral evidence, may support a more powerful conclusion: most white Americans want no further change in the racial status quo, even though they know they are not supposed to say so out loud. We do not draw that conclusion here, if only for lack of sufficient evidence. The conclusions we can draw from survey data are gloomy enough.

42. Charles E. Lindblom, *Politics and Markets* (New York: Basic Books, 1977), 210–11. See also Hochschild, *What's Fair?,* 265–72; Michael Mann, "The Social Cohesion of Liberal Democracy," *American Sociological Review* 35 (3) (June 1970): 423–39.

43. Gunnar Myrdal, *An American Dilemma: The Negro Problem and Modern Democracy* (New York: Harper and Brothers, 1944), especially Intro. and chaps. 1, 2, 4, and 45.

44. For data on disparities between the races, see Reynolds Farley and Walter Allen, *The Color Line and the Quality of Life in America* (New York: Russell Sage Foundation, 1987); for a recent overview of the situation of the worst-off blacks, see William J. Wilson, ed. "The Ghetto Underclass: Social Science Perspectives," *Annals of the American Academy of Political and Social Science* 501 (January 1989).

45. Our thanks to Clarence Stone, of the University of Maryland, and Thomas Pettigrew, of the University of California, Santa Cruz, for drawing our attention to these points. On the change in whites' atti-

tudes after schools were desegregated, see Jennifer Hochschild, *The New American Dilemma: Liberal Democracy and School Desegregation* (New Haven: Yale University Press, 1984), 179–87, and Thomas Pettigrew, "Advancing Racial Justice: Past Lessons for Future Use," in *Opening Doors: An Appraisal of Race Relations in American,* ed. Harry Knopke, Robert Norrell, and Ronald Rogers (Tuscaloosa: University of Alabama Press, 1989).

46. Persuasive evidence on this point is Robert Shapiro and Lawrence Jacobs, "The Relationship Between Public Opinion and Public Policy: A Review," in *Political Behavior Annual,* vol. 2, ed. Samuel Long (Boulder: Westview Press, 1989): 149–79.

47. They are, at least, bedrock *white* American beliefs. If blacks subscribe less to individualism as either description or prescription, then the gap between the races is deeper than most people perceive. Survey research can help to answer that question, but a careful consideration awaits another paper. On whites' ideology, see citations in note 25; J. R. Pole, *The Pursuit of Equality in American History* (Berkeley: University of California Press, 1978); and Daniel Rodgers, *Contested Truths: Keywords in American Politics Since Independence* (New York: Basic Books, 1987).

48. The most convincing and pertinent research on this question is that of Kluegel and Smith, *Beliefs about Inequality;* Apostle et al., *Anatomy;* and Sniderman and Hagen, *Race and Inequality.* None, however, considers the full array of caveats that we have found or directly compares the model models. Kinder and Sanders, "Pluralistic Foundations," casts an admirably wide net, but uses an excessively imperialistic definition of symbolic racism and focuses too much on which explanation is more compelling rather than on the distribution and prevalence of many explanations. We need research that, to put it very roughly, suggests many possible caveats to support for policies of racial change, and permits respondents to choose as many as they wish (and add others), and to rank them in order of importance.

49. For a similar conclusion, reached from a slightly different direction, see Hochschild, *The New American Dilemma.*

50. For a mathematical demonstration of this claim, which does not preclude success of some individual blacks under the equal opportunity rubric, see Edwin Dorn, *Rules and Racial Equality* (New Haven: Yale University Press, 1979), 107–40.

51. Jonathan Leonard, "The Impact of Affirmative Action on Employment," *Journal of Labor Economics* 2 (4) (October 1984): 439–63; "What Promises Are Worth: The Impact of Affirmative Action Goals," *Journal of Human Resources* 20 (1) (Winter 1985): 3–20.

52. And probably only if the political leaders do not depend on reelection to continue their political career. On this point, see Hochschild, *The New American Dilemma* 112–45.

53. Clarence Stone suggests another way to deal with the "Yes, but . . ." phenomenon: "The crucial point is not what substantive sentiment we express on opinion surveys; it is what problems we see as salient. . . . Suppose we treat the issue, not as one of how to promote equality. Instead, view the problem as one about the future capability of the workforce. . . . Once this issue is the salient one, attitudes about race and equality of opportunity become peripheral, and measures to enhance capability can be widely promoted and defended. That is why I would explicitly avoid an opinion-control-policy position. That formulation begs the issue." We are not as sanguine as Stone, but we agree that his approach seems promising. It is, however, beyond the scope of this chapter. Clarence Stone, personal communication with Jennifer Hochschild, January 25, 1989.

INDEX